THE 100 BEST TRENDS

2006

Emerging Developments
You Can't Afford to Ignore

George Ochoa and Melinda Corey

Adams Media
Avon, Massachusetts

Published by Adams Media, an F+W Publications Company
57 Littlefield Street
Avon, MA 02322
www.adamsmedia.com

ISBN: 1-59337-451-8

Printed in Canada.
J I H G F E D C B A

Library of Congress Cataloging-in-Publication Data
available from publisher.

This publication is designed to provide accurate and authoritative information with
regard to the subject matter covered. It is sold with the understanding that the publisher is not engaged in rendering legal, accounting, or other professional advice. If
legal advice or other expert assistance is required, the services of a competent professional person should be sought.
    —From a *Declaration of Principles* jointly adopted by a Committee of the
American Bar Association and a Committee of Publishers and Associations

Many of the designations used by manufacturers and sellers to distinguish their product are claimed as trademarks. Where those designations appear in this book and
Adams Media was aware of a trademark claim, the designations have been printed
with initial capital letters.

This book is available at quantity discounts for bulk purchases.
For information, please call 1-800-872-5627.

Acknowledgments

It took three agents to bring this book into being: the late Jane Jordan Browne, Scott Mendel, and Danielle Egan-Miller. We thank them all. We also thank our editor Jill Alexander, along with Kirsten Amann and Larry Shea.

Contents

CONTENTS

Introduction

If there's one thing we know about the future, it's this: it has already begun. The changes that will shape our lives in the next 10 to 20 years are already in motion—from demographic changes to technological marvels; from social trends to novel ways of doing business. The pace of transformation can be bewildering, but if we scrutinize the present, we can see the footprints of change even now. This new, updated edition of *The 100 Best Trends, 2006* is a snapshot of 100 of those footprints: the 100 most important trends now shaping the near future.

Trends are more than just fads or fashions, things that are hot now but may not survive the winter. Trends are patterns of change that have been in formation for several years and are expected to endure for at least several more years. The macarena was a fad; a multicultural population (greater cultural diversity among Americans) is a trend. *The 100 Best Trends, 2006* presents each trend in an essay that says what the trend is, gives historical background on the trend, describes the evidence for it, and sketches its major aspects and implications. This book is intended for business readers who need to know about the most important trends affecting their operating environment and customer base. It is also intended for general readers who want a better understanding of the directions in which their world is heading.

Trends arise in every category of human activity, from the most leisurely to the most purposeful. To cover this broad range, *The 100 Best Trends, 2006* is divided into 10 chapters, each focusing on one area: business and industry; demographics; entertainment and the arts; health and medicine; lifestyles; marketing; politics; religion and spirituality; science and technology; and the sexes.

Within each chapter, the trends are presented in alphabetical order by title. Some of the titles are self-explanatory; others will make sense once you delve into the essay. "Alternative Medicine" is exactly what it says; "More Bananas, Fewer Potatoes" has to do with changing tastes in the American diet.

The scope of the essays varies as the trends do, from broad concepts ("Asymmetrical Warfare," the art of fighting enemies whose size and strength does not compare with your own) to narrow social or political phenomena ("The Decline of Spelling"). Most essays focus on the United States, but some cover international trends, among them "Globalization Continues," "China Rising," and "Remembering the Forgotten Continent" (Africa). Whether the topic is scientific ("The Incredible Shrinking Science," on nanotechnology), spiritual ("Christian Cool"), commercial ("Conglomermedia"), or sexual ("The New Teen Facts of Life"), the aim throughout is to present the trends concisely in a plain, lively style with a minimum of jargon. An increase in spare time is not one of the trends discovered in our research, so the reader's time is respected here.

Trends are always changing, making this second edition a necessity. For this edition, we added many new trends, including "The Sleep Industry," "Do-It-Yourself Entertainment," "Medical Tourism," "The NASCARization of America," "Marketing to Grandma," "States in Trouble," and "Gaming the Search Engines." We also revised and updated the trends that remained from the first edition. To make room for the new material, we had the unhappy task of cutting out some old trends, even though they still had life in them. Luckily, some of them seemed close to playing themselves out. Metrosexuals, for example, have never been the same since presidential candidate Howard Dean announced himself as one.

In a time of rapid change, it helps to understand the underlying patterns of change; not only because those patterns are interesting, but also because knowing about them confers an advantage in the pursuit of prosperity and happiness. It is our hope that this new edition of *The 100 Best Trends* will help give you that advantage.

Business
and Industry

Biotech Foods: A Comeback

1 Whatever happened to biotech foods? At one time they were supposed to revolutionize the food industry. Back in the 1990s, the Flavr Savr tomato, the first biotech food approved by the FDA for sale in the supermarket, was supposed to kick off a new wave of genetically modified foods. But the Flavr Savr never lived up to its early promise. Nor did other biotechnology-enhanced horticultural crops, such as potatoes, strawberries, lettuce, and squash, which were approved by the government and scheduled for greatness. But don't count the biotech industry out of the supermarket yet. There are signs that biotech foods are about to stage a comeback.

The Flavr Savr, dubbed an "economic disaster" by the *Wall Street Journal*, was genetically engineered to have delayed maturation, so that the fruit would be easier to transport to market. But even though the tomato made it to the supermarket in 1994, consumers saw no advantage in buying the tomato, and it was taken out of circulation. "Probably the most important lesson is, the customer is always right," U.S. Department of Agriculture researcher John Radin told Scripps Howard

News Service. Heavy regulatory requirements, the difficult economics of the food industry, and scientific setbacks have further delayed development of biotech foods. So has vigorous public protest about the safety of genetically engineered food. In Europe, about 70 percent of the population are opposed to genetically modified foods, also known there as Frankenfoods.

Agricultural biotech, or agbio, has made inroads in some areas, notably corn, soybeans, canola, and cotton. In the United States, about 80 percent of all soy has been genetically engineered, along with most canola and about 40 percent of all corn. At least 70 percent of processed foods on grocery store shelves contain ingredients and oils from biotech crops. Worldwide, more than 167 million acres are now growing genetically modified plants. However, most of these crops are intended for animal feed. And setbacks continue. In May 2004, Monsanto Company scrapped plans to commercialize its genetically modified wheat, engineered to be resistant to the herbicide Roundup. Strong public opposition to genetic modification of wheat, with its symbolic associations as "amber waves of grain," likely played a role in the decision.

Nevertheless, more biotech foods are probably on the way. The Swiss company Syngenta is planning to launch its own genetically modified wheat in 2007, and a biotech banana is planned for 2006. Genetically modified papaya and squash are already on store shelves. Biotech foods are likely to prevail for both environmental and economic reasons. By developing plants that are resistant to pests, genetically modified foods lower the need for pesticides. Genetic modification can also lead to higher yields at lower cost, bringing savings to the consumer. "I remain optimistic that eventually we will use these technologies, but it's going to take time," Kent Bradford, director of the Seed Biotechnology Center at the University of California, Davis, told Scripps Howard News Service.

There are signs that the tide of public opinion about biotech foods is changing. In May 2004, the European Union (EU) ended its six-year moratorium on genetically modified foods by approving the import of Syngenta's Bt-11 corn, an insect-resistant sweet corn. The UN's Food and

Agriculture Organization is confident of the potential of biotech foods. In a May 2004 report, it said that genetically engineered crops have great promise to alleviate hunger among the world's poor. The report said too little money is being spent researching the kinds of crops and animals used in developing countries. But in the worldwide debate about whether to use biotechnology in food crops, the report came down on the side of using it.

Controversy remains. In February 2004, a study commissioned by the Union of Concerned Scientists found that DNA from genetically modified crops had contaminated ordinary corn, soy, and canola seed batches. This raised fears that genetically modified DNA will spread widely in the environment and may pose hazards. An international scientific panel appointed under the North American Free Trade Agreement (NAFTA) essentially concurred. In November 2004, the panel concluded that the unintended spread of genetically modified corn from the United States into Mexico poses a potential threat and recommended ways of stopping it. The United States vigorously disagreed.

Biotech foods will probably win the day, but how long it takes depends on how well they make their case in the public debate. "How consumers see the benefits affecting them is what will make the difference," Stephanie Childs, spokeswoman for the Grocery Manufacturers of America, told *USA Today* in May 2004.

Come Fly with Me

2 In a variety of ways, airplane flight is being transformed. As a business, it is reshaping itself to fit a more fragmented, consumer-savvy market. New varieties of airlines and destinations target regions not served by major carriers; major carriers are fighting back with new initiatives to attract business. Competition overall has increased, leading to lower or stabilized prices across the board. What's more, the entertainment factor of airline travel is increasing, making flight a source of amusement, if not fun. The jet-set status of the 1960s may be gone, but the Kate Spade uniforms, personal TVs, and especially increased on-time arrivals don't hurt.

It is a marked change from early 2003, when airline traffic was stymied. The war in Iraq and the threat of global transmission of severe acute respiratory syndrome (SARS) were largely responsible for two-digit declines in domestic and international travel, according to the Air Transport Association, as reported in the *New York Times*. Yet, by early 2004, some discount carriers posted profits in the fourth quarter of 2003, with some of them marking their success by increasing earnings and traffic or instituting cost-cutting measures.

In general, the move toward discount airlines is invigorating the industry, with three airlines—Southwest Airlines, America West, and AirTran posting profits in the last quarter of 2003 and touting more customers. Some discount airlines are like JetBlue Airways, which serve many major destinations but cut costs by not serving traditional full-meal selections, among other practices. JetBlue also prizes itself on its stylishness, advertising its uniforms as "Pradaesque." JetBlue has been successful not only financially but in terms of customer satisfaction. In the 2004 Airline Quality Rating (AQR) study (based on 2003 data), JetBlue ranked number one in airline quality. It achieved that distinction for the first time in the first year it was large enough to be eligible for the study.

Other discount airlines are spinoffs of established airlines. Among them is Song, the discount arm of Delta Air Lines, which began service in 2003. In part, Song (and some other airlines) distinguishes itself through positive attitude and style. At its inception, Song marketed itself as being "[f]ounded by optimists and built by believers" and offering to "give style, service, and choice back to people who fly." Indicators of the company's sunniness are the friendly Song "talent" (or flight attendants) and roomy, brightly colored seats of blue, purple, green, and orange. Ultimately, Song plans to serve organic meals and equip planes with leather seats and individual screens for watching movies and accessing the Internet. In all, what with the gray-and-green Spade designer outfits, Song aims to be more hip than its competitor, JetBlue.

Still other discount airlines moderate prices by establishing their hub in smaller cities that have lower operating costs, such as lower enplaning charges. Examples include AirTran, which is based in Orlando, Florida, and Allegiant Air, which is consolidating its operations in Las Vegas. Many discount airlines establish themselves by serving more medium-sized and niche locations. For example, among Allegiant Air's destinations are Las Vegas and Des Moines, Iowa. Other discounters specialize in such medium-sized locations as Lansing, Michigan, and Fort Collins/Loveland, Colorado.

The added competition has spurred major airlines to cut fares and improve service. Aiming mostly at business travelers, Delta cut its most expensive fares by as much as 50 percent in January 2005. Several other major carriers quickly matched it, including American, Continental, Northwest, and United. The major airlines are also competing by eliminating the requirement for a Saturday-night stay over on most flights, a thorn in the side for many travelers. According to the 2004 AQR study, the 2003 overall industry Airline Quality Rating showed slight improvement over 2002.

The airline industry's plans for the future include research and development programs to promote good health while traveling. In one initiative, companies including Goodrich will develop an airline seat cushion that encourages proper seating posture and decreases pressure on the veins of the lower extremities that can result in deep vein thrombosis (DVT). To attend to less glamorous needs, airlines have pledged to adopt their own and government-mandated procedures to fight infectious diseases such as severe acute respiratory syndrome (SARS).

All is not rosy for the airline industry, which remains beset by troubles as well as promise. Jet fuel prices soared in 2004 and reached near-record highs in early 2005, hurting profitability. But the case of US Airways in the winter of 2004–2005 may inspire hope. Mired in bankruptcy and plagued by problems ranging from bungled baggage operations to mechanics threatening to strike, it has so far survived despite predictions of its imminent demise. The airlines fly on.

Conglomermedia

3 Over the past half century, many parts of the media industry have undergone great consolidation, reports *The Progressive*. Between the 1960s and 1980s, huge numbers of newspapers ceased publishing, and those that remained became owned by a handful of major chains. Similarly, the book publishing industry shrank in its number of publishers and owners. The major cable TV and music industries also became owned primarily by a few conglomerates.

Consolidation increased markedly during the past decade. Previous laws that had prevented television stations from producing their own shows, kept movie companies from owning their own theaters, and limited ownership of TV and radio stations within a market and within a family of owners were relaxed. As a result, television and radio stations are now owned by a handful of corporations and private individuals. In 2004 alone, NBC acquired the entertainment operations of Vivendi Universal, putting it in possession of a major movie studio and theme parks. As of 2005, the largest media players and their properties include:

- **Time Warner**—CNN, Warner Bros., Time, AOL, WB, TNT, HBO
- **Disney**—ABC, Walt Disney Studios
- **General Electric**—NBC, Universal, Telemundo, Bravo
- **News Corporation**—Fox movie and television, Fox News on cable
- **Viacom**—CBS, UPN, MTV, Paramount, Simon & Schuster

Some proponents of media consolidation pointed to the Internet as an answer to the concerns that the media would become a monopoly.

These proconglomeration businesses said that as the Internet grew as an information medium, it opened up the media market. Individuals could establish new media strongholds, which eroded the need to impose strict ownership rules on traditional media outlets.

Media owners also pointed to the increased threat of terrorism as a call to broaden media units. The media power used to cover terrorist events like the 9/11 attack was raised as evidence of a need for more conglomermedia. Consolidated media coverage was presented as a way of ensuring public service.

In reality, the Internet is pervasive, and it is a force in decentralizing the arts. But it does not yet have the media power of the major television and film outlets, so it is not equivalent competition with them. Further, the typical media conglomerate is less focused on providing public service with its media than it is with using all of its parts to generate revenue, say by producing a movie, and promoting it on its TV and radio stations, broadcasting the movie after its release, and making recordings related to the movie on its own label. This is what the Viacom/CBS matrix—which includes Paramount, CBS, Showtime, multiple TV stations, over 150 Infinity Radio stations, and Blockbuster Video—can do.

For years, various media critics have decried the increasing concentration of media ownership in the hands of a few corporations. In his 1989 book, *Culture Inc.: The Corporate Takeover of Public Expression*, Herbert Schiller called for active political involvement that would "aim at reducing private monopoly" over the media and discourage it from being a "salable commodity." He also hoped to see "public support and encouragement of noncommercial expression and creativity" to counter the commercial media. In recent years, these movements have not occurred and show few signs of developing.

Rather, over the past two decades, the U.S. government has hastened the trend of concentrated ownership of media outlets. Among its acts have been the passage of the business-friendly Telecommunications Act of 1996, and the 2003 FCC decision relaxing rules for corporate media ownership.

These June 2003 changes are sweeping. They include increasing the proportion of television stations that companies can own, from stations reaching a total of 35 percent of the U.S. population to stations reaching 45 percent. Companies can own more local TV stations; a company can own two in a five-station market and three in an eighteen-plus market. Companies can own newspapers or radio stations as well as TV stations in markets with nine or more TV stations. Companies can own up to eight radio stations in a 45-plus station market. In all, the FCC changes mean that in the largest cities, a company may own up to three television stations, eight radio stations, a daily newspaper, and a cable operator. The decision also allows the television networks to buy more stations.

Since then, however, the new FCC rules have been tied up in court. In January 2005, the Bush administration decided not to appeal a federal court ruling that rejected the rules. The decision was a blow to companies seeking greater media consolidation, but there were no signs they would stop lobbying and litigating for what they wanted.

Whether the American public cares about the control of the media by a few players is questionable. PBS reported on a study by the Project for Excellence in Journalism that showed that people aren't bothered by the prospect of most media outlets being held by a few hands. Unless the American public gets weary of overly similar programming and credits it to the shrinking circle of media owners, that circle will grow ever tighter. Imagine the nation's media outlets owned by a single conglomerate, such as AOLGeneral ElectricNewsCorporationTimeWarnerVivendiUniversalViacom—or AGENTVV.

Creative: Not a Dirty Word

4 Everyone praises creativity, but creative people have always had something vaguely disreputable about them. If someone who is not famous says he is an actor, artist, or writer, the implication is that this person is poor: the actor waiting on tables, the artist starving, the writer living in a garret. But the stock of creative people is rising as cities and businesses realize that money can be made from them. And the spectrum of people who are considered creative is getting broader—not just artists and writers but also scientists, academics, lawyers whose craft is designing tax shelters, and even managers who think "outside the box."

A greater premium began to be placed on creativity in the 1980s, when scientists, software engineers, and other knowledge workers began to be valued for driving fields such as biotech and information technology. At that time, the business world showered its appreciation on science, but not necessarily on the arts and humanities. Increasingly, however, the trend has been to value artists and humanists as drivers of economic growth.

Richard Florida, in his 2002 book *The Rise of the Creative Class*, theorizes that creative people are crucial to the modern economy because they produce new forms and designs that can be marketed and used widely, and because they think on their own, drawing on far-flung knowledge to solve new problems. They include a "super-creative core" of people who invent new forms, such as artists, writers, musicians, academics, scientists, engineers, actors, designers, architects, editors, analysts, and general opinion-makers. And they include "creative professionals" who solve problems creatively, such as financiers, managers, lawyers, and physicians. With the net thrown this wide, Florida counts 38.3 million creatives in the country, about 30 percent of the U.S. work force. Another book, *The Cultural Creatives* (2000) by Sherry Ruth Anderson and Paul H. Ray, puts the number of "Cultural Creatives" even higher, at 50 million. Anderson and Ray's criterion is somewhat different from Florida's: they view Cultural Creatives as a distinct subculture interested in things such as spirituality and personal growth.

How to count creatives, and whether their numbers are as big as these authors say, is open to debate. But it seems certain that creative people, however counted or grouped, are important to economic growth in today's fast-changing world. We live in an era of lowered trade barriers, globalized competition, and rapid technological development. In this setting, a country's economic standing rests not primarily on cheap labor or protection of old industries, but on new ideas and the ability to thrive in changing circumstances. As this fact becomes more widely recognized, creativity will continue its shift from being viewed as the opposite of moneymaking to a condition of it.

As Florida documents, creative people tend to cluster in certain kinds of cities: those with flourishing art and music scenes, interesting history, active nightlife, ample outdoor recreation, young people, and gays. The last may be surprising, until one considers that most creative people grew up feeling like outsiders, so they value places that welcome people of different persuasions, orientations, and lifestyles. Also, creativity is fueled by contact with different perspectives, so creative people tend to appreciate diversity and avoid conformity.

With this in mind, Florida has come up with a "Creativity Index" that ranks cities according to how many creative people live there, how much high-tech industry and patent innovation exists there, and how many gays live there (the "Gay Index"). The top large city for creatives turned out to be San Francisco, followed by Austin, San Diego, Boston, and Seattle. (Despite its reputation as a Mecca for artists, New York came in ninth.) Albuquerque, Albany, and Tucson were the top three medium-sized cities, and the top three small-sized cities were Madison, Wisconsin; Des Moines, Iowa; and Santa Barbara, California. Bottom-ranked cities included Memphis, Alabama; Youngstown, Ohio; and Shreveport, Louisiana.

Being a top city for creative cities translates into jobs and money. The leading 11 Creativity Index regions generated 2.32 million jobs between 1990 and 2000, nearly three times as many as the 850,000 jobs created by the 11 lowest-ranked regions. Between 1999 and 2002, the top-ranked regions added more than $100 billion in wages, five times the $20 billion added by the bottom-ranked regions.

As demand for the services of creative people rises, so does their price: creative class salaries are considerably higher than for working-class or service-class workers. David Brooks has wittily described the culture of at least some creative class members in *Bobos in Paradise: The New Upper Class and How They Got There* (2000). Brooks's term *Bobos* stands for "bourgeois bohemians," people who combine an artistic-idealistic worldview with a taste for the comforts of money.

Not everyone agrees with Florida's views on the creative class. Steven Malanga of the neo-conservative Manhattan Institute has argued that cities should focus principally on low cost-of-business, and that creative cities generate fewer jobs than less creative urban centers. Joel Kotkin says that political leaders should emphasize family values and suburban sprawl regions rather than trying to attract what he calls "homosexuals, sophistos, and trendoids."

Despite the critics, the clout of creatives is likely to rise. As it does so, look for cities and businesses to step up efforts to attract them, both with cultural/lifestyle amenities and hard financial incentives. But don't be surprised if many artists remain starving and many writers still live in garrets. The most genuinely creative people tend to care more about what they create than whether they can make money with it—which means that a lot of their creations will bring in little or no money. And since everyone has a novel in their drawer or a doodle on their phone pad, there will always be fierce competition among creatives, keeping down their price. There will be more demand for creatives, but probably also an undiminished supply.

Globalization Continues

5 Long an unstoppable juggernaut in world economics, globalization seemed in recent years more like a 97-pound weakling. Terrorism, war, slow growth, and international disputes hindered the continued integration of the world's economies into one big free-trade zone. Nevertheless, globalization has been making a comeback. Further global economic unification is inevitable, and there are signs that the pace of it is already picking up.

Globalization has been growing since the post–World War II era, when many countries realized that they could find mutual advantage in trading freely across national borders, with a minimum of tariffs, subsidies, and other government regulations aimed at protecting native industries. The European Economic Community, now the European Union, was formed to work for economic integration of Europe. The major world economic powers formulated the General Agreement on Tariffs and Trade (GATT) to encourage free trade; GATT ultimately gave rise to the World Trade Organization (WTO), in 1995. In the decades since World War II, technology made the world smaller, with jet airplanes, satellite communications, and the Internet facilitating the spread of ideas, people, and capital around the world. In the 1990s, with the Cold War ended and free trade driving economic growth in many countries, it seemed that nothing would stop the onward march of globalization.

Then 9/11 happened. The September 2001 terror attacks prompted the United States and other countries to place new restrictions on international travel and shipping. Security and war dominated summits of world leaders that once would have focused on trade issues. The world economy, already sluggish, sank further into the doldrums, and world trade and global capital flows went into decline. Politicians looked to protect jobs in their nation's own industries rather than shoot for a distant abstraction like globalization. And the United States, once the admired leader in globalization, became an object of global scolding because of various unilateral actions. In September 2003, WTO talks in Cancún, Mexico, collapsed. The breakdown derailed the WTO's self-imposed deadline of January 2005 for reaching a new global free-trade agreement. However, the WTO decided that talks would continue beyond the deadline, and the negotiation process has gone on.

Despite all the bad news and controversy, globalization is unlikely to stop growing. For one thing, it is already here, in spades. Further, globalization does not depend only on the trade agreements of governments, but more fundamentally on basic economic principles. As Bill Mann of Fool.com puts it, "people naturally gravitate toward buying the same goods at the lowest price available." It also depends on what Thomas Friedman, in his book *The Lexus and the Olive Tree: Understanding Globalization* (2000), calls the Electronic Herd—the faceless masses of investors, traders, and multinational corporations that every day shift funds, factories, and jobs to whichever country seems best equipped to produce goods efficiently at low cost. Since the Electronic Herd and the consumer preference for buying cheap are unlikely to go away, globalization is all but certain to continue growing, despite the best efforts of trade negotiators. Antiglobalization protestors who vocally oppose every round of free-trade talks because of the allegedly toxic effect of free trade on poor nations are also unlikely to stop it. At least some antipoverty groups will find it more productive to try to influence free-trade accords in ways that benefit the poor.

According to the 2003 A.T. Kearney/*Foreign Policy* magazine Globalization Index, globalization can even survive the ebb and flow of economic activity. Despite economic tough times worldwide, in 2003, the Index reports, "other aspects of globalization sustained their forward momentum. Political engagement has deepened, and levels of global personal contact and technological integration have continued to grow." Globalization should also be measured by the regional ties that countries form. In October 2003, for example, Singapore and Thailand urged their partners in ASEAN, the regional association of Southeast Asian countries, to work together for a common market—and announced that the two of them would move ahead in tandem if no one else cared to follow their lead.

A significant new power bloc is the Group of 20-plus or the Group of 21, conceived by India and Brazil and consisting of resource-rich, economically ambitious developing nations around the world. This coalition, which is committed to free trade and has a sophisticated sense of its own interests, exerted considerable influence at the Cancún meeting before the talks fell apart.

Most Americans approve of globalization. According to a survey by the Chicago Council on Foreign Relations, 56 percent say globalization is mostly good. And despite stumbles along the way, more countries around the world are getting savvy enough to want to increase globalization as well.

Making IT a Utility

6 Few people generate their own electricity or build their own telephone poles. Instead, they rely on utilities—companies that make big capital expenditures on behalf of large numbers of customers who pay for the use of their equipment. Until recently, information technology (IT) wasn't regarded as utility material. Businesses bought their own hardware and software systems and kept them up to date on their own. Now increasing numbers of businesses have decided that IT should be a utility—and companies are making money servicing them.

Whether it is called utility computing, adaptive enterprise, Pay-as-You-Go (PAYG) IT services, or simply on-demand IT, the IT utility model is a growing trend. A July 2004 report from strategy consulting firm Saugatuck Technology, "The IT Utility: The Future of the Data Center," says, "[T]he IT Utility is the predominant driving force for change in the data center over 2004-2010." According to Saugatuck research in

2004, nearly 20 percent of companies are using PAYG IT services and 37 percent expect to be using them within two years. Andrew Doyle, senior consultant, and Merv Langby, chief services analyst, IDC Australia, wrote in the October 2002 issue of *interaction*, "In the next decade we . . . expect that IT as a utility will become a generally accepted and deployed source of IT infrastructure management services."

In an IT utility approach, a company pays for use of computers but does not own the hardware or software outright. IT is available on an as-needed, as-used basis, including processing power, storage capacity, applications, and maintenance. The advantages for a business include not only reduced costs but greater flexibility as they grow and respond to a changing business environment. Firms are less likely to be stuck with an outmoded or unnecessary IT system that cost too much to get rid of, and more likely to gain a competitive edge by acquiring just the IT that is needed when it is needed. The IT utility approach helps companies improve productivity, manage risk, and optimize allocation of IT resources within the firm, so supply better meets demand. "This is the next sea-change in business computing," said Saugatuck senior program director Mike West, director of the PAYG research program.

Utility computing isn't for all companies. It yields the biggest returns for businesses with extremely variable infrastructure and application requirements. So far, large rather than small-to-medium companies have been quickest to embrace utility computing. Often, they use a hybrid model in which they combine both variable PAYG services and in-house IT resources. Yet not everyone has embraced this solution. "Buyers are not yet thinking about a hybrid model in which external PAYG resources seamlessly supplement in-house resources," said Michael Isaac, a senior program director at Saugatuck. Dan Farber wrote in *CNET Asia* in April 2003 that not every IT function benefits from utility computing: "[T]he trick is to figure out what functions need to be more closely managed and which can be treated like a commodity service."

Despite the attractions, there is resistance to utility computing on a number of grounds. Businesses fear for their security and privacy and do not want to become too dependent on a vendor. "When you hand control of your infrastructure to another company, you can really get burned," Joe Gottron, CIO, Huntington National Bank, Columbus, Ohio, told *CFO.com*. Users sometimes resist sharing resources across departments because they think their own department may lose control. Software vendors worry about the shift to pricing and delivery models that are not based primarily on up-front payments but on long-term annuity streams. IT employees worry that jobs will be lost—a fear exacerbated by a 2004 Gartner report that utility computing would add to the job losses already caused by outsourcing.

Companies offering IT utility services, such as Hewlett Packard and IBM, face problems of their own. One is how to meter the IT utility the way electric companies meter the power used by their customers. Many on-demand services bill their customers based on the number of employees using the service times a monthly rate per user. The agreements are often similar to leasing, though with greater flexibility. But greater precision in measuring IT usage and setting rates would be useful to both provider and customer. Companies such as Evident Software are in the business of helping vendors achieve such goals.

Whatever the problems, the IT utility approach is expected to grow rapidly in the next few years. In an August 2004 interview with *CIO Insight*, Saugatuck Technology Senior Strategy Consultant Jim Cassell said, "Over time, demand for an IT-Utility environment will increase rapidly, such that by 2008 the IT Utility will be the dominant new IT deployment model."

Networked Businesses

7 The traditional model for a business is a top-down hierarchy: a chairman, under whom is a president, under whom are senior vice presidents, under whom are more vice presidents, and so on all the way

down to the guy who sweeps the factory floor. When such a company wants to expand, it adds more factories, departments, and subsidiaries, all ultimately reporting to one big boss. This hierarchical business model is as old as the Egyptian pharaohs and will probably never go away completely. But in our wired, globalized era, it is now competing with the networked business model—and that model is increasingly beating it.

A networked business is one that makes its money through linkages with partners more than through in-house, top-down operations. A networked business keeps its overhead low; outsources tasks to specialists who can do them at low cost; acts as a hub of productive exchange (for example, between customers and vendors); takes advantage of modern technology to keep its network flowing; and ignores regional and national boundaries, cheerfully hiring contractors in Singapore while soliciting customers in Denmark from its base in Hoboken.

A prime example of a networked business is the online auction house eBay, which has become a huge success by facilitating exchanges between buyers and sellers of everything from paintings to computers. Unlike a brick-and-mortar auction house, it has no warehouse of dusty goods to maintain, no fast-talking auctioneers to pay; rather, it functions as a business-web or b-web, a networked business that links suppliers, distributors, customers, and commerce service providers via the Internet and other electronic media. Prices are set by moment-to-moment negotiations among buyers and sellers, rather than by a central agency. The result is a Web powerhouse, with total sales in 2004 of $3.27 billion, up 51 percent from the previous year.

In *Digital Capital: Harnessing the Power of Business Webs* (2000), by Don Tapscott, David Ticoll, and Alex Lowy, the authors argue that participation in b-webs is a necessity for surviving and thriving in the digital economy.

Networked businesses have been most visible in e-commerce, and for good reason. The essential fact about the Internet is that it is a network, a global linkage of computer networks sharing information electronically. As such, it is of interest to the burgeoning scientific field of network theory—and it is a huge opportunity to businesses that can take advantage of its radically decentralized structure. The best way to do so is for a company itself to become networklike, connecting to customers in this direction, to suppliers or service providers in that direction, leaving itself free to concentrate on whatever its core competencies might be.

But even companies whose main business is not Internet-related are increasingly discovering the benefits of a networked business model. In a 2002 report called *Networked Pharma*, the business information company Datamonitor predicted that, by 2015, networking would be the preferred competitive strategy for the pharmaceutical industry. This is a big claim, given that pharmaceutical companies are traditionally extremely hierarchical behemoths with huge capital investments in R&D and manufacturing. But Datamonitor argues that they will improve their productivity and profitability by networking instead. Ideally, the result would be a limber, responsive, and unbureaucratic company that is neither burdened with excess production capacity in times of slowdown nor limited by tight production constraints in times when business is booming.

No major pharmaceutical company is yet fully networked, but many have taken steps in that direction, for example, through partnerships with biotech companies and contract research organizations. In 1999, the drug giant Roche launched a "virtual" organization spinoff called Fulcrum Pharma Development that conducts trials of new medicines and takes the products to market by outsourcing all facets of the drug development process. It is at heart a project management team, coordinating up to 20 contractors per project while acting as the point of contact for its clients.

Networked business models vary greatly, from ones that are thoroughly or mostly decentralized to ones in which one company functions as the central leader but forms partnerships as needed. In years to come, successful new businesses will increasingly be fully networked ones, taking full advantage of globalized connections and a telecommuting work force. Meanwhile, older businesses will increasingly become networked, in whole or in part, just to stay competitive with the upstart business-webs around them.

Shrinking Offices

8 Do the walls at work seem to be closing in? Do you bang your knee more often? Do you have to squeeze ever closer to get past your colleagues? No, you are not getting heavier. Your office is shrinking. Offices across the country have been doing so for years, and there is no end in sight.

According to research reported by the International Facility Management Association (IFMA) in June 2004, the average amount of square footage per U.S. office worker declined continuously from 1994 to 2002. All groups surveyed lost space during that time, from technical professionals (12 percent) to middle managers (16.5 percent) to executives and upper management (17 percent). General clerical staff lost the least amount of space in percentage terms—only 4 percent—but since they started from the most cramped conditions they ended up in the tiniest amount of space: 66 square feet as compared to the lordly 239 square feet enjoyed by upper management. Another study says that companies in the 61 largest metropolitan areas fell from an average of 227 square feet per employee in the 1980s to 150 to 200 square feet at present.

"The shrinking office is not a myth, but a reality, and a clear sign of the economic times," said David J. Brady, president and CEO, IFMA. "As companies have been forced to downsize their workforces and tighten their belts, many also have had to examine the productivity level and dollar value of each square foot of space they own. This might mean more workers sharing less space as they parcel off some of their real estate assets."

The trend toward smaller offices is affecting many industries. Law offices are getting smaller. According to *New York Lawyer*, by September 2002 partner offices had fallen from more than 225 square feet to about 215 square feet.

The causes behind the shrinking office trend are complex. They include economic constraints, consolidation of real estate, and changes in the workforce. More people make their living as knowledge workers in creative roles who work nomadically in several locations. They may not be at their work stations all days, but may work from home, out in the field, or at the headquarters of several clients. This reduces the need for a large permanent space for each employee.

Even though offices are getting smaller, smart employers and forward-thinking designers do not want employees feeling like sardines. A smaller space can be positive if it allows workers to collaborate more freely. This can happen if the office design emphasizes areas where people meet and circulate, exchanging ideas informally and teaming up on projects. "There will be a greater importance on what is happening in the circulation spaces and the common areas," Don Goeman, vice president of design development, Herman Miller, told TFM in May 2004. "Most of the collaborative interactions happen—typically between two people, sometimes three people—in the circulation spaces of an environment." Many businesses are trying to achieve this kind of design—bright, attractive, collaborative—in a style that is known as new urbanism or we space. "New urbanism design is about having an eye for what a community needs over what an individual needs," said Goeman.

It is also important to break the link in workers' minds between space and status. Many companies are trying to do away with the notion that every promotion means more room. According to the *New York Times* in May 2004, ChevronTexaco in Houston planned to replace its wall-and-door offices with an "open plan" layout of cubicles. "In the past, space was used as a psychic form of compensation," Richard McBlaine, president for strategic consulting, Jones Lang LaSalle, told the *New York Times*. "To a large extent that's changed."

Another way of coping with shrinking offices is to design furniture and equipment to occupy less space. Allsteel offers a pedestal with a seat cushion on top, so it can serve both as a guest chair and a storage pedestal. Many offices are using flat screens instead of bulky computer monitors. In 2004, IBM released the ThinkCentre S50 Ultra Small, its smallest desktop ever, with a central processing unit about the size of a New York City telephone book.

Companies have been creative at coping with shrinking offices, but the trend cannot go on forever. Repetitive-stress injuries, costly to the employer, may increase if workers are too cramped. Employees squeezed into ever-tighter spaces will eventually seek more breathing room in other companies, which will mean that some firms will save space only to lose valuable employees. "They can't be pennywise and pound foolish," Louis Goetz, president of Group Goetz Architects, Washington, D.C., told *BusinessWeek Online* in December 2002. Ultimately, it is in the interest of both employer and employee to keep offices from shrinking out of sight.

The Sleep Industry

9 For millions of Americans, sleep deprivation is a chronic problem. For many businesspeople, it is an opportunity. There is a great deal of money to be made from all those sleepless nights and drowsy days, and the sleep industry is hard at work serving the needs of those sleepy people. According to the National Institutes of Health, more than 70 million Americans are sleep-deprived, and given current socioeconomic conditions, the sleep deprivation trend will probably continue.

Intense demands on our time are the biggest cause of mass sleeplessness. A competitive 24/7 economy insists that companies produce faster and more plentifully, and that translates into pressure on employees to work longer hours. The high cost of living forces many people to work overtime or hold two or more jobs. Students trying to get into college or keep pace once enrolled have to work late studying and doing homework. When it is time to rest, distractions abound—computers, the Internet, cell phones, satellite dishes, home entertainment centers. According to the National Sleep Foundation, 55 percent of people ages 18 to 29 stay up too late watching television or surfing the Web.

Chronic sleep deprivation can sicken and kill people, leaving them more prone to disease and shortening their lifespans. "There is a very dangerous immune system depression that occurs with chronic sleep deprivation," Dr, Peter Birrell, a sleep research expert at the University of New South Wales's School of Psychology, told the *Sydney Morning Herald* in October 2004. "You're more likely to come down with whatever is going around from trivial minor viral infections to major problems." Sleep deprivation is especially menacing on the road. In a September 2000 study in *Occupational and Environmental Medicine*, researchers in Australia and New Zealand reported that sleep deprivation can have some of the same dangerous effects as being drunk. Coordination, reaction time and judgment all suffer from lack of sleep, and 16 to 60 percent of road accidents involve sleep deprivation. The study found that people who drive after being awake for 17 to 19 hours did worse than those with a blood alcohol level of .05 percent, which is the legal limit for drunk driving in most western European countries.

The bright side for industry is that a nation of sleep-deprived people is a huge market for sleep aids. Hotels are positioning themselves as havens for drowsy drivers (as in the Drive Revived campaign from Baymont Inns & Suites) and mattress manufacturers are emphasizing the health benefits of a good night's sleep. Far-sighted employers are providing nap rooms, with recliners and mood music, for their drowsy employees and bringing in sleep experts to offer them tips on getting better rest at home. There are low-tech solutions, such as Red Bull and other high-caffeine drinks that make their money by promising people the jolt they need to get through their day. And there are high-tech solutions, including sleep disorder specialists and sleep centers designed to diagnose and treat problems. In September 2002, *www.devicelink. com* estimated the annual growth rate for continuous positive airway pressure (CPAP) treatment devices for sleep apnea as between 20 and 25 percent.

The sleep industry also includes drugs to help insomniacs sleep. This market is potentially huge: up to 30 percent of women and 20 percent of men take medicine to help them sleep. CFO David Southwell told the *Wall Street Journal* that, in terms of the potential market, sleep is "like depression before Prozac." There are plenty of pills vying to be the Prozac of sleep. In December 2004, the FDA approved a new sleeping pill, Lunesta, manufactured by Sepracor. It competes for the insomnia drug market with Ambien and Sonata. More sleeping pills are in the works, including indiplon from Neurocrine Biosciences and Pfizer. All of these drugs are part of a new generation of sleeping pills that, unlike older drugs, are not habit-forming and do not require larger and larger doses when taken over a long term. That allows doctors to prescribe them more freely without worrying about side effects.

Some experts think the nation's sleep crisis is overhyped. "If you have kids," Dr. Jerome M. Siegel, sleep expert and professor of psychiatry at UCLA, told *Mother Jones* in January/February 2005, "you go down to six hours of sleep a night and stay there for the next 10 years, but I haven't heard any evidence that parents live shorter lives or have more illnesses than others." Yet despite the skeptics, the sleep industry is likely to continue thriving for some time.

Venture Capitalists Are Back

10 Venture capital is mother's milk to a young company. Entrepreneurial firms depend on investments from venture capitalists (VCs) to sustain them until they can go public or be acquired. But for a long time start-up companies have been gasping for the missing milk. VCs drove the dot-com boom of the late '90s, and when the stock bubble burst in 2000, many of them retreated from the field. VCs became preoccupied with saving the struggling companies that could survive, or closing down those that could not. Investments in new companies went on the back burner, making venture capital hard to come by. Now VCs are ready again to take a chance on new companies—but they will do so in a smarter way. "When money became free then investment decisions become silly," one former dot-com executive told BBC News. Money is available again, but it is no longer free.

Today, VCs are likely to be increasing funding for new companies. In 2004, venture capital investments rose to an estimated $25 billion, according to the National Venture Capital Association (NVCA), an industry trade group. In 2005, NVCA president Mark Heesen predicted that many VCs would have fresh funds to invest and would be shifting to earlier-stage investing. They would be looking for the most promising new technologies and not worrying about exiting right away. "[V]enture capitalists have the opportunity to search for those seed, startup, and early stage companies that have the potential to truly change the way we live and work in the next decade—the future FedExes, Intels and Genentechs," said Heesen. Among the hot areas for VC investment: software, the life sciences, energy, clean technology, financial services, nanotechnology, and stem cell research. Even some companies that survived the dot-com crash will return to boost the VC industry by finally going public and allowing early investors to exit at a profit.

The availability of money for investment is driving the search for innovative new businesses. "VCs have been out raising money and they need to put that capital to work," Tracy Lefteroff, global managing partner of venture capital at PricewaterhouseCoopers in San Jose, Calif., told *Inc. Magazine*. Valuations are now likely to be more favorable toward entrepreneurs. There will be a great deal of competition among VCs to be the first to bring a new idea or technology to market—and a move into "stealth mode" to avoid tipping off the competition. "There will be some very exciting investments in highly innovative spaces in

2005—ones that will make a permanent impact on the U.S. economy," said Jim Breyer, managing general partner of Accel Partners and NVCA chairman. If that happens, the effect on the economy would likely be positive, since new company formation promotes economic growth. "VCs need to get behind new companies" to propel the U.S. economy, economist Alastair Goldfisher told *Venture Capital Journal* in 2005.

Some venture capitalists are even looking beyond startups to former startups. Garnett & Helfrich Capital specializes in carving out former technology startups that have been languishing inside the larger corporations that acquired them.

Yet there will be limits on the new funding. According to NVCA, VCs will be looking for breakthrough innovations and avoiding "me-too" deals. Good ideas will not be enough. "Gone are the days when ethereal ideas got seed money, just to flesh them out," said Lefteroff. "[E]ven startup companies had better have some meat on their bones if they are to attract venture capital."

Money will be more carefully allocated. "Businesses will see financing in smaller bids and will have to prove a concept before securing more," Stephen Spinelli Jr., an entrepreneurship professor at Babson College in Wellesley, Mass., told *Inc. Magazine.* It also helps to be in the right part of the country: investors these days prefer to be geographically close to their investment. Businesses in Silicon Valley and Boston will probably have a better chance at finding venture capital.

If companies are in trouble, VCs are likely to call in a specialist in helping troubled businesses, such as Martin Pichinson, president of Sherwood Partners in Los Angeles. Pichinson can renegotiate with creditors and do what is needed to reduce the burn rate, from layoffs to putting companies in "hibernation mode." If all else fails, Pichinson, who is sometimes known as Doctor Death, can shut down the company. "It is not nice to close a company down," he told the *Seattle Post-Intelligencer,* "but if there is no money left, we close it down in the kindest, nicest way possible."

II

Demographics

Bigger Families, Younger Parents

11 While birth rates are a far cry from a century ago, when the national average was five children, the United States is replenishing itself well. The reasons are immigration and faith-based and secular birth initiatives.

To begin, the United States is in the middle of an immigration boom. The 2000 Census revealed a foreign-born population of over 30 million, nearly half of whom arrived in the 1990s. In fact, since 1987, legal immigration has averaged about 1 million a year; plus, according to conservative estimates, about 400,000 illegal immigrants. An analysis by the Center for Immigration Studies shows that nearly 70 percent of the population growth between 1990 to 2000 was immigration-related. To put this into historical perspective, during the last great wave of immigration 100 years ago, about 850,000 people entered the country each year between 1900 and 1910. The current influx of immigrants parallels that era—which means hundreds of thousands of new births.

Some native-born Americans are also working to increase the population. In fact, they have made the increased propagation of their members a priority. In the *New York Times*, political and cultural critic David Brooks cites this move toward larger families as "natalism." He says that parents are having "three, four or more kids. Their personal identity is defined by parenthood . . . they [have] concluded that parenthood is the most enriching and elevating thing they can do."

Further, Brooks observes this move toward larger families as having a spiritual component. "[T]his is a spiritual movement, not a political one," he continues. "The people who are having big families are explicitly rejecting materialistic incentives and hyper-individualism. . . . These people are saying money and ambition will not be their gods." He notes that the move toward larger families is marked by families with more established attitudes. He explains, "People with larger families tend to attend religious services more often, and tend to have more traditional gender roles." He also finds the natalism phenomenon to be prevalent in less urban, noncoastal regions that do not contain high proportions of immigrants—or put simply, red states with high percentages of white populations.

As another thinker concludes, the regional increase in population serves politically conservative causes in America well. Says Joseph A. D'Agostino, vice president for Communications at the population Research Institute, a nonprofit organization dedicated to debunking the myth that the world is overpopulated, "The self-evident truth: the future belongs to those peoples and countries that are living out the pro-life, pro-family message."

Yet some ethnic groups, even some relatively recent immigrants, view the ideal family size differently. In many states with high Hispanic immigrant populations such as California, Texas, and Georgia, the second-generation families are turning away from larger families. Even in Georgia, the state with one of the highest family sizes, the average number of family members is 4.14. An Atlanta priest attributes it to the influence of American ways of life. Says Rev. Pedro Polche of the Cathedral of Christ the King in Atlanta, "Those Hispanics who have been here for a while . . . incorporate some of the American lifestyle. . . . Couples who get married and are so focused on their careers, they hold off on having children," he said. To the family members themselves, reasons are simpler. Said one second-generation Hispanic mother, "It's very difficult to have enough money for everything children need. You can take care of your children better if you have fewer of them."

While many groups champion increased population growth, others warn that the United States must level off its numbers to maintain adequate space and resources for the hundreds of millions already living here. There is worry that the nation will grow too fast. If growth persists at a 13 percent rate per decade as it did from 1990 to 2000, the U.S. will have 666 million people in 2070.

According to the Diversity Alliance for a Sustainable America and other groups, the United States cannot remain sustainable with that increase, and even legal immigration may need to be curtailed. Not only are more immigrants taking additional money for entitlement programs, they reduce farm and living space. According to Cornell University Professor David Pimental, if the U.S. continues to lose farm land at its current rates, by 2040, this country will not be able to export food.

Still, the country keeps growing. Whether fueled by a fear of a decreasing number of native-born Americans or the relatively high birth rates of immigrants of the United States, or a simple desire for more children, the trend is more Americans, many of them born to younger parents.

The Fattening of America

12 The United States is growing larger. It is not establishing a new state; its citizens are picking up excess pounds. In fact, the nation's people have increased their weight so much that the head of the U.S. federal health agency called it the country's top health threat. According to Dr. Julie Gerberding, the director for the Centers for Disease Control and Prevention, 65 percent of U.S. adults are either overweight or

obese. Poor diet and lack of exercise are far more likely to kill Americans than any biological threat, imported menace like anthrax or smallpox, or disease like SARS.

Yet, over the past few years, Americans have tried in some ways to eat more healthfully. They have reduced the overall fat in the national diet and have eaten less meat. Despite these changes, Americans have gained weight. Even supposedly active young adult Americans, who decreased their intake of dietary saturated fats and cholesterol over the past seven years, increased their average weight by 10 pounds.

This weight gain is reflected in a rising obesity rate. According to the federal government's Weight-control Information Network, 130 million (65 percent) of American adults aged 20 and up are overweight and 61 million (31 percent) are obese. That was a marked increase from 1994, when 33 percent were overweight and 23 percent were obese. Since 1991, the prevalence of obesity among American adults has gone up 75 percent.

Now for the truly bad news. Obesity is associated with an increased risk of heart disease, hypertension, some cancers, type 2 diabetes, and reduced life expectancy, among other health problems. According to a 2005 report from the American Heart Association (AHA), a 40-year-old, nonsmoking woman can expect to lose 3.3 years of life for being overweight, and 7.1 years if she is obese. A man the same age loses 3.1 years for being overweight and 5.8 years for obesity.

The major health problems are even affecting children. According to the AHA, almost 4 million children aged 6 to 11 and 5.3 million adolescents aged 12 to 19 were overweight or obese in 2002. Registered dietician Nadine Pazner says, "We're seeing heart disease in young people, high blood pressure in children, and what we used to call maturity-onset (type 2) diabetes showing up in people in their twenties and thirties. Even kids in high school are showing up with it."

To make things worse, obesity is increasing the national health budget, which the American public ends up paying for in increased taxes. Treating obesity-related health conditions costs individuals and the health care system about $39 billion annually.

Obesity has not just increased in the United States. According to Kelly D. Brownell, Ph.D., professor of psychology, epidemiology, and public health at Yale University, "[O]besity is on the rise in country after country, as each becomes more like America." In 1997, the World Health Organization declared a global obesity epidemic.

Causes for this increased weight are varied. Americans have unprecedented access to a poor diet—to high-calorie foods that are widely available, low in cost, heavily promoted, and good tasting. There is also the unending psychological allure of food. Says Dr. Margo Denke, associate professor of internal medicine at the University of Texas Southwestern Medical Center and researcher at the Center for Human Nutrition, "Food . . . fills a growing dissatisfaction with the depersonalization of America—food is a fabulous reward that never fails."

Another problem has to do with American thriftiness. Americans don't like to waste food, especially when it is served in restaurants. Add to that the fact that restaurants today are serving larger portions and that processed foods are getting to be a bigger part of the average diet. For example, a chain-bakery blueberry muffin is 430 calories and 18 grams of fat. Its size is about 6 ounces, while the USDA lists the typical medium-sized muffin as 2 ounces. Further, a recent study showed that people do not notice the changing size of their portions. They eat more of a larger portion, particularly when it is a junk food. This practice was verified in a study organized by the Food and Brand Research Lab at the University of Illinois at Champaign-Urbana.

Not only are Americans eating more, they are eating more quickly, and this increases the possibility for sustained weight gain. Instead of moderating the dining experience by eating at home or a restaurant at a table, it is now acceptable to eat anywhere. This can mean eating in a car, on the job, in a store, at the movies, or anywhere imaginable.

It can be frustrating for those who want to adopt a proper diet to even figure out what a healthy diet is. While most nutritionists advocate fewer processed foods, many debate the correct proportions of food types, primarily proteins, carbohydrates, and fats.

Exercise and restraint are necessary to maintain normal weight levels, says Dr. Brownell, because evolution will not do it for us. The environment has changed greatly over the past 200 years, he says, but evolution has not: "[I]t takes thousands or millions of years for evolution to catch up and change our ancient genes. The environment has changed way too quickly." People used to live in an environment where food was scarce. They managed by eating large quantities of high-calorie food when they found it. Now we live in a land of abundance, and we have to learn to adapt to it. He also suggests that we can improve our health by reforming the food industry. He suggests subsidizing healthful foods and increasing the cost of unhealthful foods. Greg Critser, author of *Fat Land*, a study of the "fattening" of the population of the United States, says that it might be useful to bring back gluttony as one of the deadly sins.

But such sanctions would subvert the nation's drive to create easy abundance. According to the Department of Agriculture, says Dr. Marion Nestle, Chair of the Department of Nutrition and Food Studies at New York University, "our food supply provides an average of 3,800 calories every single day for every man, woman, and child in the country. . . . And it's roughly twice what the average person needs." According to physiologist James O. Hill, getting fat is less an aberration than "a normal response to the American environment."

Honey, I Shrunk the Middle Class

13 Under the tax cuts put into law in 2003, the already wealthy have prospered and will continue to do so. The 1 percent of Americans living on investments or who have employment that pays more than $250,000 per year receive greater tax benefits than other Americans, and the 400 richest taxpayers, who in 2003 made an average $174 million each, stand to benefit even more. Assuming that the Bush tax cuts are made permanent, more than a quarter of the cuts will go to the top one-half of 1 percent, those making $581,000 a year or more. To apply the old adage, the rich will get richer.

For a variety of reasons, the middle class in the early 21st century will be slimming down their spending. In general, fewer people will have the components that made for 20th-century middle-class comfort, such as a job that pays the bills, a residence big enough for the family, the ability to pay medical bills, and leftover funds for a car or vacation.

This widening of the distance between the well-off and everyone else continues a pattern that has been going on for over a quarter of a century. One reason for the gap is education. A study by the nonprofit Economic Policy Institute, a think tank in Washington, D.C., reported that nationally from 1973 to 1977, wages of workers with advanced degrees rose 6 percent above the inflation rate. Incomes of those with college degrees remained nearly steady, and wages of those with only a high school diploma fell 14 percent against inflation.

Linked to the increasing erosion of wages for workers without advanced degrees is the decrease in well-paying blue-collar jobs. Traditional blue-collar jobs that require little educational training job, such as manufacturing in heavy and light industry, have declined over the past quarter-century and will continue to decline over the next decades. Service jobs at all levels will increase, but most bring low salaries: an average store cashier earns $15,000 per year, without health benefits.

Not having health benefits can immediately increase costs for the uninsured. Not only do the uninsured have to pay for doctors' services, they pay higher rates than insurance companies. Particularly in hospitals, uninsured patients pay "gross charges," or list prices for medical services. Insured people get a discount from the negotiations of their insurance companies or government health programs (Medicaid, Medicare), which pay reduced rates to medical professionals, while hospitals charge uninsured people the full rate. With medical costs increasing much faster than pay raises, and with an aging population requiring more forms of medical treatment, it will be increasingly difficult for average Americans to fit medical costs into the middle-class budget.

Many other factors challenge the accepted middle-class way of life. For example, statistics show that college and advanced degrees usually result in higher salaries. But the cost of college and graduate school education, which many employers deem necessary, is increasing in cost by double-digit percentages each year. Because of increased state mandates and a highly expanding college-age population, even the usually less expensive state schools will increase tuition and yet be unable to serve all applicants in the traditional classroom educational experience. Private colleges may become prohibitively expensive for all but the well-to-do, as they had been in generations past.

Ballooning housing costs, shrinking pension plans (with uncertainty about Social Security reform), and the general rise in the cost of living also present threats to the new modern middle class. From this point early in the 21st century, it seems the great shrinking game for the bottom 99 percent of Americans has just begun.

Multicultural People

14 What do Vin Diesel, Tiger Woods, and Hispanic census figures have in common? All testify to the transformation of America from a society that is assimilationist and racially divided to one that is multicultural but perhaps less racially divided.

For most of U.S. history, the population fell into two main categories: white and black. According to the U.S. Bureau of the Census, white people were the vast majority, peaking at 90 percent from 1920 to 1950, with blacks making up most of the remainder. Asians in those days constituted less than half a percent, and Hispanics weren't even counted. White people weren't all from one country, of course; many were recent immigrants. But most of them came from Europe, and were expected to quickly abandon their native cultures and adopt a more or less uniform American one. They were expected to learn English, like baseball, honor George Washington, and believe in the Constitution and the Judeo-Christian tradition. The universality of the American way was marred mainly by segregation, which in the days before the civil rights era kept the black population apart and below. America was a melting pot, with blacks in a separate pot.

But a funny thing happened on the way to the 21st century. In the last 50 years, immigration from Europe declined while immigration from the rest of the world soared. Latin America, in particular, contributed vast numbers: nearly half of the foreign-born people in the United States today are from Hispanic countries. The Asian-American population also mushroomed, increasing more than thirtyfold, while the U.S. population as a whole grew by less than twofold. The African-American population grew more quickly than the white population, but neither grew as quickly as either Asians or Latinos. The result is that Asian-Americans are now 4 percent of the population, and Hispanics, at 13.7 percent, now surpass blacks as the country's biggest minority group. Meanwhile, in the past 50 years, whites have fallen from being 90 percent of the population to being only 75 percent. In another 50 years, estimates are that whites will make up barely more than 50 percent of the population. Soon after that, the United States will no longer have a clear majority race, but only an assortment of minorities. According to U.S. Census Bureau projections, Hispanics will constitute 24 percent of the nation's population by 2050 and Asians will constitute 8 percent.

As this trend accelerates in the coming years, many people fear the Balkanization of America. As universities expand their "Asian Studies" and "Latino Studies" departments, there is concern that children will be less likely to grow up with positive views (or any views) about George Washington and the Constitution. Islam and Hinduism are spreading, and a growing number of Americans don't even speak an Indo-European language, much less English.

However, in his book *The Monochrome Society* (2001), sociologist Amitai Etzioni offers reason to think that any fears about America's growing multiculturalism are unnecessary. Numerous surveys show that despite the demographic changes of the past 50 years, Americans of all races and ethnicities share basic values and beliefs, including a commitment to the American way. As far as basic attitudes go, says Etzioni, "[w]e are much more a monochrome society than a rainbow society." For example, one poll asked Americans whether high school students should "be required to understand the common history and ideas that tie all Americans together." Not only did 85 percent of all parents say yes, but foreign-born parents (88 percent) and Hispanic parents (89 percent) were even *more* likely to say yes. Far from refusing to learn English, foreign-born parents are more likely than the population at large to want schools to teach English to their children as quickly as possible. In most surveys of opinion on current issues, there is more similarity than difference among Asians, Latinos, blacks, and whites.

Demographic change is not likely to make the country fly apart. What it is likely to do—and is already doing—is introduce Americans to previously little known cultures. (Globalization and the Internet are helping, as trade and communication with other countries proliferate.) In recent years, music by Latino artists has gone from marginal to mainstream—with Jennifer Lopez, Ricky Martin, and Christina Aguilera all becoming household names. After 9/11, sales of books about Islam shot up, as Americans took notice—more often curious than hostile—of the growing population of Muslims in their midst. In 2002, *Flower Drum Song* was revived on Broadway, with an entirely new script that erased the stereotypes of 40 years ago and showed a new, richer understanding of Chinese-American history. That same fall, Deborah Treisman came on board as fiction editor at the staid *New Yorker* magazine, expressing her preference for voices from less well-known cultures.

While no less loyal to their adopted country than previous generations of immigrants, the new immigrants are more likely to celebrate and want to preserve their ethnic heritage. The United States less resembles a melting pot than a salad bowl now, with numerous ingredients retaining their flavor while contributing to the mix. Numerous businesses are making money by selling to ethnic markets within the United States. Witness the enterprises that are thriving by serving just the Hispanic market—everything from Goya Foods to the Telemundo and Univision television networks to the periodicals *El Diario* and *Latina*.

With all these changes happening, the question of racial identity is likely to become more complicated, and perhaps less important. Is golf champion Tiger Woods Asian-American, African-American, or what? Essentially, he is whatever he wants to be. Hispanics are not a distinct race at all: the U.S. Census Bureau notes that they can be of any race, and many Hispanics are a biological mix of European and Native American genes, often with African ones thrown in. Fifty years ago, being black almost always entailed being poor, but now there is a growing black middle class that is statistically likely to share the views and buying habits of the rest of the middle class. Furthermore, Americans of all races and ethnicities are more likely than ever to marry outside their group: since 1970, the number of such marriages has increased by 72 percent. More than 40 percent of third-generation Asian-American women, for example, marry non-Asians.

Expect more Americans in the coming years to identify themselves as multiracial or multicultural. Actor Vin Diesel gave himself the "multicultural" tag in publicity interviews in 2002, when he won box-office success as a new, rougher-edged, racially vague kind of movie spy in *XXX*. The ranks of celebrities increasingly abound with multicultural people, such as singer Michelle Branch and actress Kate Beckinsale, both Eurasian. On the Internet there are interracial dating services and online multiracial communities. Greater diversity without greater division: that is the wave of the future for America's ethnic groups.

World Population: Slowing Growth

15 Over the past 50 years, the world's population rose at a hectic pace. Global population soared from 2.8 billion people in 1955 to 6.4 billion in 2005. Throughout most of the 20th century, the world population increased each year by about 2 percent. At that rate, the population would reach 10.6 billion by 2025. By 2600, the 2 percent growth would mean a population of 6.3 trillion, an amount that would leave barely enough room for any human to turn around. If the problem of space did not occur, a lack of food would. In the book *The Population Bomb*, author Paul Ehrlich posited that the population was increasing at such a high rate that there would not be enough food to feed everyone.

Studies now show that neither of these scenarios is likely to occur. The planet Earth is not likely to have the rapid population growth it had in the 20th century. According to the U.S. Census Bureau, the world population in 2050 is expected to be only 9.2 billion, with an average annual growth rate at that time of about 0.5 percent.

Reasons for the decline in the rate of population growth are varied. A primary reason is the increase in HIV/AIDS. According to a recent U.N. report, the countries most affected by AIDS will have half a billion fewer people in 2050 than had been projected. Another reason for lower world population is decreased fertility. In the last two decades of the 20th century, fertility dropped by 1.5 births per woman. In most advanced countries, the birth rate is under the replacement rate of 2.1 births, the rate necessary to keep population stable. The birth rate in developing countries has also declined, from 6.3 to 2.9. Generally, the decline in non-AIDS related birth rates can be traced to the families' increased affluence and/or family planning.

The United States is the only developed country expected to increase its population; this increase will be due to immigration. Aside from the United States, all population growth sites over the next 50 years will be developing countries. They include Bangladesh, China, Congo, Ethiopia, India, Nigeria, and Pakistan.

Overall, the increase in world population over the next decades will come largely from the world's poorest countries. According to the World Bank Group, the next billion of the world's population over the next fifteen years will include nearly 600 million from low-income countries. About 375 million will come from middle-income countries, and high-income countries will add 30 million, or 3 percent.

Geographically, the population increase in these areas breaks down as follows, according to the World Bank Group:

- **South Asia**—310 million
- **Sub-Saharan Africa**—230 million
- **East Asia and the Pacific**—220 million
- **Middle East/North Africa/Latin America/Caribbean**—230 million
- **Europe and Central Asia**—9 million
- **High-Income Countries**—30 million

A 2001 study, published in *Nature*, forecasts a possible scenario of the world population rising to 9 billion in 2070, and dwindling afterward. The study "The End of World Population Growth," by Wolfgang Lutz, Warren Sanderson, and Sergei Scherbov, argues that there is about an 85 percent probability that the world's population will stop growing before the end of the century. The study presents a model of aging populations and ultimately decreasing numbers for the most modernized societies. Meanwhile, population rates in the countries of the Southern Hemisphere are projected to increase, resulting in substantial population redistribution. Commenting on these projected changes, John Bongaarts of the New York–based Population Council says, "The world is becoming less European, less white, less North American."

According to the World Bank, every minute 380 women worldwide become pregnant. Most of these pregnancies and births will occur in developing countries, while births in developed countries will continue to decline. According to the United Nations Population Division, 44 percent of the world's population already lives in countries where the fertility rate is below the replacement level. How these countries change and coexist will define the new world for the 22nd century.

III

Entertainment and the Arts

Decentralized Art

16 In the 20th century, New York was the center of publishing, theater, and the fine arts, and Los Angeles was the center of the film and pop music industries. But as the 21st century wears on and technology improves, both high and low arts are breaking away from traditional geographic centers. We have entered the age of decentralized art.

New technology has been the most important factor in driving this trend. Digital cameras, desktop publishing, the Internet, and other innovations are rapidly changing the two halves of any living art: production and distribution.

In most arts, production has traditionally been the cheaper of the two halves; writing, for example, requires nothing more than paper and pencil, whereas publishing requires printing presses, warehouses, and a sales force. But in some arts, even production costs can be high; the typical Hollywood film, for example, costs tens of millions of dollars to make. Enter new technology: digital video can drastically lower filmmaking costs, making it easier for movies to be made outside of Hollywood. Mike Figgis, who filmed *Time Code* on digital video in 2000, said, "It's beyond imagination what this is going to do to filmmaking. What has been an exclusive medium of high finance, banking and financial exclusivity is now going to become something that is within reach of everyone."

Technology is also decentralizing the distribution half of the arts. The Internet has made it possible in principle for everyone to be a publisher, art gallery owner, record company, and movie exhibitor. By posting pictures on the Internet, a painter in Montana can exhibit her works to as large a potential art-buying audience as one in Manhattan. A writer can attract more readers on a popular online literary journal than in some print ones. Film distribution on the Internet is still in its infancy, because high-quality digital prints of feature-length films come in huge files, difficult to transmit electronically. But producers of short films are increasingly in demand on the Web, and several low-budget, non-Hollywood films have gone on to surprisingly big box-office returns on the strength of Web publicity (most memorably, *The Blair Witch Project* in 1999).

Podcasting is another form of decentralized art made possible through technology. Podcasters use a computer to record an audio show and post it to a Web site from which listeners can download the program to an iPod or MP3 player. A form of do-it-yourself radio, the popularity of podcasts has been growing quickly, with subjects from fishing and wine to music and religion (nicknamed "Godcasts").

Technology has even affected the link between production and distribution in a way that promotes decentralization. In previous periods, because long-distance travel and communication were slow and expensive, the best way to achieve access between writers and publishers was by placing them in physical contact. Hence, the arts tended to cluster in one or a few locations—publishers in New York and movie studios in Hollywood. But the widespread availability of e-mail, cell phones, and express shipping means that a writer in New Mexico and an illustrator in Florida can easily collaborate with a publisher in Dublin, who can outsource distribution to a global sales force. Though most of the major trade publishers are still in New York, other publishers can increasingly be found elsewhere, including religious and health publishers (Health Communications in Florida, Tyndale House in Illinois). Hollywood itself is barely located in Hollywood anymore: many big-budget American movies today are filmed in Vancouver or eastern Europe, often with foreign financing and aimed heavily at foreign audiences.

Technology is not the only factor encouraging decentralized art. Cities throughout the world have realized the importance of the arts in promoting economic development. The arts attract creative people who drive economic growth and bring in tourism and recreational dollars. From Bilbao, Spain, where the Guggenheim Museum has spurred revitalization, to Detroit, Michigan, now sporting a new symphony hall, city planners are looking to the arts for urban renewal. One effect of this trend is to increase the number of the world's artistic centers, further decentralizing the arts.

Is decentralization a good trend for the arts? With millions of Web sites in the world, would it increase the world's total aesthetic merit if each Web-site owner posted his own poems/films/yodeling for the world to enjoy? Maybe not—but then nobody is going to wade through all those millions of galleries in search of the rare gems. There will always be a need for critics, reputable publishers, hoary museums, and name-brand conglomerates to serve as filters directing audiences to artwork they are likely to enjoy. Corporations that are in the filtering business (such as movie studios) usually have deep pockets for marketing and distribution, and all that money will serve as a brake on decentralization, persuading even an upstart artist to sign with a big record label or movie studio. But even in the filtering side of the arts, decentralization is taking place. Movie fans are now as likely to look for guidance to someone like Harry Knowles—publisher of the independent movie-criticism Web site Ain't It Cool News (*www.aintitcoolnews. com*)—as to TV ads or reviews in major newspapers.

Despite the benefit decentralization brings—most notably, bringing art to more people in more geographic locations—something of value might be lost in the process of breaking up old geographic centers of art such as New York or Los Angeles. A side effect of centralization was the aesthetic cross-pollination that resulted from having artists living close together, debating over coffee and swiping ideas from each other's studios. But the Internet makes possible a digital version of this effect, as artists debate in chat rooms and swipe from each other's Web sites. Meanwhile, decentralization encourages the rise of new regional centers of the arts, such as Austin, Texas. As artistic decentralization continues, many other locations will soon join Austin.

Digital Hollywood

17 Hollywood may have a taste for novelty, but in its basic technology, it has long opted for something exceedingly old. Since the invention of the movies more than 100 years ago, the cinema has relied on the same equipment: chemical emulsion on celluloid film. But in the biggest cinematic revolution since the advent of talkies, that equipment is now being replaced by digital technology: technology based on the conversion of information into ones and zeroes.

This transition has been happening in every phase of the movie business, though not all at the same pace: the shooting of movies (production); the fine-tuning of movies with special effects and editing (postproduction); the dissemination of movies from studios to theaters (distribution); and the showing of movies to paying audiences (exhibition). Most movies are still shot on 35 mm celluloid film, which has a depth and richness that until recently was difficult to attain with other formats.

In postproduction, the pace of change has been faster. Even movies that are made on 35 mm film are now routinely digitized so they can be more easily edited and spruced up with special effects. Editors now rearrange digitized pieces of film on computers, rather than having to fuss with physical snipping and cementing of celluloid. Digital effects have transformed special effects in ways both obvious and invisible. Everyone knows that the Hulk is a computer-generated creature, but when a car is digitally erased from the background of a medieval epic, only the filmmakers know about it.

The slowest transition has been in distribution and exhibition. Even though movies are regularly digitized in postproduction, they are just as regularly converted back into old-fashioned celluloid prints for shipping to theaters and projection on movie screens. The studios would love to save money by releasing their movies to theaters as digital files sent via satellite or network lines; however, the vast majority of theaters are not yet equipped with digital projectors. At current prices, converting a screen to digital projection costs about $150,000. True, the theaters might gain bigger audiences if digital projection turns out to be a draw. But that gain may not be enough to offset the cost of conversion. Since the studios are the ones that stand to save the most money (right now, they spend $1.36 billion a year to produce and distribute celluloid prints worldwide), exhibitors say the studios should pay for the conversion. Still, many experts think the transition to digital distribution and exhibition will be complete by 2010, if not sooner.

For the film industry, the shift to Digital Hollywood presents both risks and opportunities. When the day comes that movies are routinely shipped as digital files, piracy may become as big a problem for film studios as it now is for the music industry. Already the studios are working on encryption systems and other techniques to protect digital products from being stolen.

Theater owners will get a windfall by using their digital projectors not only to show movies but to present souped-up ads before the movies (goodbye, old-fashioned slide shows; hello, digital displays) and offer videoconferencing. The nation's biggest theater chain, Regal Entertainment Group, is already doing that with digital projectors in many of its theaters.

Film producers may benefit more than anyone from Digital Hollywood if they can eliminate their greatest source of tension on the set: actors. The 2002 film *SIMONE* imagined the rise of a computer-generated star who looked fully human, got rave reviews, but demanded no salary, limo, or air-conditioned trailer. At present, even fantastical computer-generated creatures, such as Gollum in the *Lord of the Rings* movies, require human actors to supply their voices and block out their movements. Still, filmmakers are taking small steps to supplement human performances with digital ones, and producers are increasingly replacing or supplementing real sets with computer-generated ones. The 2004 blockbuster *The Polar Express* was notable for its complete reliance on both digital actors and digital sets. Coming attractions: Hollywood continues to go digital.

Do-It-Yourself Entertainment

18 People have long had home equipment with which to entertain themselves, from the family piano to the radio, stereo, and TV. But in recent years, home entertainment centers have become ever more elaborate and versatile: able to provide dazzling shows once reserved for theaters and concert halls. This is the age of do-it-yourself entertainment.

At the center of most home entertainment complexes is the television. The development of high-definition television (HDTV), plasma TVs, and LCD sets has made television more appealing, with larger screen size, better image quality, and less bulkiness. These innovations will become even more widespread as prices continue to fall; HDTV sets, for example, will soon bridge much of the price gap that separates them from conventional sets. Every home entertainment center needs peripherals for the TV: a DVD player, a VCR, perhaps a TiVo or digital video recorder (DVR) to record shows. The up-to-date home entertainment center will probably have great stereo sound, with a CD player that takes advantage of that sound to play music.

Though one room is typically the heart of a home entertainment center, the circulatory system of that center may spread throughout the house. In many cases, the entire home is becoming wired for entertainment. People are making it so they can listen to their digital music collection from anywhere in the house, or even programming some rooms for one kind of music and other rooms for other kinds. Video images and photographs can similarly be broadcast wherever there is a monitor.

Some people establish a genuine home theater, using a rear projection TV or a video projector that projects a super-sized image from the front. When done well, such a room gives all the pleasure of a real movie theater without the expensive concession stand. Katie Hafner of the *New York Times* set up a home theater in her garage for under $3,000, and after much ado with wiring and contracting, concluded in a May 2004 article, "[I]nstalling a home theater yourself is no trivial undertaking."

The only serious rival to the television as home entertainment center is the computer. According to a 2003 poll conducted by Harris Interactive Inc. for Microsoft Corp., nearly half of those surveyed said their computer is more important than their television (43 percent). Almost two-thirds said their computer is more important than their CD player (63 percent), stereo (61 percent), or DVD player (59 percent). "We were blown away with the number of people who are using the computer as their center of entertainment," said Hal Quinley, group president, Harris Interactive. "These results indicate people look to their computer as a TV, DVD player, stereo, and CD player combined." The poll also showed that people are more likely today to move their computer out of the office and into social rooms such as living room or den (63 percent). Of those polled, 28 percent use a computer in the living room specifically.

The computer industry is capitalizing on consumers' increasing interest in computer as show place. Manufacturers such as Dell and Gateway are embracing the idea of the "digital living room" as a way of expanding their market. In 2005, Hewlett Packard released its digital entertainment center, which, said Michael Stroud of AlwaysOn-Network.com, "fits neatly into an AV rack, replaces a DVR, DVD, CD player and two TV tuners, and can store an entire music, video, and photo collection on its massive hard drive." Though the product is expensive, less costly competitors are likely to emerge soon, pushing down prices. According to analyst Tim Bajarin of Creative Strategies, quoted by Stroud, there may soon be cheaper, more dedicated digital entertainment centers that will have some PC components (for example, high-speed processor, hard drive, and TiVo-like capabilities) but will be priced much lower than what is currently available.

As the computer becomes more central to home entertainment, people will increasingly edit or create that entertainment on the computer itself. People are already burning CDs and DVDs, editing photographs, and making movies with digital video. If there are budding filmmakers in the house, they may not restrict their productions to viewings in their own house, but seek some kind of distribution and release—for example, selling DVDs of the film online and mailing them to buyers. Thus their movies, created in a home theater, can end up showing in other people's home theaters.

Pirates of the Internet

19 The word pirates conjures up images of 17th century rogues, sailing in black-painted ships, armed with cutlasses, boarding Caribbean ships and relieving them of treasure chests. But 21st-century pirates are likely to be armed not with cutlasses but computers. The treasure they steal is likely to be digitized information, and the pitching sea on which they find it is the Internet. Nor are these pirates adorned with savage-looking eye patches. They are likely to look like suburban teens, or perhaps the reader of this book.

So far, digital pirates have become best known for stealing music. Using file-sharing software such as KaZaA, LimeWire, Morpheus, and BearShare, about 60 million Americans have downloaded music free-of-charge on the Internet and traded it with other pirates. (The phenomenon is also called peer-to-peer, or P2P, networking.) File-sharers are unlikely to see what they are doing as wrong: Sonya Arndt, a fourteen-year-old pirate in California, told the *New York Times*, "It shouldn't be illegal. It's not like I'm selling it." Music companies and recording artists have another view: record labels are suffering from the loss of sales, performers from the loss of royalties. In September 2003, the empire struck back, as the Recording Industry Association of America (RIAA) sued 261 people for up to $150,000 per song for allegedly downloading music illegally. The strategy certainly intimidated the people who were sued, but it also gave a public relations black eye to the recording industry, which looked like a cyber-age bully, trying to shake millions of dollars out of middle school students. However, the music industry has continued the campaign, suing thousands more computer users in the years since.

Digital piracy is already spreading to other areas. For piracy to exist, all that is needed is a valuable commodity regularly conveyed along a poorly protected route. In the 21st century, the poorly protected route is the Internet, and the valuable commodity is digital information: music, movies, TV shows, software, corporate secrets, bank accounts, and war plans. As more types of data are routinely shuffled through electronic networks (or can be easily uploaded onto a network), and as the technology for getting to the data becomes more widely available, the opportunity for piracy increases.

Hollywood movies are a prime example. Until recently, a digital file containing a high-quality, feature-length film has been too big and cumbersome for the ordinary home PC user to download. But as broadband and compression technologies become better and more widely available, consumers are increasingly swapping free movies as easily as they had been swapping free songs. According to a 2004 survey by online research company OTX, nearly one in four Internet users had illegally downloaded a movie online, prompting the Motion Picture Association of America to warn against a "growing global epidemic" of movie piracy over the Internet.

Like the music industry, future victims of digital piracy are likely to crack down with detective work and legal action, but that will probably only fuel technological efforts to evade detection and legal vulnerability. In 2002, the music industry succeeded in shutting down the file-sharing system Napster, which used a central index server that made it vulnerable to a lawsuit. But another generation of file-sharing programs, such as LimeWire and BearShare, sprang up to take its place, and these did not use central servers. Some, such as Blubster, use encryption software, circuitous routes through proxy servers, and other technological tricks to make it harder for the music industry to find and identify pirates. Some pirates are resorting to darknets, private file-sharing networks that are difficult for outsiders to crack.

With digital pirates always improving their armaments, perhaps the best way to battle them is to join them, by helping anyone who wants digital commodities to get them in the cheap and easy online format that makes piracy attractive. Apple's iTunes Music Store is doing strong business by offering legally downloadable songs at low prices. Low price is still more expensive than free, but many consumers will pay a small premium for legality, especially if the sellers throw in greater convenience and service.

Then there is the prospect of an entirely new business model: the recording industry could continuously offer all its songs to all comers, so that anyone with an Internet connection can hear any song, anytime, in streaming audio. The price would have to be right, and a system for collecting fees and distributing the proceeds would have to be developed, but if such a system evolved, music piracy might become as obsolete as Caribbean pirates stealing pieces of eight. To battle their own pirates, movie studios and other purveyors of digital goods will have to come up with their own solutions. In the meantime, the pirates of the Internet will probably continue to sail the digital seas.

Stop the Presses—No More Newspapers!

20 The institution known as the daily newspaper is in danger. Most people do not buy or even read the morning or evening paper anymore. According to a study by the founder of *American Demographics Magazine*, the decline has been occurring for 20 years. In 1985, 63 percent of 25- to 34-year-olds bought newspapers. By 1995, that figure had fallen to 56 percent. By 2000, it had plummeted to 35 percent. Findings indicate that people may buy occasional or Sunday newspapers, but not daily papers. According to a 2004 study done through Columbia University's Graduate School of Journalism, English-language newspaper circulation has declined 11 percent since 1990. "We're in a period of change and dislocation," said Tom Rosenstiel, director of the study.

Owing to decreased readership and lower profits, the number of newspapers has decreased. Recent numbers put the number of dailies at about 1,400, from a high of about 2,500 a century ago. In addition to lower revenues and reduced staff, there are specific markers of the decline in newspaper publication. One is the reduced number of high-quality enhancements, such as the in-house editorial cartoonist. As of 2004, there are perhaps 90 full-time editorial cartoonists on U.S. dailies, which represents a decline from a 20th-century peak of more than 200 cartoonists.

To stem further reductions, newspaper editors and owners are attempting to adapt the format to attract more readers. Some newspapers have ceased publishing newsprint copies and instead appear only online. Other newsstand newspapers charge for online access; some, like the *New York Times*, charge per back issue article. In that way, newspapers turn the Internet into a private pay library.

Another move is to produce free newspapers targeted to a specific audience, such as commuters. As of early 2005, there are examples in New York City, Philadelphia, and elsewhere. As explained in material from *Metro*, a Philadelphia free daily, the idea of a free newspaper targets people who are not regular newspaper readers, but who may respond to a reduced-size paper that has an easy-to-follow (and carry) tabloid format. As the *Metro* information sheet says, focus groups revealed that people do not like the process of carrying the newspaper to the garbage for pickup. The lighter tabloid will save trips to the trash bin.

Tony Ridder, chief executive officer of the Knight-Ridder chain, reports that his company may launch tabloid editions of its papers, which include the *Miami Herald* and the *Philadelphia Inquirer*, and also free editions. Said Ridder: "We think that a tabloid size has a lot of appeal, and there's a track record in various places that indicates that really works and can boost circulation." For example, tabloids would counter traditional newspapers, like the *Washington Post*, which has seen a 15 percent falloff in its circulation over the past decade, to just over 700,000 on weekdays.

Despite efforts to reinvent the medium, the newspaper may be doomed. Writing for TechCentral Station, an online forum on technology and markets, economist Arnold Kling deemed the numbers so grim he predicted "the newspaper business is going to die within the next 20 years. Newspaper publishing will continue, but only as a philanthropic venture."

Kling's concern was triggered by data from the Newspaper Association of America (NAA), which calculated spending on newspapers by age group. The highest spending relative to the general population came from 65- to 74-year-olds, who spent 136 percent of the national average on newspaper subscriptions or single-copy purchases. The lowest spending on newspapers came from the 18- to 24-year-olds, who spent just 25 percent of the national average. Catering to the interests of young adults is not likely to improve the newspaper as a source of information about the day's events. For a recent MTV poll on young adults and newspapers revealed that 18- to 24-year-old respondents did not read newspapers because they focused on politics rather than music, which was their main area of interest.

Indeed, most advocates do not suggest reforming the newspaper to fit a demographic group. Instead, they promote the teaching of reading in the primary grades. It is believed that once students become able readers, the desire to read newspapers will follow. But it is a long road to literacy. Perhaps even more chilling was an analysis done by the Paris-based Organization for Economic Cooperation and Development (OECD). Among 18 industrialized nations, OECD found, the United States ranked dead last in the literacy of 16- to 25-year-old high school graduates who did not go on to further study. Six in 10 of the high school graduates read below a level considered minimally necessary to cope with "the complex demands of modern life." Reading the newspaper every day would help.

Web Lit

21 For some time, a popular topic at cocktail parties has been whether the computer would ever replace the book. No, goes one line of thought, people will always want to be able to crack spines and flip pages; yes, goes another line of thought, people will increasingly do everything on the computer. While this debate has gone on, it has quietly been made more complicated by the proliferation of a new kind of literature: writing created, distributed, and read on computers, without necessarily ever being committed to print. If you want to read this literature, you won't find it on the printed page—and in that sense, it has already replaced the book. Welcome to the world of Web Lit.

Web Lit is not one genre but many: the online journal, the e-zine or Webzine (an online magazine or newsletter), the e-text or e-book (an electronic book), the blog. It includes the personal stories and articles posted on subject-specific Web sites, such as those that specialize in, say, diabetes, and feature a place for readers to give their accounts of coping with the illness. It includes the online-only material offered by the Web sites of periodicals like *Newsweek*: the full-length interviews and columns that are available only on the Web. Some Web Lit venues are direct replacements of print venues. Some print journals, for example, have responded to rising costs and shrinking subscription lists by giving up print publication altogether and moving online. Other venues would probably not exist were it not for the World Wide Web. They include a few household names—such as *The Drudge Report, Salon,* and (in the humor market) *The Onion*—along with millions of lesser-known or wholly unknown sites.

Web Lit includes online fiction magazines, some of them highly respected, such as *McSweeney's*, associated with the writer Dave Eggers. Some online magazines specialize in literary fiction, others in genre fiction, such as science fiction, fantasy, and horror. The benefit for writers is an increase in the number of markets to which they can submit; the downside for readers is the increase in the number of writers who probably should never have been published. Nevertheless, some online journals have built up a readership based on the good taste of the editors and the quality of the writers. Popular online journals include *The Blue Moon Review, Intertext, Monkeyplanet,* and *Zuzu's Petals Quarterly.*

Most online fiction journals have had trouble turning a profit, though some have tried innovative approaches to getting paid. *Mind's Eye Fiction* came up with the idea of letting readers read the beginning of a story for free, then, if they liked it, having them pay to read the ending. Recognition in the form of awards has been rare, but there has been some progress, such as the establishment of the storySouth Million Writers Award for Fiction, which considers only stories published in online publications.

E-books are another growing form of electronic literature. Some e-books begin life as a print book. Project Gutenberg has made a specialty of converting books that are in the public domain into electronic form. Since many of these volumes, such as the novels of Mrs. Humphry Ward (circa 1900), are out of print, they would virtually go out of existence were it not for this conversion to e-text. Other e-books begin life in electronic form and remain there, unless a reader wants to buy a Print-on-Demand (POD) copy of the book. The independent publisher iUniverse has made a business out of helping writers self-publish in this new digital age.

One form of Web Lit that has recently received a great deal of attention is the blog. Short for Web log, a blog is an online personal journal. A typical blog combines personal observations, commentary on current events, and links, but blogs can take unusual turns. One blog by writer Michael Dagley at *http://buddydon.com* morphed into an online, chapter-a-day novel. New software made it possible for anyone to build his or her own blog without knowing programming code, while some Web sites specialized in letting people post their own blogs. One such site, Blogger.com, trumpeted the democratic nature of blogs with its slogan "Push-Button Publishing for the People."

Democracy is characteristic of Web Lit in general, making it part of the broader trend of decentralized art. In principle, anyone can post his or her fiction or commentary to the Web, though in practice it takes a combination of talent, grit, marketing savvy, and luck to build traffic to one's opus. Web Lit has also brought changes to the style and format of literature. These changes include the creation of new forms, notably hypertext fiction, which is characterized by multiple paths through the same text, multiple endings and beginnings, interactive features, maps that the reader can navigate, and audiovisual attachments. There are also more subtle changes, such as a taste for short sentences and paragraphs and bite-sized sections with subheadings; these changes have already been influencing the world of print lit. One online journal, *Story Bytes*, specializes in very short stories—as short as two words long. Jakob Nielsen et al., in an article for *www.sun.com*, argues that Web content should have only 50 percent of the word count of its paper equivalent.

As Web Lit grows and evolves, it will likely continue to spawn new forms and exert a growing influence on literature in general.

The Year-Round TV Season

22 Americans of a certain age remember the excitement of the fall television season. Every autumn, the cover of *TV Guide* was resplendent with foliage, the airwaves full of new sitcoms, dramas, and variety shows. New episodes of those series aired throughout the winter and spring, to give way to reruns in the summer. It was as regular as the life cycle of some primordial moth. By contrast, today television's life cycle is in chaos. It is hard to tell when one season ends and another begins. We are living in the year-round TV season.

The drive toward the year-round TV season has been going on for some time. Cable networks have long improved their competitive chances against the broadcast networks by premiering shows in off months, including the summer, when reruns formerly ruled. Some of these shows became major hits, including HBO's *Sex and the City*, which debuted in June 1998, and *The Sopranos*, which premiered in January 1999.

To stay competitive, the broadcast networks began premiering shows of their own in off months, including the big hits *Who Wants to Be a Millionaire?*, *American Idol*, *Survivor*, and *The O.C.*, all of which got their start in the summer. In January 2004, Fox went further, announcing a deliberate move to a year-round TV season. "When May is over, our new season will begin in June," said Fox Entertainment President Gail Berman. "We are not seasonal programmers. We are 12-month-a-year programmers." In fact, Fox's 2004–2005 season was not so much 12 continuous months but three distinct pulses: summer, then the period after the baseball playoffs in November, then January. It included *The Simple Life 2* in summer, *The Rebel Billionaire* in November, and the new season of *24* in January.

Other networks have experimented with changing the start time of the fall season. In 2004, NBC announced that it would start its 2004–2005 TV season in late August and early September, building on the

Summer Olympics telecasts to promote its new lineup. ABC held the new seasons of *Alias* and *NYPD Blue* until January 2005.

Changes like these require even bigger changes behind the scenes. The traditional development and production schedule has to be altered, though it may relieve some pressure for producers if there is less demand all at once for the same pool of actors, writers, and crews. Some observers have feared that viewers will not be able to keep track of their favorite shows or follow the complex new schedules, but others disagree. "With TiVo, PVRs, and even the lowly VCR, viewers are perfectly capable of determining what they want to watch, when they want to watch it," wrote Belinda Acosta of the *Austin Chronicle* in June 2004. "If they miss something, there's always repurposing, reruns, and DVD sales and rentals." Frazier Moore of the Associated Press believes the networks even benefit from confusing schedules. He wrote, "[J]ust because the schedules seem to run riot doesn't mean there isn't a higher plan: Keep viewers occupied by keeping them befuddled. Then they'll forget to look elsewhere. Like on cable."

Even with the move toward the year-round TV season, the broadcast networks face daunting challenges. Their ratings have been eroding for years, and Americans have an ever-growing number of other cable, satellite, and DVD options for their viewing pleasure—not to mention plenty of other choices of amusement, from video games to iPods. The move toward the year-round TV season will probably continue as the networks seek those wandering audiences.

IV

Health and Medicine

AIDS Across the Continents

23 In the coming decades, acquired immune deficiency syndrome (AIDS) is expected to expand its reach over the world's continents. It has already been a scourge in the United States, where based on Centers for Disease Control (CDC) data, the cumulative number of AIDS cases through 2003 was 929,985 and the cumulative estimated number of AIDS deaths was 524,060. These numbers have already been dwarfed by the scale of the epidemic in other countries, and the global devastation is expected to grow. According to the Joint United Nations Programme on HIV/AIDS (UNAIDS) 2004 Report on the Global AIDS Epidemic, 38 million people worldwide are presently living with the Human Immunodeficiency Virus (HIV) that causes AIDS and 20 million people have died from AIDS.

Over the next decades, HIV/AIDS will present itself in various ways geographically and demographically. Because the disease is contracted more often through heterosexual encounters, the number of women with the virus will rise. Sub-Saharan Africa, already the site of the highest incidence of HIV/AIDS, will be the region with the greatest growth in the number of cases of the disease. In 2003, sub-Saharan Africa had 3 million new infections, bringing its overall total to 25 million afflicted. HIV prevalence rates appear to have become stabilized in the region, but that is mainly due to a balance between rising AIDS deaths and a continuing increase in new infections.

Some African countries, including South Africa, Uganda, and Senegal, have instituted health and public policy programs that have decreased the prevalence of HIV in pregnant women and others. Among their methods of attack are promoting condom use and strengthening rules for blood collection. In general, programs using these and other safeguards have been successful. In Cambodia and the Philippines, HIV prevalence rates have been reduced or have stayed at low levels.

Yet, in some cases, moves to reduce cases of infection have met cultural roadblocks. Across all affected continents, there is resistance to using condoms. Reasons include the condom's awkwardness, possible discomfort, and perceived unmanliness. In Uganda, where over the past several years the spread of AIDS has been cut by a nationwide public policy program of abstinence or delayed first sexual encounters, some young women are complaining on economic grounds. They indicate that forsaking sex or marriage with financially stable men deprives them of financial support for their families.

In recent years, pockets in other geographic regions have seen sharp growth in incidence of AIDS. For example, UNAIDS reports an estimated 7.4 million people in Asia are infected with HIV. According to UNAIDS, India has the largest number of people living with HIV outside South Africa, 5.1 million. In Indonesia and Vietnam, HIV/AIDS rates are increasing, and it is the leading cause of death in Thailand. Increasing the spread of the disease in China are unsafe practices such as reusing drug-injection needles and lack of sanitation in blood donation.

The disease is also spreading rapidly throughout Eastern Europe and central Asia. HIV/AIDS has been contracted by about 1.3 million people there. As in many other countries, only a small fraction of HIV/AIDS patients are receiving antiretroviral medication. In some countries such as Ukraine and Tajikistan, spread of the virus is made worse by lack of information about the disease, particularly for young adults.

In Latin America, an estimated 1.6 million people have HIV. Among the hardest-hit countries are those in the Caribbean basin, notably Haiti and the Bahamas. Overall, this region's high HIV prevalence rates are second only to those in sub-Saharan Africa. But medical and public policy programs in the region are reducing hospitalization rates by providing drug therapies. Through several multinational coalitions throughout the region, countries are developing stronger HIV/AIDS programs and negotiating better prices for antiretroviral drugs.

An estimated half million people are living with HIV/AIDS in North Africa and the Middle East. As yet, treatment facilities reach only a small fraction of patients. Among countries with HIV/AIDS epidemics is the Sudan. High incidence of unsanitary injected drug use and unsafe practices in prisons account for some of the increase in HIV/AIDS cases.

In the United States, Europe, and other Western industrialized nations, HIV/AIDS incidence continues to grow and in many cases, can be linked to a return to unsafe sexual practices. Some experts believe that the wide availability of highly active antiretroviral therapy (HAAR) may be contributing to a less serious commitment to AIDS prevention.

Throughout these regions, another way AIDS treatment is compromised is by false medicine. For example, in recent years there have been rumors of cures or unorthodox treatments that turn out to be dangerous, such as nonworking vaccines in Nigeria that promoted instead of slowed the spread of HIV/AIDS.

For the future, the UNAIDS report stresses the importance of instituting "large-scale protection programs" for all citizens, from those with high-risk behavior to knowledgeable members of high-income nations to the population as a whole. These programs, along with facilities and medications for treating HIV/AIDS, are crucial to reducing the wider growth of the epidemic.

Alternative Medicine

24 For medical and practical reasons, complementary and alternative medical treatments will rise throughout the 21st century. As defined by the National Center for Complementary and Alternative Medicine, a U.S. government agency, complementary and alternative medicine "is that group of diverse medical and health care systems, practices, and products that are not presently considered to be part of conventional medicine." Complementary medicine includes practices used in addition to traditional medicine. Alternative medicine includes practices used instead of traditional treatment, such as folk medicine, herbal medicine, diet fads, homeopathy, faith healing, New Age healing, chiropractic, acupuncture, and naturopathy.

According to a report by the Institute for Alternative Futures, complementary and alternative approaches to health and medicine are among the fastest-growing branches of health care. For example, over 150 million consumers used herbs, and other alternative health substances, with sales totaling $17 billion in 2000. The Institute projects that by 2020, at least two-thirds of Americans will use some form of alternative approach to health care. To confirm growing U.S. interest in alternative medicine, an executive order in 2000 formed the White House Commission on Complementary and Alternative Medicine Policy. Further, a group of physicians and lay experts testified to the U.S. Congress that already proven mind-body therapies could substantially reduce the number of doctor visits and save over $50 billion annually. They might also reduce ever-increasing expenditures on prescription drugs.

Alternative therapies also appeal to people because they provide a source of control over one's health. According to a survey in the late 1990s published in the *Journal of the American Medical Association*, most of the over 80 million Americans who used some form of alternative medical treatment used the therapies to prevent rather than treat illness.

Increased use of the Internet will continue to fuel knowledge and use of alternative medical practices. Despite the White House Commission on Complementary and Alternative Medicine's caution that voluntary standards are needed to maintain the quality of Internet information on alternative medicine, tens of millions of Americans seek health and medical information online, often at alternative medicine sites.

Among the most popular of alternative substances is the herbal supplement, and its place in the Food and Drug Administration hierarchy suggests the flux in which the substances exist. Like other alternative products, herbal supplements are not regulated as drugs by the Food and Drug Association, but instead as foods. As such, if they are shown to be unsafe, the FDA can take them off the market, as it did with the herb found in some weight-loss and bodybuilding supplements. The FDA has also stressed the need to label products accurately and package them without additives.

Over the next few years, the U.S. government will study some of the most popular supplements to increase scientific knowledge about them, such as analyzing their active ingredients and how they work in the body. They hope to determine whether the ingredients can be standardized for public use.

Among alternative approaches that have gained the interest of the medical community is the ancient practice of Tibetan medicine. Dating from the 4th century B.C., Tibetan medicine uses plants, minerals, and animal organs to treat acute and chronic conditions. The practice, built upon the Four Classics of Tibetan medicine, is being used in parts of China and is being studied by modern scholars and medical professionals. The Institute for Alternative Futures projects that by 2010, there will be 24,000 physicians and other health care professionals trained in Asian medicine.

In addition, other types of alternative medicine are expected to become more prominent. For example, estimates are that there will be 103,000 chiropractors in practice by 2010. Generally, says the Institute's report, this will dovetail with a move toward health care that includes a large wellness component. It will have varieties of types of self-management for disease prevention. Says Pat De Leon of the American Psychological Association, "Health science has reached a point where it is no longer accurate to talk about psychology versus biology; the mind versus the body; or nature versus nurture. These processes are inextricably linked."

Along with growing consumer interest in alternative medicine is increasing pressure on insurance companies and employers to pay for it. "Consumer trends will continue to drive changes in health-care delivery and demand for benefits in terms of complementary health care," George DeVries, founder and CEO of American Specialty Health, a San Diego-based complementary health care network, told *San Francisco Business Times* in January 2005.

Do-It-Yourself Health Care

25 Health insurance costs have been rising at double-digit rates for years, and such growth is expected to continue for some time. Health insurance companies blame much of the rise to the development of costly new pharmaceuticals and technologies. Fewer health care providers and lower payments to hospitals also increase costs to the consumer. In response, consumers and providers are seeking new ways to afford good health. Traditional health care constructs, such as indemnity or fee-for-service (or point-of-service) plans, HMOs (health maintenance organizations), and PPOs (preferred provider organizations), may be headed for a makeover to cut costs. As they change, others will attempt more unconventional solutions to health care. Some of the proposed solutions are conservative variations on belt tightening, while some reimagine the doctor-insurance-patient structure. Nearly all involve making health care more consumer oriented, or in plain terms, turning health care into a do-it-yourself endeavor.

Over the next years, alternative forms of health insurance will probably continue to involve self-selected partial service. In this way, health insurance of the future, unless nationalized health insurance is initiated, will involve limiting coverage to match one's needs or funds. This will bring health insurance more in line with home and automobile insurance. One employer-based health plan involves alternating between self-payment and traditional coverage. The pay-as-you-go plan is particularly appealing to healthy young people, who have relatively limited health care bills. Many plans are already adopting variations on this health care model that offers more choices but less reimbursement.

However, such self-directed health insurance comes with risks. One is the shortcuts people take to lessen health care costs. For example, rather than paying to see a doctor, some people go straight to a medical lab for testing. The process eliminates physician costs, but does not provide treatment advice, which one gets only from a medical doctor. Another problem is grossly inadequate coverage masquerading as full-fledged health care. The *Wall Street Journal* cited an employer-sponsored health insurance that charged only $10 to $20 per pay period but had a maximum payout of only $1,000. That amount is far less than the cost of any hospital stay or series of specialized medical tests.

One possible counter to the high cost and time spent on doctor visits is visiting a doctor virtually. These visits, which range up to $25 each, are online meetings with a doctor that let the doctor dispense medical advice without seeing the patient in person. Another way people reduce health costs is by using at-home testing. Instead of paying for preliminary testing, there are already a number of tests for conditions such as pregnancy, ovulation, cholesterol, hepatitis, and HIV. To the pharmaceutical companies that produce the tests, they're a bonanza, toting up over $1 billion in annual sales.

Another alternative to traditional health insurance is the discount health medical card. The sponsoring organization offering the card arranges for its members to receive discounts from 25 percent to 80 percent on medical, dental, vision, chiropractic, and pharmaceutical services with providers linked to the plan. Online nurse service is also available on some plans.

Given the government's high participation in the health care industry, many politicians have various plans for reform. Some politicians and tax reformers suggest that the health care system could be simplified through the introduction of medical savings accounts. Like IRAs, which encourage and provide tax benefits for saving for retirement, medical savings accounts will encourage people to save for medical needs. Instead of paying into a health care plan, people can contribute to a medical savings plan that they use only when needed. Unused monies carry over on a per-year basis.

For patients who have ample health care funds, tiered health care will ensure high-quality treatment. According to Robert J. Blendon and Catherine DesRoches of the Harvard School of Public Health in *Issues in Science and Technology Online*, "[T]he new approach to cost containment, which asks individuals to pay more for their own health care, is going to lead to tiering, in which those with higher incomes will be able to afford a wider range of health care services than much of the middle class and those with lower incomes." For example, according to Dr. Clark Howard at *www.clarkhoward.com*, hospitals are already courting well-heeled patients by offering luxury accommodations. Luxury rooms generate prestige for patients and funds for hospitals like Cedars Sinai, Los Angeles.

In 2003, the U.S. government spent $1.7 trillion on health care. This translates into $1 out of every $6 or $7 of the U.S. budget going toward some type of government coverage for about half of all Americans. The other half is covered by employers, private insurance, or not at all.

In coming years, one of these sources of coverage will become dominant. If it is employer- or private-based coverage, the patient will become more responsible for the quality of his or her own health care. In some ways, it will allow for more personal choice, and health care forecasters believe it will be just what take-charge baby boomers want. But for those who can't or do not have the resources to care for themselves, the future may mean no health care.

Despite the importance of the issue, experts fear a future of health care inaction. According to Robert J. Blendon and Catherine Des-Roches, "Based on the experiences of the past decade, the biggest challenge facing the U.S. health care system . . . is the continued failure of decision makers to reach a consensus on how to address the major health care problems facing the country."

Everybody's Bionic

26 Bionic surgery is the wave of the future. Moving far beyond pacemakers, surgeons in the next few decades will be able to replace weakened or nonfunctioning body parts, such as hearts, eyes, lungs, kidneys, muscles, and even the brain. The Six Million Dollar Man and the Bionic Woman never had it so good.

Already, some health-related implants are used routinely. One is arthroplasty, or hip replacement surgery. Each year, according to ABC News, more than 400,000 people in the world with hips disintegrated by arthritis or osteoporosis undergo hip replacement. By 2030, it is estimated that there will be 272,000 hip replacements done in the United States alone, due to the aging population

At the other end of the spectrum are replacement surgeries that would be more commonplace now if supply could match demand. These surgeries call for human organs of which there is limited availability. For example, according to findings in *BusinessWeek Online*, there is already a shortage of 100,000 hearts available for donation each year. As with other organ replacement, the demand for hearts is likely to grow more intense as the baby boomer generation gets old.

For the future, the search is on for workable human-made replacement parts, and in particular, for a heart. Thus far, many mechanical hearts have been designed and have become much more efficient than the pioneering Jarvik mechanical heart of the 1970s. Many of the latest versions have borrowed from technology used by NASA's space shuttle and have developed small turbines for pumping blood. While the turbine hearts are now used as bridge devices in operating rooms for patients awaiting transplant, scientists believe that the turbine heart will eventually be used for full heart replacement.

Other future improvements to implants may involve refinements in size and delivery. One is simplifying the implant's power supply. In the early 1990s, researchers developed what *BusinessWeek Online* terms a "so-called inductive system" that sends electrical power through the skin. It eliminates the need for an outside power source. This through-the-skin process also will be used for other types of implants, such as vision-enabling brain implants.

Within a few decades, some chronic medical conditions will be treated with computer chip implants. When implanted in the brain and spinal cord, the chips being developed are meant to ameliorate many nerve and muscle disorders, such as amyotrophic lateral sclerosis (ALS). At the University of New Mexico's Artificial Muscle Research Institute, scientists are developing polymer-metal composites for use as substitute muscles for patients with muscle-deteriorating diseases such as muscular dystrophy. Other products are also under development to repair bladder function in the incontinent, as are artificial parts including kidneys and blood vessels.

Restoring the senses is the goal of some implants. At Johns Hopkins University Medical Institutions and elsewhere, researchers are developing methods to restore vision and hearing to people. This technology involves restoring sight by implanting in people's eyes light-sensitive chips that yield a multiple-pixel image. Other vision systems, such as that developed at Dobelle Institute, Inc., in Commack, New York, send images by video camera to an electronic-circuit card inside a person's brain. As silicon chip technology increases chip power, artificial vision may eventually compare to that of the human eye, and one researcher suggests that artificial eyes may be workable by the 2020s.

Optobionics recently completed a series of clinical trials in which they implanted a two-millimeter silicon chip in the eye in patients with the degenerative eye disease retinitis pigmentosa. The results show impressive restoration of vision. The microchip may later be used for other vision loss ailments, including age-related macular degeneration. Other researchers are developing bionic eye implants of solar cells. These act as artificial eye cells, converting light into images that can be processed by the brain. If they prove workable, the cells are expected to be most suitable for patients whose rod and cone cells are damaged (the cells that sense light) but whose retinas can still connect eye and brain.

Other physical conditions are being treated with artificial body parts, such as artificial hearing implants to restore hearing and electronic muscle stimulation for muscles in paralyzed arms and legs. Before the first quarter of the 21st century ends, researchers are also predicting the use of artificial kidneys and lungs. Also by that time, predict the British Telephone Labs, artificial brain cells should also be available. An artificial brain, however, is not projected to be developed until 2035.

In addition to developing new types of artificial parts and implants, researchers are creating "intelligent implants." According to Garth Ehrlich, executive director of the center for Genomic Sciences at the Allegheny-Singer Research Institute in Pittsburgh, interviewed for ABC News, researchers aim for the smart implants to reduce the possibility of dangerous infections. For example, an artificial hip embedded with microelectronic mechanical systems (MEMs), is under development. The MEMs can detect the presence of destructive bacteria and trigger the release of antibodies stored within the implant. According to Ehrlich, implants such as these may be available within several years.

Amidst the development of artificial parts is much biomedical engineering research for devices that interact with the human body to ward off infection. Researchers at the University of Arizona Biomedical Engineering Program are developing medical devices that grow new replacement organs once implanted in the body. In one instance, they are using polymers to develop new blood vessels used during coronary artery bypass graft surgery that will work with the body's own defense system, which usually fights the implant as a foreign entity.

Because of stringent U.S. Food and Drug Administration policy, many of these implant systems and much ongoing research are done in Europe. In *BusinessWeek Online*, Dr. Bartley P. Griffith, director of Pittsburgh's McGowan Center for Artificial Organ Development, says, "The U.S. standard is that we're not going to use devices that might do harm, no matter how gravely ill the patient is." But some experts suggest that a reappraisal of European methods may lead to U.S. easing of current restrictions on implant devices.

In an age of bionic reconstruction, the phrase "100 percent natural" will lose its cachet. Instead, people will seek to be "100 percent functional," many of them with the help of artificial spare parts.

Female Physicians on the Rise

27 Watch out, the next woman you meet may be your doctor. For an increasing number of scientifically minded women, the medical profession is a stable, rewarding, flexible career choice. Since the late 20th century, the number of female doctors in the United States has risen substantially. From 1975 to 1995, the percentage of female physicians in the United States more than doubled. By 2010, analysts expect the number of female physicians to constitute 33 percent of the profession. Already by 2003, 45 percent of medical students were female.

The racial and ethnic breakdown of female doctors roughly reflects the makeup of the country. Of the 205,903 female physicians cataloged by the American Medical Association in 2001, 44 percent listed themselves as white. Four percent were black; 3.4 percent were Hispanic; and 11 percent were Asian. American Native/Alaskan Native accounted for .08 percent, and 3 percent noted themselves as "other." Thirty-four percent listed no race or ethnicity.

Not surprisingly, differences between male and female physicians have emerged. Studies have shown that female doctors are more likely to spend more time talking with patients than do their male counterparts. In part, the practice reflects differences in the way the sexes perceive the medical profession. In a poll of first-year medical students conducted by the American Psychiatric Press, women said that the most valuable quality a doctor could have was compassion, while male students said it was competence.

Female doctors are also more interested in reforming the health care system. For example, according to an American Medical Women's Association survey, 90 percent of its members approved of universal health coverage. This puts them at odds with the mainly male members of the American Medical Association. Female physicians have said they support change in the health care system even if it means a reduction in their earnings.

In addition, female physicians generally structure their careers in ways that more clearly reflect a need for balance between family and work. Over half of female physicians are employees, reports the American Medical Association. As such, they have more regular hours than self-employed physicians, most of whom are male. Females also tend to choose specialties that involve high contact with people and lower incidence of complicated surgeries. According to the *Journal of the American Medical Women's Association,* nearly two-thirds of those choosing to specialize do so in obstetrics/gynecology and pediatrics. Other specialties, many of which pay more but allow for limited interpersonal activity, attract a small number (20 percent) of females.

Female physicians generally earn less money than their male counterparts. According to the U.S. Census Bureau, female physicians make 63 cents for every dollar their male peers earn. The causes of this gender gap may include women's choices of specialization and their intent to balance family and profession. But a salary divide holds even when researchers control for such variables. For example, a study in the June 2004 *Archives of Otolaryngology—Head & Neck Surgery* found that within academic otolaryngology, female physicians made 15 to 20 percent less than male physicians, even after taking into account professional practice hours, hours spent in surgery, type of practice, and years since residency.

For the future, the increased number of female doctors may result in many changes both subtle and obvious in the medical profession. As doctors seek ways to balance family and medicine, the number of part-time practitioners may increase. As the number of female physicians increases, communication between doctors and patients will improve, with one likely result a greater patient role in medical decision-making. Women doctors may also encourage a greater focus on women's health issues, both in their attention to women's health problems and by initiating more studies on women's diseases. More female doctors working as employees may invite the ownership of medical practices by big medical/business consortiums, which would further lessen doctors' control of their practice. Obstetrics/gynecology and pediatrics may become female-dominated specialties, while other specialties may become more male-dominated. Females may comprise a larger number of primary-care physicians, but because women are less likely to establish practice in rural areas (where school systems and housing are less favorable), the rural regions of the United States may be inadequately covered.

According to the Association of American Medical Colleges, the proportion of women medical residents increased from 28 percent of residents in 1988 to 38 percent in 1999. One outcome is certain: the number of women in the medical profession keeps increasing.

Gene-Based Drugs

28 Since time immemorial, pharmaceuticals have been discovered in roughly the same way: try out a little of this fungus, weed, or other strange substance and see what it does in the body. Today, the first real challenger to this method has arrived: pharmacogenomics, or gene-based drugs.

Pharmacogenomics is the development of pharmaceuticals based on knowledge of the human genome, the entire set of human genes. In pharmacogenomics, drug discovery begins not with a fungus or weed, but with a human gene, preferably one that is known to be somehow associated with a disease. Once scientists pinpoint how the gene is linked to the disease, they can use that knowledge to develop a tailor-made remedy. For example, if the gene codes the manufacture of an important protein, but an individual is sick because he or she has a defective copy of that gene, scientists can use the gene in the lab to manufacture the protein that the patient is missing. That is a pharmacogenomic remedy—one based not on hit-and-miss searches for wonder drugs, but on rational development of treatments for diseases based on knowledge of the genome.

Another aspect of pharmacogenomics is developing drugs that are customized for patients who have a particular genotype, or set of gene variations. This is based on the premise that patients with one genotype may respond differently to therapies than patients with a different one. Genentech's drug Herceptin, for example, one of the first pharmacogenomic products, is designed to treat breast cancer in women who express the HER2 gene. AstraZeneca's drug Iressa works well for lung cancer patients with certain genetic mutations in their tumors.

In several years, scientists believe it will be possible for people to order fairly complete reports on their genetic makeup, giving them information on what medicines or foods can help them ward off the diseases. When genetic knowledge becomes great enough, DNA scientist Leroy Hood told the *New York Times*, medicine will go from being one-size-fits-all to being "predictive, preventative, and personalized."

In some cases, pharmacogenomics may result in gene therapy treatments, in which patients receive a replacement gene or some other alteration in their genetic material as a remedy for disease. So far, progress in gene therapy in humans has been slow and unsatisfying, but if researchers can overcome technical obstacles, it may become an important part of pharmacogenomic treatment.

Completion of the Human Genome Project, with its mapping of the entire human genome, has been an important step forward for pharmacogenomics. Even while the project was still in process, academic and corporate research centers were lining up to analyze the data to find out what genes do in the body and how they do it. But don't expect to see your local pharmacy shelves flooded with pharmacogenomic products by tomorrow. The Committee on Genomics and the Public's Health, a government-sponsored panel of experts, reported in October 2004 that completion of the Human Genome Project has so far made little difference in health care. The process has been slow for several reasons, including ignorance and cost questions. Another is the misfit between the wealth of information and the speed with which scientists and pharmaceutical companies can apply it. Scott Morrison of Ernst & Young has said that as the information becomes more user-friendly, "[i]t will then turn into an engine that increases the quality and number of new drug targets and brings down drug development costs."

A bigger problem is whether the current business model for drug development is compatible with pharmacogenomic research. Right now, companies spend vast amounts on drug development, and to make a profit they count on big blockbuster drugs that reach lots of disease sufferers. But the kind of pharmacogenomic drug likely to be discovered in the short term will probably have a small market: patients who are made sick simply by having a missing or defective copy of some gene. More common diseases, like cancer, depression, or arthritis, are usually more complex in origin, involving several interacting genes, and the chances that they will be conquered soon by a pharmacogenomic wonder drug are slimmer. So drug companies may not want to bother with the kind of pharmacogenomic drugs that are doable now; and they may not want to wait for the lucrative kind that will be available later.

Eventually the day may come when patients will go to their doctor with all their genetic information on a chip, and the doctor will examine the chip and prescribe appropriate gene-based remedies and preventive measures. For added convenience, consultant Roger Shamel has argued, the doctor may even have a "custom gene machine" in his office that churns out the remedies while the patient waits. We are probably still decades away from such scenarios, but other benefits of pharmacogenomics are already here and picking up steam.

Generics R Us

29 In the pharmaceutical industry, the big dollars and publicity campaigns go to new brand-name prescription drugs: Prozac in the 1980s; Viagra in the 1990s; and Nexium in the 2000s. Aggressively marketed to doctors and patients, these drugs quickly became omnipresent, displacing older remedies for the diseases they target. Because the new medicines are protected from competition by patents, their manufacturers can charge as high a price as the market will bear, and, since people will spend anything for their health, the market will usually bear a lot. So drug prices rise steadily, increasing the already bloated sum spent by Americans on health care.

Against this juggernaut expect to see a growing preference for generic drugs among everyone who has to pay for them: the federal government; private insurers; corporations that provide health benefits to employees; retail pharmacies (which earn a bigger profit margin on generics); and individual consumers. A generic drug is a medicine that has the same active ingredients as a given brand-name product and has been approved by the Food and Drug Administration (FDA) as being bioequivalent (achieving the same concentration in the blood). However, the generic is usually 30 to 80 percent cheaper. During a brand product's period of patent protection or market exclusivity (usually 20 years), no one is legally permitted to come out with a competing version of the same ingredient. But once that patent/ exclusivity period lapses, all bets are off. Provided the FDA gives its approval, any manufacturer can make a generic version and slash the price to attract customers.

The power of generic competition has been increasing in recent years and is likely to keep doing so. Already the rate at which brand companies lose market share to generics upon patent expiration "is greater than anything we've seen in the last fifteen years," Michael Yellen, senior portfolio manager for AIM Global Health Care Fund, San Francisco, told the trade magazine *Pharmacy Practice News*. According to Yellin, "A branded company can lose 70 to 90 percent of revenue on a drug within the first three to six months" after patent expiration. A case in point is the antidepression drug Prozac, which lost much of its market share when a generic version of its active ingredient became available early this century.

The public at large was once suspicious of generics, viewing them as inferior in quality as well as in price. That view is changing, in part due to a concerted effort—by insurers, pharmacy chains, and the generic drug industry itself—to spread the word that generics are just as good as the brand-name product. Pharmacy chains are likely to promote the cost savings of generics through fliers and circulars; insurers typically offer lower copayments if patients use generics. Doctors, too, are more willing to prescribe generics.

Companies that produce generic drugs, once rocked by price wars and poor business decisions, are now more likely to be stable corporations with healthy profit margins. They may offer not only no-name generics but branded products that combine generic molecules with value-added features, such as an extended-release formulation.

Despite the attractiveness of generics to those who make them and buy them, they are extremely unattractive to one group: brand drug manufacturers. Brand manufacturers have long done everything possible to block generic competition: supporting legislation to extend patents, filing new patents on old drugs just before the old patents expire, mounting court battles and regulatory challenges, and cutting deals that pay would-be generic competitors to keep their products off the market. Increasingly, these tactics are coming under fire from government officials, corporate lobbyists, and citizens' groups sick and tired of the high price of drugs.

The Federal Trade Commission (FTC) has cracked down on unlawful anticompetitive practices in the drug industry. The Medicare Modernization Act of 2003 contained provisions to reduce the barriers to generic competition. In a high-profile case, Bristol-Myers Squibb settled a lawsuit with the Attorneys General of the 50 states, territories, and District of Columbia in which they alleged that the drug manufacturer illegally delayed generic competition to its cancer drug Taxol (generic name paclitaxel). In the settlement, Bristol-Myers Squibb agreed to pay $12.5 million to reimburse cancer patients overcharged for the drug from 1999 to 2003.

The brand drug industry will not go away; indeed, generic drugs couldn't exist if brand companies didn't create new products that will eventually lose patent protection. But brand companies will most likely have to focus more on innovating new products—aided by the discoveries of pharmacogenomic research—and less on blocking generic competition. Indeed, some brand companies, concluding "if you can't beat 'em, join 'em," are licensing rights to produce generic versions of their drugs, a practice called "authorized generics."

One irony of the increasing presence of generics is that their prices are rising; they are not as cheap as they were back when people didn't think they were any good. However, market forces will probably keep their prices from getting too high, since their whole appeal rests on being cheaper than the brand.

Hormones All Around

30 From childhood to old age, hormone use is increasing in the United States. There are many hormone treatments that are prescribed by physicians and treat medical conditions, such as hormone replacement therapy during menopause and steroid therapy for asthma or serious inflammatory conditions. Better known are the equally widespread self-help hormones. They are the treatments that people give themselves to bring them closer to their physical ideal, whether 20 percent taller, stronger, or younger. Growth hormones help short children get taller, anabolic steroids make athletes stronger, rejuvenation hormones make the senior citizen feel middle-aged again. Sometimes effective, sometimes dangerous, they are mainly easy to buy and even if it's prohibited for the desired use, usually you won't get caught. It's a modern union of self-improvement, capitalism, and drugs.

Anabolic steroids have called baseball records into question and prompted public apologies from Major League players. But they aren't just for pro baseball players anymore. According to the Hormone Foundation, studies have shown that the problem of anabolic steroid abuse among children is common. While these hormone-like substances related to testosterone are prescribed for promoting tissue growth in muscle, as many as 6 percent (or one out of fifteen) of adolescent boys and 1.9 percent of girls reported using these steroid drugs without a prescription. In some areas of the United States, the use is even higher.

A national study conducted by the National Institute on Drug Abuse's Monitoring the Future group, reported increased lifetime use of steroids among 8th, 10th, and 12th graders. The annual study finds that 2.5 percent of 8th graders, 3.5 percent of 10th graders and 4 percent of 12th graders have taken anabolic steroids at least once in their lives, according to data through 2002.

Aside from being prohibited for use in sports and potentially ruining a pro career, are there any reasons for not taking anabolic steroids?

There are the health problems. In adults, the problems range from acne to hair loss to increased cancer risk. For young people, there is stunted growth. For both, there are genital disorders; see *www.thesite.org* for details on testicular shrinkage and reduced sperm rate.

For those over 50 years old who are feeling their age but still want to feel their oats, there is bioengineered human growth hormone (HGH). To fight the natural drop in the body's HGH levels, which begin at age 25 or 30, HGH injections promote muscle growth and bone density. They also restore energy and a sense of well-being—all the characteristics one took for granted in youth.

HGH is produced in the body by the pituitary gland and is the hormone that makes us grow. Doctors began prescribing it about 35 years ago for children who were in need of a growth boost. The injections are now taken by older people who want to embark on an antiaging program and have the ability to pay for the treatment, which costs many thousands of dollars per year.

Although the Food and Drug Administration approved HGH for "deficient" adults in 1996, many conventional doctors say that using HGH simply to return to age 25 doesn't properly constitute the correction. Still, hundreds of thousands of people take HGH, many of them the over-50 crowd. Generally, they report good things from the hormone. Doctors who offer it are more circumspect. In *USA Today*, Dr. Murray Susser, a Los Angeles-based physician with a celebrity clientele, says, "It's off-label use, it's legal, and people have the choice. It's only misuse if I lie to them. I say to people who are taking it, 'It's experimental, it may help, but I don't know for sure.'"

Even the Christian market weighs in favorably on at least one hormone. According to *www.themarriagebed.com*, which specializes in "Sex and intimacy for married Christian couples," the favored hormone is oxytoxin, the "bridge between touch and sex." Oxytocin is vital to the physical aspect of marriage because "it makes us feel good about the person who causes the oxytocin to be released." This is one hormone that doesn't have to be bought. According to the Web site, we just have to "[L]ook for opportunities to touch."

Hyper-Testing

31 Americans are in love with medical tests, and the love affair will intensify in years to come. From the old-fashioned tuberculosis pin-prick to newfangled genetic tests, patients will continue to subject their bodies to laboratory analysis for the sake of preventing and treating disease. However, the trend toward hyper-testing is not open-ended: the market will weed out unnecessary tests, leaving the ones with the best chance of being useful.

The factors driving hyper-testing are many. Medical science is discovering new facts about the causes and early stages of disease, allowing them to devise tests that can detect the presence of illness early. This work is aided by the findings of genomic research, which is beginning to pinpoint the genetic causes of many diseases. Fear of malpractice litigation drives many doctors to order tests freely to rule out even remote possibilities, lest they be sued later for missing them. And patients are living longer and adopting a more take-charge attitude about their health, so that they readily request tests they have heard or read about.

Nevertheless, there are also factors working against hyper-testing. The managed care industry and the corporate and government payers that foot much of the bill for health care in America have no interest in seeing unnecessary testing multiply. By refusing to pay for every pro-cedure, they will apply a brake to hyper-testing. Sufficiently worried patients will pay out of pocket, but even they will avoid tests that are pricey and unnecessary.

Body scans are a case in point. In the early 2000s, for-profit body scanning health centers opened nationwide, selling the opportunity to detect illnesses such as cancer or heart disease early. Patients would get their bodies, in whole or in part, scanned by state-of-the-art comput-erized tomography (CT) or magnetic resonance imaging (MRI) equip-ment without the need for a doctor's referral. Patients flocked to these centers, spending hundreds or thousands of dollars to get themselves scanned. But the fad was short-lived. Physicians and journal articles warned against the scans, saying that they were unreliable. In many cases, the scans needlessly frightened patients with false positives that took time and money to disprove. In other cases, they missed real problems, creating a false sense of security. Insurers refused to pay for the procedures, and even with falling prices, patients stayed away. Today, most of the scanning centers have closed.

Despite the decline of body scanning centers, numerous other kinds of medical tests are on the rise. There are mammograms, prostate exams, bone density exams, pap smears, and colonoscopies. There are genetic tests of several kinds: prenatal diagnosis of a fetus (to check for Down syndrome and other genetic diseases); carrier identification for couples whose families have a history of recessive genetic disorders such as cystic fibrosis and Tay-Sachs disease; tests to check if an individual is genetically predisposed for a late-onset disorder such as cancer or Huntington's disease.

Many medical tests take the form of baseline testing, preliminary assessments meant to establish a point of comparison for the future. For skin cancer prevention, many people resort to baseline photographs of suspicious moles on their skin. Whether taken by themselves or their physicians, the photographs allow them to check for changes that might indicate cancer. A growing number of athletes use baseline neuropsychological testing—a measurement of an athlete's cognitive status before the season—so that if they suffer head injuries their physicians can monitor their recovery from concussion and make return-to-play decisions. And baseline testing of employees for use in drug testing programs is now common in some workplaces.

Testing does not end at the doctor's office. At malls, drugstores, and health fairs, numerous screening tests are available from blood pressure and pulse reading machines and electrocardiograms to checkups for sugar, cholesterol, and body fat.

Some forms of testing are more equal than others. Executives may be sent by their companies for an all-expenses-paid comprehensive medical exam to make sure they are in top physical condition. At the University of Florida Shands Executive Health Center, established in Gainesville in 1999, executives get everything from a cardiac stress treadmill test to flexible sigmoidoscopy (to screen for colorectal cancer)—with relaxation massage, breakfast, and lunch thrown in. In the words of its Web site, the Center offers "complete head-to-toe medical examinations organized in one visit within a luxurious and comfortable setting designed to make the most of your time."

As medical knowledge grows and Americans become more informed, expect hyper-testing to continue. But beware of putting all your money into the next body scanning craze. Tests themselves are subject to testing.

Medical Tourism

32 Increasingly, Americans who need specialized medical services or body parts are traveling abroad for them. Hospital-based sites in Cape Town, South Africa, Malaysia, India, and Iran have well-appointed "medical tourism" sites where patients choose to visit and receive the services of European- and American-trained physicians. Such trips are generally not covered by typical health care plans; instead, the cost is borne by the patient. Because the patient is privately paying, he or she provides unencumbered resources for the medical center and/or the government. This kind of transaction makes international patients highly desired by foreign nation, particularly by less prosperous ones.

In turning to medical tourism, the patient is literally "outsourced"— packed off and sent to another country on any of a number of executive packages that offer, besides the medical services, many high-end amenities. A Web site in Thailand boasts "roundtrip airport transport, welcome massage, cell phone, half-day Bangkok orientation tour, two round trips to hospital with hospital outpatient registration and process orientation plus 24/7 assistance for your entire stay in Thailand"! Medical practices that can be outsourced include angiogram, caesarian delivery, and breast augmentation, and run, on average about half the cost of the practice in an American hospital. Even sex changes are available in some overseas hospitals. In addition to the low cost, the foreign countries sell themselves as luxurious getaway sites. The Thailand Web site proclaims, "We can schedule shopping excursions, river tours, ancient site tours, trips to nearby beaches . . . all around your medical appointment schedule."

The Cape Town, South Africa, medical tourism practice presents itself in terms that are equally grave and cheery. The Web site offers Mediscapes, "Cape Town's Original and Trusted Specialists in all Medical, Surgical and Recovery Packages for Serious Peace of Mind. As Seen on Discovery Channel!"

Relatively new to the medical tourism industry, India now involves both government agencies and tourist-related businesses to promote the idea. The alternative practice of Ayurvedic medicine, which is now increasingly popular in the United States, is offered to some notice in the state of Kerala, or "God's Own Country," as its corporate slogan goes. Owing to the predominantly western clientele, Kerala and other states in India also practice traditional western medical practices.

Various countries in the Middle East are active in medical tourism, including Oman and the United Arab Emirates. Making a particularly strong effort to attract western patients/tourists is Iran. No Middle East country can compete with Iran in terms of medical expertise and costs, announced Iranian Health Minister Masoud Pezeshkian. "Iranian medical facilities are unique in the region, providing a massive potential for medical and health tourism," he said as the country pledged to expand its tourism, including medical tourism, programs. To cite an example of the draw of Iran as a medical tourism site, Pezeshkian said that an open heart surgery would cost on average $18,000 in Turkey and $40,000 in U.K., while any heart patient can have the surgery for less than $10,000 in Iran and can afford to spend the rest on touring the country.

Even some Western European sites offer medical tourism packages. One is Munich Airport. At the airport's Munich Medical Center, the Web site promises a bustling site for medical tourism "where physicians and dentists have clinics within easy reach of the terminals and a beer garden." Patients from other countries fly into Munich, have tests or treatments at the airport, and then fly home—often in a single day. The Munich Airport Clinic has two surgery rooms and 13 beds. Individually designed packages can include diagnosis, inpatient or outpatient surgery, hotel accommodation, transfer to a partner clinic for long-term treatments, and sightseeing programs for patients and their families. The clinic will even collect patients at the aircraft and take them through immigration. Specialties include orthopedics, hand surgery, plastic surgery, endocrine surgery, minimally invasive surgery for various conditions, ophthalmics, ear-nose-throat medicine, urology, gynecology, gastroenterology, and treatment of cardiovascular conditions.

The areas affected at the end of 2004 by the tsunami have announced that they have reopened for medical tourism. The Phuket (Thailand) Health and Travel Company Limited, in alliance with Bangkok Phuket Hospital, reported in early 2005 that "much of life is back to normal again . . . [and that] work at the hospital is now back to normal and ready for tourists that want to use medical service like plastic surgery, dental treatments, or eye LASIK at a fraction of the price in most western countries."

Sometimes the travel is less glamorous. It involves the selling of a kidney, cornea, or lung by an impoverished citizen of a developing country. In a foreign country, such as Brazil, a poor donor who needs the money agrees to sell his or her organ to medical middlemen. The donor is then flown to another site, in this case, a South African hospital. There the donor meets the recipient, who is sometimes an American. In the hospital, the American receives the kidney transplant. To effect this operation, the patient has paid the medical middlemen who made the event happen. The middlemen keep nine-tenths of the tens of thousands of dollars the patient paid. The donor gets one-tenth of the payment for his body part.

With waiting lines in America for kidneys and other body parts extend several years, the recipient is often exhausted by health problems and had already been told by doctors to get hold of a kidney, as the woman in the *New York Times* said, "any way I could or expect to die." She does, at a cost of $60,000. In the end, the recipient's life is extended, the donor's health often diminished, and the middlemen enriched.

More Alzheimer's

33 Currently, there are approximately 4 million Americans who have Alzheimer's disease and as the population ages, the number is expected to rise to 14 million by 2050. NewsTarget.com calls it more serious than obesity as a health condition that strikes individuals and affects the national health care budget. The Web site reports, "There's a cost crisis looming on the U.S. health care system, and I'm not talking about obesity: it's Alzheimer's disease. Health experts expect a massive increase in Alzheimer's patients in the next few years, and treating the disease is astonishingly expensive."

Alzheimer's is actually a group of symptoms that often accompanies a disease or condition. It is a major public health problem for the United States because it has such a huge impact on individuals, families, the health care system, and society. Scientists estimate that for the 34 million Americans 65 and older, the percentage of people with Alzheimer's doubles for every five-year age group.

Currently, the 34 million Americans 65 and over accounts for 13 percent of the total population of the U.S. The percentage of people over age 65 will increase rapidly over the next few years as the "baby boom" generation reaches 65. In addition, the group of people over 85—the group with the highest risk of Alzheimer's disease—is the fastest growing segment of the population. By 2050, 14 million older Americans are expected to have Alzheimer's disease if the current numbers hold and no preventive treatments become available.

Like most other major diseases, Alzheimer's is increasingly represented by federal and state-funded programs. National funding bills have been enacted since the 1990s, to bipartisan support. In Texas, for example, where the Texas Alzheimer's-related Web site claims 280,000 state victims, there is the Alzheimer's Disease Program, established by legislative mandate in 1987 to provide information and support to Alzheimer's patients, their families, and long-term care providers. House Bill 1066 established the Texas Council on Alzheimer's Disease and Related Disorders to serve as the state's advocate for persons with Alzheimer's disease and those who care for them.

There are also more business-based programs to promote services for Alzheimer's patients. Although there is no set pharmaceutical treatment of Alzheimer's disease, there are Alzheimer's-related recognition programs for pharmacists who deal with the disease. One, instituted by U.S. Pharmacist, is the Annual Pharmacy Recognition Award. It recognizes the contributions of four pharmacists who have "implemented initiatives that have enhanced the quality of care of Alzheimer's patients either directly or indirectly or have improved the competencies of caregivers or health care providers."

Many medical studies are being done to pinpoint the cause of Alzheimer's and to effect treatment and cure. Scientists studying the brain at the University of Chicago hospitals are learning how the removal of cholesterol and the proper delivery of fatty compounds are vital for the healthy function of the brain in an effort to understand how these processes gone awry can lead to Alzheimer's disease. Despite the fact that the brain is 70 percent fat, scientists have known little about how fats, or lipids, are metabolized and transported within it. The interest intensified several years ago with the surprising discovery that an increased risk of Alzheimers disease was linked to a natural genetic variant of a key fat-transporter molecule called apolipoprotein E, or apoE. Other studies, such as one appearing in *Neurology* magazine and reported in *OnMedica*, suggests that older patients with a diastolic blood pressure below 70 mm Hg are 20 percent more likely to develop Alzheimer's disease than those with normal readings.

There are also concerted moves to effect eating-and-lifestyle public health practices to curb the incidence of Alzheimer's. Popular magazines such as *Newsweek* promote the eating of superfoods such as broccoli and green leafy vegetables. They also point to the positive effects of mental exercise, as on a job.

Ecological researchers have unearthed other possible culprits for the widespread prevalence of Alzheimer's in the 21st century. According to *www.commondreams.org*, the incidence of Alzheimer's in the United States is disproportionate to the rest of the world. The United States contains 25 percent of all Alzheimer's cases, even though we represent only 4.6 percent of the world's population. Europe is experiencing half our rate of disease. For Americans over 85 years of age, 50 percent are thought to have Alzheimer's.

Pointing to causes other than personal lifestyle choices, environmentalists have uncovered a possible link to Alzheimer causes. Aluminum by itself may not cause Alzheimer's, but in combination with the radioactive products of the phosphate fertilizer industry, it could be wreaking havoc on our health.

A national epidemic, a public health imperative, and a business opportunity, the rise of Alzheimer's disease will continue.

More Diabetes

34

Diabetes is on the rise, particularly type 2 adult-onset diabetes. According to the Centers for Disease Control and Prevention (CDC), from 1980 through 2002, the number of Americans diagnosed with diabetes more than doubled, from 5.8 million to 13.3 million. Further, the increases occurred across all sexes, ages, races, and levels of education. Across the country, over 800,000 new cases are diagnosed each year. According to the American Diabetes Association, more than 18 million Americans, including both diagnosed and undiagnosed cases, are currently estimated to have diabetes. In addition, at least 16 million more Americans have prediabetes or impaired glucose metabolism, a condition that increases a person's risk for developing type 2 diabetes.

Tied to the rise in diabetes is the increase in obesity. As the number of Americans with diabetes increased by millions, so did the number of obese Americans, who are those 20 percent or more above their normal weight. The rate of obesity in the United States increased by 74 percent since 1991, as measured by body mass index (BMI) by the CDC. According to the National Council of Health Statistics, the percentage of obese Americans more than doubled between 1976 to 1980 and 1999 to 2000, from 15 percent to 31 percent of Americans. According to the federal Weight-control Information Network, 61 million (31 percent) of American adults aged 20 and up are obese. Additionally, 65 percent of U.S. adults are either overweight or obese. Research has found that 80 percent of people who develop type 2 diabetes are obese.

Diabetes mellitus is a disorder of metabolism, or how the body uses digested food to create energy. The disease is marked by the inability of the body's cells to take glucose from the body's blood, which it would normally do for growth and energy. Diabetes is the fifth leading cause of death in women, and the sixth leading cause of death in men. The disease is the leading cause of amputation, blindness, and kidney failure in adults.

There are simple ways to combat the onset of diabetes. A National Institutes of Health (NIH) study found that people with prediabetes who lost 5 to 7 percent of their body weight and ate and exercised moderately were able to forestall or prevent the onset of type 2 diabetes. A study presented by the Defeat Diabetes Foundation, Inc., suggests that a high intake of dietary fiber may promote enhanced insulin sensitivity and may help to prevent type 2 diabetes. Physicians and researchers at the CDC reiterate that a more healthful lifestyle is good prevention for diabetes.

A reduction in diabetes would save the nation money. According to the National Diabetes Information Clearinghouse (NDIC), the United States spent $132 billion in one year on treating diabetes, directly and indirectly. The costs included disability payments, time lost from work and premature death, hospitalization, treatment supplies, and medical care.

From an investor's standpoint, however, diabetes management is a moneymaking venture. "Diabetes is a great disease from a business perspective," David Kliff, publisher of *Diabetic Investor*, told the trade magazine *Retail Pharmacy News*.

The Solar Threat

35 Sunshine and health have been linked for as long as parents have ordered their children to go out and get some sun. But that long association is coming to an end. Increasingly, sunshine will be seen not as a boon to health but as a threat.

With the degradation of the protective ozone layer of the atmosphere, the sun's ultraviolet rays have become more potent. As that trend continues, and as U.S. society ages, cases of skin cancer will increase. Already the number of new cases of melanoma, the most serious of skin cancers, has more than doubled since 1980, with the number of cases currently rising about 3 percent per year. In 2000, over 50,000 new cases of melanoma were detected. By 2010, the American Academy of Dermatology projects that 1 in 50 Americans (or about 2.8 million) will develop some form of melanoma. In addition, there will be even more cases of less-threatening skin cancers such as squamous cell and basal cell cancer. In fact, throughout the Western countries, melanoma is the fastest-growing of all cancers. Additionally, although melanoma is already a leading cancer among young people, it is expected to become more prevalent among them in the future.

Given how treatable skin cancer is (it can be cured in 95 percent of cases), the medical community and consumer businesses will continue to develop medical and over-the-counter innovations to fight the disease. At both preventative and treatment levels, there is much money to be made in new developments.

As of now, prevention involves avoiding exposure to the sun, or limiting it to periods when the sun is less strong. Prevention also entails wearing sun protection factor (SPF) sunscreen of 30 and protective clothing when in the sun. People should also stay alert for weather reports that predict the global solar UV index will be 3 or more: that level of radiation can damage sensitive skin. A solar index of 6 or more is even more menacing: for sensitive skin, sunburn can begin in 25 minutes or less under those conditions.

New standard practices to monitor the skin may include regular visits to the dermatologist, in which the doctor keeps a running photographic survey of a patient's skin; these may become as commonplace as mammograms and prostate exams. Do-it-yourself skin cancer tests and special mirrors for self-viewing may become popular, as they can detect potentially problematic spotting.

Consumer products serving the needs of potential cancer patients include clothing made from fabrics designed to shelter the body from sunrays. Such clothing is available today, but from limited outlets and aimed primarily at travelers. Over time, an increasing number of clothes for everyday wear will be made from UV-resistant material or will be treated by UV-resistant sprays. This will bring clothing up to par with eyeglasses and sunglasses that routinely have UV-screening properties ground into them. Self-tanning cosmetics will be even further refined to be more natural and less drying to the skin, and tanning salons may be reimagined so that they impart a suntan to the user without using techniques that damage the skin.

To answer growing medical needs, the numbers of plastic and reconstructive surgeons will increase, with many specializing in post-skin cancer reconstruction. In the public health arena, health classes along the lines of today's CPR sessions will train people to detect the differences between ordinary discolorations and skin cancers.

It is unlikely, but possible, that there may be a healthful cultural change. The next generations could adopt a preference for a non-sunkissed look. The healthy, preferred look could be one's everyday coloring, even if pale, as long as it has no skin discolorations caused by the sun. In the 19th century, some women avoided the sun to maintain their pale beauty. Now everyone may avoid the sun for a longer life.

The Status Syndrome

36 As if germs and cancer weren't enough, humanity now faces a new medical scourge: low social status. The last few years have seen growing acceptance of the idea that being low on the social ladder, independent of other factors such as diet, smoking, and access to health care, leads to shorter lifespan and poorer health. This is what British epidemiologist Michael Marmot calls "the status syndrome" in his 2004 book of that name.

Marmot gathered the evidence for the status syndrome over three decades of research. In his Whitehall studies, he followed the health of British civil servants from the 1970s onwards. The studies showed that those with the lowest job grade, such as messengers and doorkeepers, were three times more likely to die at any given age than the administrators in the highest grade of the organization. Even after controlling for risk factors such as obesity and smoking, nearly two-thirds of the difference in mortality from coronary heart disease remained unexplained.

Marmot has found the status syndrome in the United States as well. For every mile traveled on the Metro line from the southeast section of downtown Washington, D.C., to well-to-do Montgomery County, Maryland, life expectancy rises about a year and a half. By the time you get off, he told the *New York Times* in May 2004, there is a "20-year gap between poor blacks at one end of the journey and rich whites at the other."

Other studies have confirmed the existence of the status syndrome, and many more are now exploring it. "The whole issue of health disparities is very hot now," Nancy Adler, professor of medical psychology, University of California, San Francisco, told the *Times*. "There is a meeting every other minute." The research runs the gamut from monkeys to movie stars. American researcher Robert M. Sapolsky showed that dominant baboons usually have lower rates of stress-related disease. Canadian researcher Donald Redelmeier analyzed the life spans of actors who won Oscars, their costars, and the losing nominees. He found that winning an Academy Award added nearly four years to an actor's lifespan.

The status syndrome is not caused by wealth or poverty in absolute terms, but by relative differences in wealth among people in a society. In the United States, the gross domestic product per person (GDP) is about $34,000 and the life expectancy is 76.9 years. But in Japan, which has a lower GDP of about $25,000, the life expectancy is longer, 81.3 years. Behind Japan's better health may be the smaller gap between rich and poor and more satisfying social arrangements.

"Where you stand in the social hierarchy—on the social ladder—is intimately related to your chances of getting ill, and the length of your life," writes Marmot. Even small differences in status may affect health. For example, people with doctorates live longer than those with master's degrees.

The reason why low status causes poor health, Marmot believes, is the diminished control and fewer opportunities for full social engagement that come with being lower on the totem pole. People on top suffer stress too, but the stress is more within their control, and they have more ways of getting support from other people. Low-status people are more likely to feel overwhelmed by stress, which can result in higher levels of the stress hormone cortisol, which can put them at greater risk for heart disease, stroke, and diabetes, according to *New Scientist* in June 2004. Most people have a morning rise in cortisol after waking, but the Whitehall study showed low-status workers have a higher morning rise than higher-status employees.

There are other possible explanations. Redelmeier believes that individuals with higher status typically have more people who are invested in maintaining their health and reputation, from an agent to a personal trainer. American sociologists John Mirowsky and Catherine E. Ross argue that educational attainment and the skills and abilities acquired during the educational experience drive most of the connection between social status and health.

Are there any ways to fight the status syndrome? One therapy is political: try to reduce the income gap between classes. In the United Kingdom, Marmot points out, the difference in life expectancy between the highest and lowest social classes rose from about 5.5 years in the 1970s to 9.5 years by the 1990s, perhaps as a result of the Thatcherite government's conservative policies. After seven years of liberal Labour government rule, the gap is narrowing and is now about 8 years.

Individuals can improve their own resistance to the status syndrome by planting themselves in a small community and a relatively flat organization where there are not too many levels of social status towering above them. Being your own boss—either a small-business owner or a freelancer—brings stress of its own, but it can at least help avert the stress of kowtowing to superiors. A strong network of social support can also help reduce stress.

In the coming years, expect much more research, and more ideas, about how the status syndrome works and how to treat it.

Telemedicine

37 In the 20th century, the doctor's house call died. In the 21st century, it returns—on the computer and videophone. Doctor-patient visits are just one type of the telemedicine trend that is revolutionizing the practice of medicine. For the average patient, telemedicine is an online consult with a doctor before approving a prescription to be filled online. For another patient, just out of cancer surgery and already at her home, it is a video monitor that relays vital signs and images of the patient that allow a nurse at a medical center to monitor her progress. The nurse also uses the phone lines to check the patient's blood pressure and manage her pain levels.

Telemedicine services are particularly useful in regions that are medically underserved by physicians and hospitals. Rural and underpopulated regions where people have to travel long distances to doctors have been introduced to telemedical service with success. As reported in *Pediatrics*, a study of a telemedicine program in rural California for children with special health care needs reported high levels of satisfaction in the teleconsultations.

The ease of telemedicine also makes the practice appealing to any patient with travel difficulties, whether in rural or nonrural areas. Those facing long-term at-home rehabilitation are likely candidates for telemedical monitoring. Several companies, including HealthTech Services Corporation of Northbrook, Illinois, and Viterion TeleHealth, LLC, of Tarrytown, New York, produce telemonitors for use at home. These monitors allow physicians to track a patient's vital signs while also reducing the number of times a patient must visit the doctor's office.

Thus far, telemedicine has proven a good fit for physician and patient. Studies have shown that such telemonitoring reduces patients' visits to emergency rooms and also allows many people to keep living in their homes rather than transfer to a nursing home. Keeping patients from entering nursing homes will become increasingly important as the baby boom generation enters retirement years. At *www.Journal-News.com*, Craig Lehmann, dean and professor at the School of Health Technology and Management at Stony Brook University, said, "As the baby boomers reach that golden age when they fall under Medicare, you can't afford to be putting people in nursing homes and not managing them better, because it's going to break the bank."

Some physicians have been reluctant to participate in telemedicine for fear of not being reimbursed by insurers and being overwhelmed by patient demands. Those were the concerns of physicians at the University of California-Davis Health System when it began offering online physician-patient consultations in 2001. But as of 2005, according to Health Data Management, the health system has online consultation reimbursement contracts with 80 percent of its nongovernmental payers, and the number of messages from patients has been manageable. Studies at the institution have shown that payers and employers are willing to reimburse for online consultations because of lower costs overall for participating patients.

Telepsychiatry has also grown widely over the past decade. According to a survey by *Telemedicine Today* (done in conjunction with the Association of Telemedicine Service Providers), there are 25 telemental programs in the United States. Those responding to the survey report an aggregate total of about 8,640 consultations per year. Compared to the number of consultations done in 1994, there was a tenfold increase.

Telemedical procedures with humans and robots are also becoming more common in medical practice. In addition to using robots in operating rooms to assist physicians, surgeons are already beginning to use robots to do surgery on distant patients. In 2001, a surgeon in New York used a computer and robotic tools to remove the diseased gallbladder of a 68-year-old patient in Strasbourg, France. University of Nebraska-Lincoln researchers have developed miniature camera-carrying robots that can be inserted into patients for laparoscopic procedures. The robots would broadcast images of the patient's interior to a remote surgeon, who could control them by radio. That would allow emergency surgery in all kinds of hard-to-reach locations—for example, a battlefield or a rural car accident scene.

Robots are also being used to assist patients in long-term rehabilitation. A recent study using a robot developed at the Massachusetts Institute of Technology (MIT) showed promise in patients undergoing stroke rehabilitation.

According to *Telemedicine Today*, many hospitals and medical schools are using telemedicine to connect rural and urban physicians or to provide continuing education to physicians and health care professionals.

To maintain medical standards, state and national governments are proposing legislation and regulations for electronic medical practice. Governments and health care providers are also making decisions on reimbursement rates.

Given the possibility that telemedicine may mean lower costs and increased medical attention, it is likely to be accepted as part of the health care system. In 1997, Dr. Rick Satava, professor of surgery at Yale University School of Medicine, in New Haven, Connecticut, told *General Surgery & Laparoscopy News*, "The barriers [to telemedicine] aren't technical any longer, but social." But with other elements of our social life becoming computerized, resistance is crumbling fast. If people can order a car and fall in love over the Internet, a telemedical doctor will be able to diagnose, rehabilitate, even operate on them. "It's clearly inevitable," said Dr. Satava.

A Touch of Plastic Surgery

38 Cosmetic surgery is becoming more affordable and more common. According to the American Society of Plastic Surgeons (ASPS), over 6.6 million people underwent cosmetic surgery in 2003. Among the most popular procedures for females (who make up about 85 percent of the total) were nose reshaping (354,327), liposuction (282,876), breast augmentation (236,888), eyelid surgery (230,672), and facelift (117,831). The top five nonsurgical cosmetic procedures in 2002 were Botox injection (1,123,510), chemical peel (920,340), microdermabrasion (900,912), laser hair removal (587,540), and sclerotherapy (511,827).

It is also becoming more popular for men, with hundreds of thousands of men receiving nose reshaping, liposuction, eyelid surgery, hair transplantation, and ear surgery. Nonsurgical procedures included chemical peel, Botox injection, microdermabrasion, lower hair removal, and collagen injection. Further, cosmetic surgery continues to increase in numbers for men, growing by 10 percent in 2004 alone. For men, the facelifts, liposuction, penile enlargement, and other procedures are considered ways to remain competitive, not necessarily (as with some women) to attain a beauty ideal. "Men feel that doing some of these procedures gives them a foot up in the business world, a competitive edge," said Dr. Marla Ross, a dermatologist. Ross also said the age range of her patients has widened, with most of them between 35 and 55.

But some things never change: According to the American Academy of Facial Plastic and Reconstructive Surgery, nearly equal numbers of men and women say they get plastic surgery to look younger.

Americans are also having more fun with their plastic surgery. In general, the process of plastic surgery is becoming much less a hidden act than a cause for celebration. To wit, some of the trends noted in the 2003 survey of the American Academy of Facial Plastic and Reconstructive Surgery (AAFPRS) are:

- 36 percent of plastic surgeons saw a couple that underwent surgery together.
- 25 percent saw a mother and daughter who had surgery together.
- 31 percent saw a patient who received plastic surgery as a gift.

In addition to these findings, researchers note that plastic surgery patients generally travel dozens of miles from their residence for treatment for reasons of pleasure, not fear of discovery or need to find a specialized physician. Instead, patients report that they travel far away to create a vacation-like atmosphere for the surgery, some taking advantage of plastic surgery travel packages.

Amidst this open atmosphere for plastic surgery, there are many varieties of naysayers. Of these people, there is a sizable group who voice their opposition to what they see as the misplaced search for worth through one's body. Instead of pumping themselves up, they undergo character-building bootcamp. Jerry Hill, B.S. Kinesiology, Temple University, Certified Renegade Strength and Conditioning Specialist and former United States Marine is the founder of FitForce Camp. Through his Fitness Training Camps, participants regularly lose pounds and inches and feel strong, powerful, and according to Hill, on occasion, invincible. FitForce Camp specializes in providing a choice for those who are enraged at what the industry continues to sell. For more information on Hill and FitForce Camp, visit *www. fitforcecamp.com*.

Among medical practitioners themselves, there is also the blaming of the media for problems related to plastic surgery. The electronic newsletter of the American Society of Plastic Surgeons, *Plastic Surgery Today*, faults the current spate of reality makeover shows with stoking unrealistic expectations of what cosmetic surgery can do. Unrealistic or not, these expectations lead the number of people seeking cosmetic surgery to continue to grow, and perhaps for cosmetic surgery even to become safer and more successful in creating aesthetically pleasing results.

Whether it becomes safer or not, some medical practitioners will fault the practice nearly completely. Voicing the greatest disapproval are the British. To British psychologists, the need for cosmetic surgery is less a question of hope than of lack of fortitude. According to Ros Taylor, a chartered psychologist practicing in London, said, "The growing popularity of cosmetic surgery probably means that we are deeply superficial," she told the BBC News Web site. She continued, "Nowadays, cosmetic surgery is easily accessible, but it may not change your life, and it could be that people who are considering it need to look at other confidence issues first."

Up with Health Care Costs

39 The dominant health care trend of the late 20th century will continue well into the 21st. Health care costs to consumers will rise markedly each year, and larger numbers of Americans will be unable to afford traditional coverage. However, increases are likely to be in lower double-digit percentages than in the past several years. According to the actuarial firm Milliman USA, health maintenance organizations expected to raise their rates 11 percent in 2005, while preferred provider organizations expected to increase their rates 12 percent. That was a slight improvement over recent years, but still the sixth consecutive year of cost increases in the double digits.

Reasons behind the rise in health care costs, Milliman reports, include an aging population; rising rates of certain chronic or ongoing conditions, like obesity, diabetes, and asthma; the high cost of medical malpractice litigation; shortages in health care workers; reduced use of managed care; cost shifting from government to private insurers; costs of HIPAA compliance; and consumer demand for more performance-driven health care coverage. The American Association of Health Plans adds that increased government benefit mandates and duplicative regulations added $20 billion to overall health premiums.

Even as costs rise, so do the number of Americans who have no health insurance—45 million at present, including 8 million children. In addition, many Americans are underinsured, as the coverage that is available to them increasingly becomes circumscribed. Unions are dwindling, many jobs are part-time without benefits, and the days of the industrial worker with full Blue Cross/Blue Shield coverage are numbered.

Is this a problem for the United States? To some thinkers, it is not. Some public pundits (particularly some radio talk show hosts) have said that there should be no health insurance at all, and certainly none offered or regulated by the U.S. government. If a person cannot pay for services out of pocket, he or she should not receive them.

However, other groups are working with insurance companies and the government to expand possibilities for coverage and make it affordable for the uninsured. For example, the House of Representatives passed the Small Business Health Fairness Act (S. 545). It was designed to allow small business owners, who are increasingly unable to afford health coverage for their workers, to form national alliances through their trade or business associations that allow them to purchase national health care plans for themselves and their employees. Currently, these trade/business associations represent 80 million workers. Another group, Communicating for Agriculture & the Self-Employed, advises making it easier for individuals and small businesses to get coverage by increasing their bargaining power with insurers and health providers and making tax credits and vouchers available to low-income citizens. It also suggests expanding the types of coverage available, such as low-cost policies with limited coverage.

But the forces driving costs upward will continue and will hit providers hard. According to the Centers for Medicaid and Medicare Services, health insurance premiums and the medical expenses that drive consumer costs upward will continue to rise dramatically between now and 2010. Among the health services projected to have the highest increases are hospital care; physician services; outpatient prescription and over-the-counter drugs; and nursing home and home health care. However, administrative costs of health insurance organizations increased at a slower rate than health insurance premiums since 1998. Administrative expenses increased on average by 6.2 percent, while the average insurance rate increased by 8.4 percent.

These increases are expected to affect both private and public health providers. For example, Medicare cost increases and spending are expected to rise from $252 billion in 2002 to $456 billion in 2010. State-run health programs will also be affected. In 2003, the Hawaii Medical Service Association (HMSA) asked for an average rate increase of 11.5 percent to cover increasing expenses. It was the largest increase for the state's most popular health plan in more than a decade. Other states face similar shortfalls.

Several forces will affect private providers as well. Among them is the underwriting cycle where health care premiums grow faster or slower than underlying health care costs. Because underpricing was standard in the mid-1990s, higher prices will ensue during the early century to regain profits for insurers. Another trend will be for private companies, which pay for employees' insurance coverage, to try to encourage employee health through incentives for healthy lifestyle improvements.

The rise of most quotidian elements of health care expenditures will bring the greatest increases for the largest number of Americans. One is prescription drugs. From 1995 to 2001, the average annual rate of increase for prescription drug expenditures averaged 15 percent per year—higher than for any other type of health expenditure.

From all corners—the patient with coverage, the patient without coverage, public providers, and private providers—the call is the same: Help!

V

Lifestyles

The Colors of Money and Other Ways to Prevent Counterfeiting

40 Money has gone Technicolor to save the nation from counterfeiters. The Treasury Department is protecting U.S. currency. In May 2003, U.S. Treasury Secretary John Snow announced a move to redesign the dollar notes, beginning with the $20 bill. The aim is to keep the nation's currency a "worldwide symbol of security and integrity" by "protecting [it] against counterfeiting and making it easier for people to confirm the authenticity of their hard-earned money." The $50 bill followed in 2004; the $100 in 2005.

The redesign is marked by the use of different background colors for different denominations. In addition, a watermark, security thread, color-shifting ink and microprinting mark the new bills and make them more difficult to counterfeit. Further, the Treasury Department will introduce new designs for currency every seven to 10 years.

Treasury Secretary Snow called the security measures "The New Color of Money." On Capitol Hill, the Advanced Counterfeit Deterrence Steering Committee calls it a "comprehensive counterfeit strategy."

Writing humorously about the large-scale redesign, an assistant professor of history at the University of Georgia called it "Euro envy," recalling colorful European currency.

According to the U.S. Department of State, technology now makes digital counterfeiting easier and cheaper than it was even a decade ago; it now accounts for nearly 50 percent of counterfeited bills. Still, the government maintains that rates for the counterfeiting of U.S. currency are low. Worldwide it is between only 0.01 and 0.02 percent. U.S. law enforcement authorities note also that three counterfeit bills are passed for every counterfeit bill that enters the currency system.

The passing of counterfeit checks is also an ongoing problem. According to the National Check Fraud Center in Charleston, South Carolina, check fraud alone reaches $10 billion a year. The check counterfeiting process can work in different ways including printing fraudulent checks using office-supply store equipment, purchasing a payroll check and using it as a template for counterfeiting, using stolen identities, and collusion with a company insider. The Provident Bank of Maryland reports that sophisticated computer programs let criminals create corporate payroll checks that are nearly impossible to distinguish from the real thing. However, the massive move toward electronic bill paying is reducing the number of checks written, so that counterfeiters will need to abandon checks and go back to straight currency.

Of course, in one way or another, counterfeiters may always be around. In movies, big-time crooks will still walk through airports with briefcases full of counterfeit cash. Protest counterfeiters will still operate, like those of the Action Against Racism of Cleveland (ARA) against the Salvation Army called the "Queer Dollars Campaign." To voice opposition to antigay policies of the Salvation Army, the ARA printed fake three-dollar bills and stuffed them in Salvation Army red kettles.

Other small-time crooks will also survive, working at such low levels that they may fail to be investigated. One such lawbreaker calls himself a "low-tech counterfeiter" who works only in one- and five-dollar bills, which are less likely to be either redesigned or targeted by major counterfeiters, who work in $20 and $100 denominations. (Mr. Low-Tech

redeems his fake money at vending machine and laundromats, perpetu-
ally carrying around a tote bag for the change he collects.) For him, the
future looks rosy because the government now has no plans to redesign
$1 bills.

In its pursuit of more substantial counterfeiters, the U.S. Department
of State notes that the conviction rate for counterfeiting prosecutions is
about 99 percent.

Community-Building

41 Old-time science fiction often depicted the inhabitants of
the future as living in isolation: Winston Smith, persecuted for being
in love in *1984*; the astronauts hurtling far from earth in *2001: A Space
Odyssey*; even George Jetson, who walked Astro on a little treadmill
outside his lonely high-rise. But what was the future is now here and is
more characterized by community-building than by isolation. In real
space and cyberspace, in ways large and small, people are bent on
restoring, strengthening, and creating the human links that make for
social connectedness.

The spread of gated communities—planned neighborhoods
enclosed by walls or fences—is the most visible sign of the trend toward
community-building. The number of gated communities nationwide
has increased from about 2,000 in the 1970s to more than 50,000 in the
early 2000s; according to one estimate, about one in eight Americans is
now living in these settings. Desire for additional security is one driving
factor, as is an interest in excluding outsiders of various sorts: Edward
J. Blakely and Mary Gail Snyder, who analyze this trend in *Fortress
America*, call it "forting up." But the desire for a more close-knit community within the walls of the fortress is also at work. Ironically, says
Setha Low, who analyzes gated communities in *Behind the Gates*, such

settings are statistically no safer than other suburbs—so if security is what residents are looking for, they may not get as much as they would like.

Even if they are not behind gates, Americans are increasingly living in some kind of common interest housing developments, governed by homeowner's associations. Such developments can end with homeowners feeling oppressed by restrictive rules, but they can also foster feelings of community. Celebration, Florida, a small town founded by Disney Corporation near Disney World explicitly to promote a sense of community, continues to aim for what planners call a "spirit of neighborliness," with plenty of front porches, park benches, and communal events.

Even in New York City, legendary for its lack of neighborliness, greater numbers of people are turning their apartment buildings into small towns, with lots of sociable amenities, from gardens and recreation rooms to concerts and classes. One building, the St. Tropez at 340 East 64th Street, has a party room, movie nights, body-sculpting classes, and brunches. "We . . . want to keep a sense of cohesiveness," Robert Metz, editor of the building's newsletter, told the *New York Times*. In part, the still-potent memory of 9/11 has been driving the trend in New York City toward greater social connectedness, but it is part of a larger trend nationwide.

A less-common but more radical arrangement, the intentional community, has also been increasing. An intentional community is one in which people live together and work cooperatively to fulfill a common purpose or express a set of shared values, whether spiritual or secular. Though some people think this kind of development died out with the communes of the 1960s and the cults of the 1970s, their numbers have been rising since at least the 1990s.

In cities and towns of all kinds, a salon movement is growing, in which people meet at a prearranged time—in cafés, bookstores, houses, or churches—to converse on various topics. The Socrates Café network, which has fostered philosophical discussion since the mid-1990s, now has 200 salons operating nationwide. Political scientist David Niven told *Reader's Digest* that "thoughtful contact with others in a salon" is a way to fulfill the need for "a feeling of connection."

The Internet has made it easier for people to "meet up" in salons or other venues. In fact, *meetup* is now a term for a gathering that is prearranged online but takes place offline, in a real café or other public place. Meetup.com is a service that organizes such gatherings on specific topics of interest—"about anything, anywhere." Over a million people have used the service to sign up for meetups.

A weirder, more frivolous version of the same phenomenon is the "flash mob"—a large group of people who use the Internet to arrange to meet in some location, perform some action, then disperse. The action is often pointless but amusing, such as quacking like a duck. But it can be more purposeful. In 2004, an estimated 3,000 people came to a free, surprise U2 concert under the Brooklyn Bridge. They had learned about it on the Web or by word-of-mouth.

More serious still is the "smart mob," a leaderless group of people who use technology (the Internet, cell phones, e-mail, Wireless Fidelity [Wi-Fi]) to maintain a community and/or organize and accomplish some purpose. (Howard Rheingold analyzes these groups extensively in *Smart Mobs: The Next Social Revolution*, 2002.) Not only are such groups increasingly important to election campaigns and political movements, but they are also building new forms of community, part virtual, part real.

Then there is the plethora of communities that are wholly virtual: people who have never met in person but who interact electronically on listservs, chat rooms, forums, multiplayer online games, and dozens of other virtual communities. The online auction site eBay, for example, is effectively a community in which people interact as if at a huge open-air flea market. Virtual communities even interact with other communities. In 2002, the *New York Times* reported that a check forger connected to a Macintosh sale on eBay was caught when the victim enlisted the help of Macintosh users through the close-knit world of Macintosh electronic bulletin boards. When the criminal was caught, one bulletin board message said: "I LOVE YOU GUYS!!! *group hug for mac users everywhere.*"

In some ways, virtual communities are even stronger than real ones. In *The Monochrome Society* (2001), Amitai Etzioni remarks, "If there is a snowstorm or you are sick with the flu, not very mobile, or afraid of the streets, you may not make it to your local country store or senior center. But you can always log on." Yet, virtual and real communities are not either-or. Increasingly, the growth of one is reinforcing that of the other—and both are part of a long-term trend toward stronger social connectedness.

The Decline of Spelling

42 For many Americans, spelling has become as casual as fashion. It is practiced laboriously for serious occasions, like writing tax forms, but for everyday practice, such as work or e-mail, it is sidestepped. This attitude is very different from that of our neighbor Canada, which worries about having its hard-won spelling distinctions subsumed by American or British spelling. Americans don't worry about spelling as an element of national identity or as any problem at all. Instead they blithely dismiss spelling, as did one U.S. blogger, "It's overrated. I'm fine as long as I have my Monte [sic] Python tapes."

Because poor spelling in adults isn't seen as a national problem, there has been little call for reform. Instead we regale ourselves in stories of famous historical figures who couldn't spell, and go on with our lives.

But the case for children is different. Families and schools view spelling as a reflection of good educational practices and concerned parenting. When kids can't spell well, it's seen as an educational disaster, and parents look to the schools for a source to fault. One mother from Illinois found fault with the school's lack of emphasis on spelling and overemphasis on building self-esteem. She explains, "When my oldest boy was in first grade his teacher told the kids, 'It's not how you spell the words, as long as they look like how they sound.' [So y]ou get sentences like, 'I ait the kow beecus it was ded.'" And sometimes, the schools' attempts at reinvigorating spelling curriculum fall short.

For example, a few years ago, the Milwaukee, Wisconsin, public school system issued a publication touting its high standards. The document included references to "rigourous" requirements and "proficiencey" exams.

In addition, there are other culprits responsible for the spelling debacle. One is the misspelling made in e-mail, where words and phrases are shortened and misspelled at will. More prominent and troublesome is the computer spell checker. Useful but overused, it has infused nonspellers with confidence. But the application is highly fallible, allowing correctly spelled but nonsensical words to slip through.

While bestsellers like *Eats, Shoots and Leaves* about punctuation and other books on the English language may continue to be published, as they have for the past two years, so will haphazard spelling. It will be fought by the millions who think spelling distinguishes and helps to sustain society. As cultural critic James J. Kilpatrick points out, "Spelling is not merely a tedious exercise in a fourth-grade classroom. Spelling is one of the outward and visible marks of a disciplined mind."

Distance Learning Grows

43 In the 21st century, America will have more students of all ages. There will be the record enrollments of "echo boomers," the children of baby boomers, who were born between 1979 and 1994. There are the children of the millions of new immigrants. There are varieties of adults, from immigrants who want to learn languages and skills for employment to an entire generation of baby boomers who want to return to school.

Enrollment in public and private colleges and other institutes of higher education is expected to rise to 17.5 million by 2010. This represents a 20 percent increase since 1998. In addition, some states are expected to have heightened percentages of enrollment. According to the Western Interstate Commission for Higher Education, California, Arizona, Colorado, Washington, and Nevada will increase enrollment by 25 to 35 percent by 2008.

Community college enrollment is set to increase greatly, particularly for older students. According to the National Center for Education Statistics (NCES), the number of community college students over age 25 is expected to increase 9 percent from 1999 to 2010.

The projected growth rates of enrollment reflect the exponential rate of college attendance over the past century. Since 1930, reports the Commission on National Investment in Higher Education, higher education enrollment in the United States increased seven times, while the overall population only doubled. The University of California says 65 percent of high school graduates now enroll in college.

To accommodate the huge demand, distance learning will become increasingly popular. Distance-learning expert David W. Butler says, "Distance or open learning . . . is in a strategic position to bring about the first overhaul of the teaching/learning process in 400 years, since the creation of the university concept in medieval Europe." According to Butler, distance learning is defined by the following: a student and instructor "geographically remote" from each other; the use of electronic and other "educational media"; and the use of "two-way communication between teacher and learner."

The number of students involved in distance learning has already increased greatly over the past decade. In 1998, 710,000 students were enrolled in distance-learning courses. In 2002, the number increased to 23 million. Fifteen percent of all higher-education students are taking distance-learning courses, which is an increase from 5 percent in 1998. The International Data Corporation (IDC) projects that distance learning will grow by 33 percent during the first years of the 21st century.

According to experts in the field, distance learning will be particularly strong in some areas, including career areas expected to grow in the early 21st century. According to the U.S. Bureau of Labor Statistics, some of the areas of projected growth include teaching, computer-software engineering, nursing, accounting, and marketing.

Providers of distance learning have included Western Governors University, an online university developed by a consortium of eighteen governors, and the University of Phoenix Online. Others have included Suffolk University, Wayne Huizenga School, AIU Online, the University Alliance, the Art Institute Online, American Graduate School of Management, and the University of Liverpool.

Many states have established local support centers to encourage distance learning and offer counseling and technological aid. For example, Northern Arizona University allows students to attend lecture courses online and has a distributed learning program consisting of more than 30 degree programs with 900 courses and 4,700 students.

Educational experts also believe that the general concept of distance learning will evolve and change. Formerly it was a synchronous learning experience of students and teacher at different sites experiencing a class at a certain time. Now the educational model is different. More likely the distance learning class is an asynchronous distance-learning system, where classes can be taken and participated in through computer and Internet access. Universities and colleges that offer distance learning will also have to redefine student classifications to include those who attend the school offsite.

Distance learning need not be all or nothing. Blended learning is a hybrid approach that combines classroom and online learning. It offers some of the conveniences of online courses without the total loss of face-to-face contact.

Along with public and private colleges and universities, the U.S. government is also involved in distance learning. Acknowledging the growth in the number of students seeking higher education in the 21st century, the government is supporting private-public partnerships that include college-level coursework. Through the U.S. Department of Education's Distance Education Demonstration Programs and the Learning Anytime Anywhere Partnerships program, distance education providers can offer increased federal aid because the restrictions placed on them are being reviewed and changed.

The U.S. military uses distance learning. The U.S. Army is developing a distance-learning system to serve the army in the United States and overseas. By 2010, there will be 745 classrooms at more than 200 sites to teach 525 courses virtually at their home stations, according to *Army LINK News.*

Still, there has been criticism of the distance-learning process from educational groups. The National Education Association said that distance learning costs more than on-campus courses, and the College Board has said that distance learning puts students without computers at a disadvantage. Another education expert says, "Face-to-face with a talented professor in a classroom is still the best way to learn."

The education experts may be right, but the reality is that face-to-face learning is simply not available to all those who want it, whether because of money or time. For these students, distance learning is another educational option. Former Secretary of Education Richard W. Riley has called education "the key civil right for the 21st century." For many, distance learning will help extend that right.

Dust Thou Art—But Not in the Ground

44 It remains true in America that nothing is certain but death and taxes. Disposition, the term used by the funeral industry to describe the final handling of the deceased's remains is another matter. While most American bodies are interred in religiously affiliated or nondenominational cemeteries, a growing minority is being cremated. According to the Cremation Association of North America, cremations as a percentage of total deaths in the United States rose from 25 percent in 1999 to 33 percent by 2004. Further, the association projects that cremation will be chosen by 37 percent of Americans by 2010 and 44 percent by 2025.

One reason for the growing numbers of cremation is its increasing acceptance by churches. As a spokesperson for the Episcopal Church in the United States explained, cremation may be chosen for both economic and environmental reasons, and the fact that the Church as a body is more accepting of the practice. As spokesperson Dennis Downes says, "I think there is probably a growing sense that what is important is the spirit."

Cremation is also being accepted by the Catholic Church in the United States. It has been permitted by the Church since 1963, but just how many Catholics are choosing cremation in the 21st century is a guess. Anecdotal evidence, however, suggests the percentage of Catholic cremation is lower than the national average.

Geographically, the percentage of Catholic cremations varies widely and is closely tied to state trends. Rates are highest in the far western states but substantially lower in the South, where more faithful seem to reverence the traditional funeral and burial.

Because of this sharp rise in cremation, the "death-care professional" is offering "many more opportunities with cremation, including memorialization and innovative approaches," said Jack Springer, executive director of the Cremation Association of North America (CANA).

According to CANA, people are devising various personalized rituals for dispensation of cremated remains. Reflecting these changes, many cemeteries are building or expanding their columbarium, a place where ashes are kept. In addition, cemeteries are discussing the building of a scatter garden or burial sites for ashes. Many church cemeteries already provide such a garden and marker for the dead. Some families are even choosing to take ashes to a location that was important to their loved one. Urns that are biodegradable, which easily disintegrate in water or freeze and shatter when a helium balloon carries it to a certain height in the atmosphere, make that even more possible. Despite these innovations, "most cremations are still being [buried] in the cemetery," said Nancy Cole, office and business manager for Carroll Memorials in Fredericksburg, Virginia.

The realities of space and buyers' preference mean that cemetery owners are revamping how the business is run. In previous times, families bought large lots, with as many as 20 burial sites, Episcopal Church spokesperson Dennis Downes said, but "there are very few families that do that any more. Generally people will buy one or two sites or maybe three or four: very rarely more than that, and that is largely to do with the mobility of our society."

Still others are rejecting the ecologically unfriendly process of embalming and sealed coffin burial entirely. They are adopting green burial. One such burial ground is the 350 acres left as a nature preserve in Florida. It has no embalming fluid, steel-lined coffins, or concrete vaults. As owner John Wilkerson knows, traditional cemeteries are incredible resource consumers—some 800,000 gallons of formaldehyde-based embalming fluid and 40 million board feet of timber get deep-sixed in America's million-plus acres of graveyards each year. Unlike conventional urban cemeteries, biological deserts that can pack upward of 1,200 bodies into an acre, the deceased at Glendale Nature Preserve will be tucked discreetly here and there among the returning trees, while the wildest areas on the farm will remain grave-free.

With its low overhead (no grass to mow and no pesticides to spray), Glendale can charge less for plots and funerals—about $2,000 total—and still generate a tidy sum for long-term stewardship. But Wilkerson had more than money on his mind when he dreamed up the idea. "My daddy told me before he died, 'Don't ever let our farm get turned into a trailer park,'" he says. "And 'ever' is a long time."

Others have similar practical views. The concept appeals to retired Detroit auto worker Ford Sims, 67, of Destin. He hopes Glendale will be his final resting place so his six children will not have to spend their inheritance to bury him. "I've learned that it's fairly expensive to just die," Sims said. "From my perspective, if you put me six feet under in a gunny sack, I'm happy."

Gamblers R Us

45 Gambling in America is everywhere. It's far beyond the luxe casinos of Las Vegas and Atlantic City. It's off-track, online, on the water, at the convenience store, at the track, in the mail, at the hall. It also comes in many varieties: slots, cards, lotteries, horses, dogs, video screens. It brings in revenue for states and privately run gambling businesses. And for most of the tens of millions betting means, as comedian Drew Carey says, "another walk to the ATM."

For the record, two decades ago, commercialized gambling existed in two states. Today, various forms of gambling occupy 48 states—only Hawaii and Utah remain free of gambling. In 2003, the gross revenues from gambling were $72.9 billion—more money than Americans spend on movie tickets, theme parks, spectator sports, and videogames combined.

Some forms of gambling are being revitalized. Currently, one of the fastest growing betting systems is slot machines. About 40 million people played slots in 2003. Playing is expected to increase over the next few years, owing to machines created by leading mathematicians, and game, light, and sound designers that get the player's heart rate going and take money from him, willingly. "[Y]ou can lose money faster on a nickel slot machine than at a $10 blackjack table," said Nigel Turner, scientist at the Center for Addiction and Mental Health in Toronto. To antigambling voices, slots are the "crack cocaine" of gambling. With a time span of six seconds for each pull on the slot handle, a person plays ten games per minute, 600 per hour; and at $2 per spin, it is $1,200 per hour. And newly designed slots with licensing connections to Carey himself or George Lucas's *Star Wars* are meant to attract a younger audience in their thirties.

Governments continue to expand the use of gambling. They continue to increase revenue from it, but find most of their ballot initiatives to increase state gambling voted down. During the past year, there were

45 gambling-expansion proposals (bills, referendums, etc.) in 29 states. Out of 45 separate attempts to expand gambling, only three states succeeded. The remaining 42 proposals were defeated. Voters want no more gambling expansion. Combining racetracks and casinos (termed "racinos") is the newest rage, particularly while interest in the horse and dog racing industry continues to decline.

Many social critics disagree with the government embrace of gambling to resolve overspending problems. Economist C. Ford Rudge, writing in the *Minneapolis Star-Tribune*, says, "Gov. Tim Pawlenty, like many members of the Legislature, wears his religion on his sleeve. He is also a supporter of gambling, euphemistically called 'gaming.' Why does a good Christian like the governor support spending taxpayer dollars to build a casino? The answer is not redeeming: It's about money and ambition. Pawlenty made a pact with his own devil: the Taxpayers League of Minnesota."

Citizens who oppose state-sanctioned gambling point to the fallacy of the bounteous revenues supposedly coming from taxes. A newspaper article against legalized gambling in Rhode Island said, "Yearly expenditures by the 21 towns in New London County jumped by $58 million more than they would have without the casinos, reported the Southeastern Connecticut Council of Governments. These costs, offset by only $14 million from a state fund maintained by slot machine revenues, were required to educate the children of casino workers, deal with increased traffic and provide other municipal services. Increased taxes and debt made up the difference between the extra $58 million cost and the $14 million received from state taxes on the casinos.

According to the American Gaming Association, which represents the non-Indian gaming industry, commercial casinos paid $4 billion in taxes in 2002. Lotteries, all state-run, generated $18.638 billion. Only two states allowed no gaming whatsoever: Utah and Hawaii.

Religious groups oppose gambling as a political policy or personal choice. According to Dr. James Dobson's Focus on the Family Web site at *www.family.org*, "Focus on the Family opposes all forms of legalized gambling for both moral and pragmatic reasons. We believe the net societal effect of our government's embrace of gambling has been disastrous."

Studies nationwide shed more light on the problem of gambling addiction. Between 4 percent and 5 percent of adults nationwide struggle with some form of gambling habit, according to a 1999 study by the National Opinion Research Center.

There are variables that exacerbate the problem of gambling, from age group to profession to geography. Living within 10 miles of a casino doubles the odds a person will develop a gambling habit, according to the Research Institute on Addictions at New York's University of Buffalo. In addition, according to the State of Illinois Department of Aging, senior problem gambling is rising. And American soldiers have been and continue to be active gamblers, and some are problem gamblers. The long stretches of inactivity and potential for physical injury lead soldiers to find calm through the ritual of card playing and betting.

Whether at casinos or slots, gambling will continue. Whether used as a stress relief or in the hopes of getting rich quick, people will always believe they can beat the odds.

More Bananas, Fewer Potatoes

46 As America ages and becomes more diverse, we are becoming less the fast food nation than the supermarket society. According to the Economic Research Service (ERS) of the Food and Drug Administration (FDA), the population of the United States will continue to grow, from 281.4 million in 2000 to 331.9 million in 2020, but age and ethnic changes will alter what and how Americans eat.

We will still spend a lot on food: The additional number of people will increase food sales by $208 billion from current numbers of $800 billion. But increasing numbers of people of Hispanic and Asian descent are projected to mean possible increases in some food areas, like citrus fruits, and declines in other, such as potatoes and dairy. In addition, the aging population will eat less fried food, cheese, and sugar. The popularity of eating out may erode as well, given age and demographic changes. Not only do Hispanics and Asians eat out less frequently on average than other dominant U.S. ethnic groups, the increased number of over-60 Americans are more likely on average to dine at home than they did when they were younger.

Short-term changes in food include more diversity and high quality in produce and in-store prepared foods. Running neck-and-neck with the desire for nutrition-rich produce is the desire for pretty food. To that end, gardeners and grocers now regularly grow or stock sweet potatoes, multiple varieties of sweet and hot peppers, slender pole beans, and curly deep green chard and rabe. In addition, some foods long considered ugly and unappealing have gained new cachet as they are reinvented with a new name and called functional food. Foremost in this movement is the prune, now called the dried plum, and praised for its usefulness as being high in antioxidants. Blueberries are similarly praised for their high quantities of antioxidants.

People are also more aware of the chemical compounds of other everyday fruits and vegetables. For example, apples have long been touted for their healthful properties, and there is now scientific proof for them. One study shows that apples are the most concentrated food source of flavonoids, a group of phytochemicals, natural substances that protect against cancer and heart disease, and may block the ability of certain viruses to grow and spread.

Lowly squash, too, is full of healthful properties. Winter, acorn, Hubbard, and butternut squash are more concentrated in several nutrients than summer squash. Its dark color is a hint that winter squash is an outstanding source of carotenoids, a family of antioxidants believed to enhance immunity and heart health as well as play an anticancer role. Winter squash is also a good source of vitamins A and C, potassium, iron, riboflavin, and dietary fiber.

Awareness of food properties is also growing. People want to know what their favorite foods contain and what changes they have to incorporate into their diets. They are particularly interested in healthful foods, or what one food writer calls "medifoods." "You can't open a magazine or newspaper without seeing information about blueberries as antioxidants, pomegranate juice as an antioxidant, foods as medicines," said Karen Caplan, president of the specialty produce company Frieda's in Los Alamedos, California.

In their continuing quest for healthful foods, Americans are incorporating the cuisines of non-Western countries. In this way, Asia is a center for inspiration and health leadership: New-to-America robiotic dairy drinks, energy drinks, and enhanced waters have all been long established in Asia. For example, Red Bull was on the market in Thailand for many years before an Austrian company licensed the concept. And soy is finally being accepted in the West but it has for centuries been part of the Asian diet.

Various healthful food preparation techniques are gaining vogue. One is as simple as eating food en brochette, or on skewers, grilled. Another is the raw food movement. Known about for years, eating raw is gaining popularity. Raw-only restaurants continue to open, and more people phase out cooked foods, for health and anticruelty purposes. "Raw food is living food," says a raw-food restaurant owner. However, heat of less than 120 degrees doesn't "kill" the bacteria in the food. So raw-food enthusiasts can use a heat dehydrator, an appliance that blows hot air on food until it "cooks" to a safe temperature.

There is also the powerhouse known as organic and near-privately grown food. Organics have been growing greatly. The industry has grown 24 percent a year from 2001 to 2003. Artisan breads have also become popular. Artisan bakeries exist as stand-alone stores or as suppliers to high-end supermarkets.

For restaurants, the lasting trends appear to be the intermixing of cuisines and the desire for personalization. In *Restaurants USA* magazine, restaurant owners spoke of the desire—for health, age, or social reasons—for smaller portions, or else portion presentations that can be shared easily. Simply prepared, flavorful food is also a lasting preference for American eaters. They don't want only childhood comfort food, but fresh food prepared in inventive ways. And American stand-bys will continue, such as the steakhouse. With over 6,000 in operation, it is part of the American menu.

In sum, people want to eat smart, well, and fast. In the kitchen, that means more cooking oneself, but with some help. "We are so time-crunched that people want things that are portable," said Karen Caplan of Frieda's. "For example, a friend of mine made a terrific squash casserole by combining already cut-up butternut squash with some butternut squash soup. But she bought all the ingredients already prepped. I think there's a resurgence of interest in home cooking. We don't want to buy everything ready-made, but that doesn't mean we don't want some help."

More Hidden Segregation

47 The civil rights movement made its mark a half century ago, but schools, neighborhoods, and cities across America have become more effectively segregated than they had been in decades. According to a study of desegregation done by Harvard University, while U.S. public schools are becoming steadily more nonwhite, with minority student enrollment approaching 40 percent of all U.S. public school students, classes are more segregated by geography and economics. Money may not buy happiness, but it can get children into a good school system.

The desegregation of black students, which increased continuously from the 1950s to the late 1980s, has now receded to levels not seen in three decades. Black students are experiencing the most rapid resegregation in the south, triggered by Supreme Court decisions in the 1990s, and have now lost all progress recorded since the 1960s

There is also large-scale school segregation for the groups that have seen the most dramatic population growth over the past few years—Hispanics and, to a lesser extent, Asians. Hispanic students are the most segregated minority group, with steadily rising segregation since federal data was first collected a third of a century ago. Hispanics are segregated both by race and poverty, and a pattern of linguistic segregation is also developing. Hispanics have by far the highest high school dropout rates. Asians are the most integrated and the most educationally successful group in American schools. Interracial schools, particularly ones that have high success rates for college admission, are uncommon.

Part of the problem with schools lies in the segregation within metropolitan areas, traditionally home to many immigrants. At the end of the twentieth century, the majority of blacks remained severely segregated from whites in major cities and the surrounding regions. (According to the U.S. Census, metropolitan Detroit is the nation's most segregated area.) Due to the persistence of high-volume immigration, Hispanic and Asian segregation from whites has increased, although it is still best characterized as moderate.

In some ways, the root of the racial inequity is simple: wealth. White people are able to accumulate more of it because they have more worthwhile investments, such as their homes in better neighborhoods. And once money is passed from generation to generation, it can accumulate. Because neighborhoods are racially segregated, African Americans' homes do not grow in value as fast as whites' homes do. According to historian Thomas Shapiro in *The Hidden Cost of Being African-American: How Wealth Perpetuates Inequality*, housing segregation costs African Americans tens of thousands of dollars in home equity. Homebuyers look for amenities commonly found in predominantly white neighborhoods. They pay extra for parks, convenient shopping and attractive views. Parents pay huge premiums for what they perceive to be good schools, using easy-to-observe markers, such as students' race. These preferences raise the costs that first-time homebuyers face when they try to buy houses in mostly white neighborhoods. Inequality has grown because each new generation has been willing to pay a higher premium for these amenities. The market doesn't punish discrimination; it rewards it, and continues it as parents pass inherited wealth to their children, who keep settling in privileged, segregated communities.

One public policy analyst suggests that revamping the inheritance tax system might even out inequities between the races—the privileged and less so. But such an overhaul is not expected in the near future.

There are less overt examples of perpetuating racial inequality. One is a community's lack of interest in changing a nonintegrated school system. For example, one upper-middle-class woman said she was unconcerned with troubles in the local public school because she never intended to send her children there. Author Shapiro points out that her indifference—and that of others like her—is just one more obstacle in the path of people trying to improve local public education

As the director of the Harvard desegregation study said, "Dr. [Martin Luther] King would not have been celebrating today; he would have been marching again." And as one Detroit teacher noted about her segregated city, "We're still dealing with stuff we were dealing with during the civil rights time."

The NASCARization of America

48 When President George W. Bush needed a regular Joe to testify to his merits as a candidate for reelection, he could have turned to a plumber, fireman, or real estate agent. But he turned to former National Association for Stock Car Auto Racing (NASCAR) driver Darrell Waltrip, who stumped for him in both the 2000 and 2004 campaigns. Waltrip brought a rough, amiable manliness to the ticket, refusing to talk about politics and emphasizing Bush's character. "I'm not an issue guy," said Waltrip. "I know the man." It was an effective line—and another sign of how influential NASCAR has become. More and more, America is being NASCARized.

NASCAR was founded in 1948 to organize and promote stock car racing, where the cars look more like ordinary vehicles than souped-up racers. NASCAR events such as Florida's Daytona 500 were soon popular attractions in the South and Midwest, but were slow to penetrate beyond those areas. Then, in the 1990s, NASCAR racing grew into a national pastime. NASCAR's Nextel Cup championship became the most popular racing series in the United States, attracting more than 6 million spectators in 1997. In 2002, 17 of the top 20 U.S. sporting events, as measured by attendance, were NASCAR races, and the events were second only to football in television viewership. NASCAR racers like Dale Earnhardt became household names. NASCAR merchandise turned into a preferred Father's Day gift. By the early 2000s, there were an estimated 70 million NASCAR fans in the country.

Those numbers were high enough to make NASCAR fans a political force. Politicians began aggressive courting of "NASCAR dads"—conservative, white, working-class fathers who tend to vote Republican but might swing either way. In the *Dallas Morning News* in September 2002, Colleen McCain described a NASCAR dad (a term coined by pollster Celinda Lake) as "a working-class man who places more emphasis on values than on party labels." Those values included manliness, family, God, country, small government, gun ownership, and opposition to gays.

In the 2004 presidential election, both parties did their best to NASCARize themselves. Senator Bob Graham went so far as to sponsor a racing pickup truck and emblazon it with the slogan "Bob Graham for President." That tactic didn't get him the Democratic nomination, but the eventual nominee, John Kerry, tried to appeal to NASCAR voters by emphasizing his military roots and going hunting. However, he became better known for going wind-surfing, which perhaps appealed to wind-surfing dads, but not NASCAR dads. Meanwhile, the Bush campaign held a multistate NASCAR tour featuring seven of NASCAR's best known drivers, including Waltrip, and many more NASCAR owners and drivers endorsed Bush. Bush won handily. There was a strong perception that the NASCAR vote had been crucial for him, along with the "moral values" that had influenced that vote.

NASCAR voters had proved their power, and where power goes, devotees follow. NASCAR is increasingly becoming less of a sporting subculture and more of a national cultural influence. People across America want to NASCARize themselves—to look, act, and believe like the sort of person who goes to stock car races. The NASCAR dad is the latest incarnation of the cowboy, the American noble savage, embodied in the past by everyone from Natty Bumpo to John Wayne. We can't all exhibit the earthiness and toughness of the ideal NASCAR dad, but we can at least buy a hat like his.

NASCAR is even becoming a term of praise. Jeff Zucker, president of NBC, lauded incoming nightly news anchor Brian Williams by telling Peter Johnson of *USA Today*, "No one understands this Nascar nation more than Brian." Williams himself boasts of owning part interest in a dirt-track stock-car team. Frank Rich of the *New York Times* saw it as a sign that the television news industry is starting to become NASCARized—and correspondingly supportive of the president. "If full-scale NASCARization is what's coming next," Rich wrote in December 2004, "there will soon be no pictures but those promising a mission accomplished, no news but good news."

How will the NASCAR vote affect future elections? Right now, Republicans have the edge in appealing to NASCAR fans, 70 percent of whom are Republican. Democrats may cut into that lead, but they will have to overcome the obstacle identified by Democratic strategist Dave "Mudcat" Saunders, who told BBC News: "Rural southern men, they're going to vote Bush because there's a perception that Democrats are a bunch of wusses." Whoever wins the NASCAR vote in future, the NASCARization of America will continue for some time.

The New Thrift, or Haute Penny-Pinching

49 In coming decades, the greatest generation of U.S. consumers will become tightwads—and proud of it. One reason why baby boomers and their children are becoming more thrifty is necessity. There is less money to go around now and for the future. Most salaries are not keeping pace with inflation, making for less discretionary income. In fact, the standard of living has declined steadily since 1970. After adjusting for inflation, the median income of families with children and headed by adults under 30 dropped 32 percent between 1973 and 1990. Median household income fell by $500, or 1.1 percent, in the single year between 2001 and 2002.

Secure jobs are fewer; a high proportion of new jobs are in low-paying sectors, such as service, or are held on seasonal or contract terms. The costs of three major pulls on the family pocketbook—a new house, college, and health care—are growing at a pace much faster than inflation. Today's pension plans are less generous than they were for workers entering the market 50 years ago—if they are available at all. This makes the current widespread stability of seniors seem less likely for the next generations.

Add to these elements the fact that the gap between rich and poor is growing. Not only is the salary of the average CEO 282 times more than an average worker's pay ($26,000), it has grown much more over the past generation than a worker's salary. On average, an executive's salary is 20 times higher than it was in 1980, while the median salary of the average worker has doubled.

To live with these realities, young and middle-aged Americans will do what their parents and grandparents did from the start: make do with less. But they will do it in their own way. They will make it seem like it was their plan all along.

Those who consider saving money the center of a frugal lifestyle will take the way of the tightwad. Already there are movements to live frugally and several spokespeople who focus on introducing big spenders to a new life. For example, in her bestselling book *The Tightwad Gazette*, its sequel, *The Tightwad Gazette II*, and her newsletter, Amy Dacyczyn offers advice and pointers that show how to imitate the success she has had raising six children on her husband's $30,000 salary. In general, the advice centers on reusing or reimagining everything that might be discarded, or as she puts it, not "living stupidly." In different otherwise hard-nosed books, saving money takes on an aura of holiness, and becomes a way of simultaneously empowering oneself and serving God.

Another path to spending less is to embrace simplicity as an aesthetic. Such people may want to save money as much as the tightwad but will simply call their actions a movement toward simplifying. Magazines like *Real Simple* make the act of simplifying into a lifestyle choice and a sign of good taste. Features about women who have faced complications such as surgery or divorces show how to find peace through simplifying one's life. Tips for making household tasks less time-consuming and buying cheaper domestic goods address the practical side of simplifying, while advice on right and wrong responses to social situations addresses the moral component. Counselors offer advice on setting priorities, such as living on a budget. While mass-media endeavors like *Real Simple* may offer more attitude than practical solutions, they introduce the idea of living simply as a pleasurable choice.

While middle age and the years of senescence to follow may jolt people into a simpler lifestyle, frugal living clearly has appeal for younger adults as well. Testifying to this interest are Web sites such as *www.frugaliving.com*, which offers books and resources on such subjects from fixing it yourself to growing your own food. Another site, *www.allthingsfrugal.com*, is the home of *The Pennypincher E-zine* and *Tightwad Tidbits Daily*, while *www.thefrugalshopper.com* offers tips and deals to help you "hold on to your hard earned money."

In the early 21st century, living simply remains an alternative lifestyle, but it will become a mainstream practice over time, when it has to. By the third decade of the 21st century, a frugal way of life will become widely practiced and accepted. By then, millions of baby boomer senior citizens will have to find ways to live without some of the financial safety nets they had expected, and younger generations will find that acquiring consumables is not all it's cracked up to be.

The People's Environmentalism

50 While federal pro-environment programs and regulations either are unchanged or are being reduced during the early 21st century, national interest in preserving the environment remains high and is expected to continue. A recent national poll said three-fourths of Americans responding named the environment as a "high priority" issue. Four of five respondents considered themselves environmentalist or sympathetic to environmentalism. The language of environmentalist issues, from global warming to recycling, has become second nature to most Americans.

Private involvement in environmentalist causes is also booming. The number of environmental groups has grown from a few hundred in 1970 to more than 8,000 in the early 21st century. These groups also receive significant financial support. According to the National Center for Charitable Statistics, which monitors nonprofit fundraising, individuals, companies, and foundations gave an average of just under $10 million per day to environmental groups in 1999.

As in politics, the groups that form to make environmental statements are varied. Activists will continue to have divergent political views and religions but will unite under a shared cause. Already active are partnerships between secular environmentalists and religious institutions. According to Worldwatch Research Director Gary Gardner, "This collaboration could change the world. . . . Environmentalists have a strong grounding in science. Religious institutions enjoy moral authority and a grassroots presence." Together, he believes, they have force in changing public policy. Among pairings of scientists and religious institutions in the name of environmentalism are the Episcopal Power & Light that allows U.S. customers to buy renewable energy electricity and the Interfaith Coffee Program, which sells coffee grown under environmentally sound conditions to its congregants.

Individual items will continue to be focal points for activists of all sorts. For example, hybrid cars that run on a combination of gas and electric power have gained popularity, thanks to a mix of film celebrities, business leaders, politicians, and religious communities who bought the car. Buyers included movie stars Leonardo DiCaprio and Cameron Diaz, the New York City government, and Republican Utah Senator Robert F. Bennett. Some Americans are simply opting for buying smaller SUVs that are more environment-friendly than larger models. Causes for such purchases range from resisting climate change to decreasing dependence on finite natural resources to fighting terrorism.

Activist organizations will continue their work, each serving the environment differently. Greenpeace will continue its activist techniques to warn the industrialized world of its dangers to the environment. Among the conditions it protests are toxic waste, acid rain, and uranium mining.

Since the 1970s, the long-range "deep ecology" movement has been active, attempting to broaden the way people think about the environment. Begun by Norwegian philosopher and mountaineer Arne Naess, the deep ecology movement is contrasted with what Naess describes as the practical, short-term results-oriented "shallow ecology" movement. In its statement, the deep ecology movement "involves redesigning our whole systems based on values and methods that truly preserve the ecological and cultural diversity of natural systems." Its leaders accept all human models but reject the "industrial technology model" of human convenience and comfort and instead support common harmony with other beings and other cultures. Among the environmentalists affected by this philosophy have been former vice president and author of *Earth in the Balance* Al Gore.

Greenspirit, a government and industry consultancy started by Greenpeace founder Patrick Moore, promotes what Moore calls a "rational" environmental policy for the 21st century. Moving toward an economy of sustainable energy, managing the world population, controlling urban sprawl, and stabilizing or reversing deforestation are among its aims.

Along with environmental groups that wish to change a nation's thinking about the Earth, there are groups that will try to convince the public about the shared advantages of conservation. For example, the Nature Conservancy uses hands-on conservation programs to study and preserve nearby geographic areas. In one of its projects, at California's Cosumnes River Preserve, thousands of schoolchildren collect natural artifacts and plant trees. Other groups, like the Malpai Borderlands Group, a group of ranchers based in Arizona and New Mexico, enter into ranching and open space partnerships that preserve wildlife and ranches. Matt Magoffin, a member of the group, points out that "environmentalists are fighting with ranchers, but we both want the same goals."

In the 21st century, conservationists may turn more to corporate donations. Increasingly, corporate donations are looked on favorably, particularly as major companies like beverage giant Starbucks have become involved in conservation projects and funding initiatives. To the charge that corporate money is somehow tainted, a National Audubon Society executive remembered what someone told him: "'The only thing wrong with tainted money is there t'aint enough of it.'"

While the grass-roots environmentalism will continue and grow throughout the early 21st century, so will professional forecasters. Public policy institutions will project and promote environmental changes for the future. In 2003 the Pew Center on Global Climate Change released a report called *U.S. Energy Scenarios for the 21st Century*, which outlined possible avenues for U.S. energy supply and use from 2000 and 2035. It pointed to the need for new public policy, increased investments, and the immediate action to achieve long-term goals—in short, a complete climate change policy.

Even as environmentalism attracts new followers, it is also spurring a growing backlash. Michael Crichton's 2004 novel *State of Fear* depicted the environmental movement as a web of greedy, ignorant fear-mongers. Bjorn Lomborg's nonfiction book *The Skeptical Environmentalist* (2002) has set out a scientific case against many environmentalist claims.

Despite such naysayers, environmental activism, from practical initiatives between big businesses and activists to buyers of hybrid cars, will continue to mark the 21st century. People will see their environment changing and will want to do something about it, with or without government involvement.

The Pricing-Out of College

51 According to the College Board, people who have a college degree make $1 million more during their lifetime than high school graduates. So in the 21st century, most people will continue to try to attend college. But the costs are already astronomical and are expected to increase. For those able to save, $12,000 is the yearly sum needed to send nine-year-old Junior off to college in less than a decade. For those starting with a newborn, it's $279,000 divided by eighteen. And for the eighteen-year-old entering college in the fall, the four-year price tag is $120,000. Because an increasing number of Americans will not be able to foot the entire college bill themselves, the coming decades will see people borrowing more money, demanding creative financing programs from colleges, attending nontraditional educational outlets, and dropping the stigma from not attending college and skipping the ordeal entirely.

For years, college costs have risen at rates that are higher than inflation or other economic indicators. For example, according to the

National Center for Public Policy and Education, tuition at four-year public colleges and universities during the years 1992 through 2001 rose faster than family income in 41 states. In 2004, the College Board reported that average tuition for undergrads at four-year public universities had shot up 10.5 percent in just the past year. And while federal and state governments have increased their support of student financial aid, the increases have not kept pace with the costs of attending college.

Further, other traditional sources of aid have not matched increases in costs. For example, Pell Grants, a long-standing source of need-based funding, now covers a smaller portion of tuition at four-year colleges and universities than it did in the mid-1980s. And while institutional aid (from the colleges) amounts to $13 billion each year, an increasing amount is being awarded on a non-need basis.

State aid, in particular, has been greatly affected by recessionary periods. In most cases, states compensate for recession-driven short-falls in their budgets by raising tuition. Over the past years, this has occurred widely across the United States and is expected to continue.

To compensate for these increased costs now and in the future, many parents will borrow more money. Students themselves will also rack up more college debt. From 1989 to 1999, the average cumulative debt by seniors at public colleges and universities increased greatly among all income groups, and in particular within the lowest income quartile. For students, debt grew from $7,629 to $12,888. Growth in loans has greatly outstripped growth in grants. According to the College Board, grant aid has grown by 84 percent over the past decade, while the quantity of education loans has increased by 137 percent.

For those who want another road to education, more students in the future will seek alternative learning sources. For example, millions will seek a degree education online, where colleges specialize in subjects that can be taught by distance learning—that is, without great classroom involvement. Two-year college enrollment is also expected to increase, as are many forms of practical training, such as paralegal training or various types of computer training. But whatever the path is to improvement, the numbers don't lie. Parents will continue to have a larger and larger portion of their budget earmarked for education because they think it is worth it. Whether it is or not, college will take a higher percentage of the family's current take-home pay and the student's future earnings upon graduation. The lifetime of education promised by college may yield a lifetime of promissory notes.

Remodeling as a Way of Life

52 For the foreseeable future, remodeling of all kinds continues on in the American home. And the trend is toward bigger, better, and more comfortable. What was once home sweet home is now being remodeled into home perfect home, using everything from do-it-yourself projects to complete tear downs.

Homeowners and rental-property owners in the United States spent $176 billion and $57 billion, respectively, on remodeling and repair projects in 2003, according to a 2005 report by Harvard University's Joint Center for Housing Studies. The record $233 billion in total spending on such projects accounted for 40 percent of all expenditures on residential construction and more than two percent of U.S. economic activity.

According to the Harvard report, the most popular home-improvement projects in 2003 were "high-end" ones, such as a major remodeling of a kitchen (defined as one that costs $10,000 or more), bathroom ($5,000 or more), or the addition of a room. The National Association of Home Builders (NAHB) describes the key to kitchen remodeling today is to impart personality and compatibility with the architectural design for the rest of the house. "It's all in the island," is the further proclamation from a NAHB Web site. In current kitchens, it will be styled to fit the kitchen and family personality. And there will continue to be the consolidation of kitchen, eating nook, and family room into one design expanse.

If the kitchen is all about community, the bath is a space for luxury and escape. In their remodeling plans, designers are incorporating designs such as his-and-hers vanities, oasis-type tubs, and ornate moldings to create a spa-like atmosphere.

Remodeling the basement into a subterranean entertainment area is growing in popularity. According to National Association of Home Builders research director Gopal Ahluwalia, the "upscale downstairs" is a budding trend. Among new-home buyers, he said, "the two things they want to do immediately are install a deck and finish the basement."

So while basements are not the number one remodeling trend, they are a sizable piece of the $215 billion remodeling industry. This is a sizable amount considering that only 68 percent of all homes in the United States have basements.

As for other types of remodeling, the derided practice of demolishing a small house and erecting an outsized McMansion on the same property is also continuing. Thanks to the booming economy and a dearth of available land in some fast-growing cities, McMansions continue to proliferate. While the average square footage of a single-family home built last year was 10 percent larger than a decade earlier, the average lot size declined by the same percentage, according to the U.S. Census Bureau. "In every older upscale suburb, it's an issue right now," says Marya Morris, senior research associate with the American Planning Association in Chicago.

Demographic as well as economic conditions suggest that this remodeling trend will continue. Baby boomers are remodeling at a feverish pace and are responsible for more than half of all expenditures. Unlike previous generations, boomers will be active remodelers even as they approach retirement.

The younger generations are no remodeling slouches, either. In perhaps a sign of things to come, Generation Xers, born between 1964 and 1975, are spending more on average than baby boomers did when they were in their 30s. Both baby boomers and Gen Xers plunked down an average of $2,200 in 2003. More than two-thirds of monies spent went to professional contractors; the rest went for do-it-yourself projects.

One reason homeowners keep improving their houses is that they generally recoup their investment. Findings indicate that in metropolitan areas that were in the top 50 nationally in terms of house price appreciations between mid-2002 and mid-2003, the cost recouped was much higher than the average of 86.4 percent.

Along with the positive information about recouping costs, there are truths to the home remodeling project that have not changed. Everything does take longer than the estimates (twice as long, according to the National Homebuilders Association). But with home ownership in America at 69 percent in 2004, immersion in one's home will continue.

Tutoring Galore

53 For fun, remedial learning, and profit, tutoring is now big business. Aside from in-school tutoring, there are also thousands of tutoring centers across the United States, some for-profit, some not-for-profit, some faith-based. There are also tutoring training programs that set people up to become part of an existing tutoring program or to establish a tutoring program for themselves. In short, tutoring has come a long way from the local Y or the settlement house. Now it's big business.

According to Edventures, Inc., a Boston-based educational consulting firm, tutoring was a $4 billion business in 2003. It was over $4.5 billion in 2004 and is expected to run to $5.2 billion in 2005. Higher expectations, low test scores, and mounting competition for admission to top-tier universities is boosting student enrollment at tutoring centers across the country. For example, at Kumon Math and Reading Centers, which has nearly 1,700 centers and over 180,000 students in the United States, Canada, and Mexico, enrollment has increased by 55 percent over the past four years. As a result, the company is opening up to 150 new centers in 2005 to meet the demand.

"Supplemental education programs are gaining momentum across the country, especially among elementary school children," said Mark Mele, vice president of franchising with Kumon. "In fact, more than 60 percent of students enrolled in Kumon Math and Reading Centers are in the second through sixth grades, with fourth graders comprising the highest enrollment."

According to Entrepreneur.com, the tutoring segment received a particular boost when the government passed the No Child Left Behind Act of 2001, designed to improve student achievement. As a result, tutoring companies in the K-12 levels had 2.7 percent growth in 2003, up from a 1 percent growth in revenue in 2002, reports Edventures. "Schools are paying for tutoring programs to get their kids' scores up to meet the No Child Left Behind targets," explains Deborah Stipek, dean of the Stanford University School of Education. "So there's an industry that's developing to provide schools with tutoring in test taking.

To bring students up to standards set by the No Child Left Behind Act, the tutoring is subsidized by government funds. As Paul and Sarah Edwards note in Entrepreneur.com, "While the students you would typically work with are those whose parents can afford to pay for this service on their own, a growing area of tutoring is subsidized under federal law. These tutoring subjects are the children in public schools who are falling behind under the No Child Left Behind Act and children with learning disabilities."

There are also tutoring programs aimed at teaching fundamentals and self-esteem, such as the Learning Fun Center in California. Started by two graduates of Temple University, who found public school education lacking in its ability to prepare students for entry into the world and who learned from work at established tutoring centers such as Sylvan, the center operates from a philosophy that well-rounded, happy children make the best and most successful students.

To enhance their child's school performance, parents can enroll them in any of a variety of often expensive tutoring programs. Commonly known elementary- and middle-school level programs include Sylvan Learning Centers and Huntington Learning Centers. Beginning in elementary school, private tutoring is also highly popular, especially with good students who are seeking an edge. When a Westchester County, New York, tutor told an accomplished student he was tutoring, "You really don't need this," the child replied, "No, my mom loves tutoring, and I have to have more."

College tutoring choices begin early. In addition to the established Kaplan and Princeton Review courses, there are other storefront professional tutoring and academic counseling firms. In addition, there are many private tutors, who advertise by local newspaper or over the Internet. Most note their strong educational background; some promise specific results. For example, according to the Internet-advertised College Coach, test scores will improve markedly—an average 180 points on the SAT, and 6 on the ACT.

To find the right tutor, not every tip comes from word-of-mouth. There are national online referral programs that recommend tutors in the areas of expertise desired. One national referral program is TutorsTeach.com. Operating since 1999, TutorsTeach.com, according to its Web site, can use its database to "find hundreds of qualified teachers and tutors specializing in a wide range of subjects at every level." Providing a similar service is the national TutorNation.com. "For the past six years," its Web site says, "TutorNation.com has [brought] . . . in-person, e-mail and live online tutoring across North America . . . in more than 400 academic and nonacademic subjects . . ."

Increasingly, tutors for all levels of education are being outsourced. Elementary school students in Florida, California, and Texas were tutored online by tutors born and located in India. In fact, one of the largest tutoring firms, careerbuilder.com, offers not only online tutoring 24 hours a day, seven days a week, but provides content for and teaches for crucial regional or national tests.

To promote the needs and training of tutors across the disciplines and grade levels, there is the National Tutoring Association. As its mission statement reads, "The National Tutoring Association (NTA) is a nonprofit member serving association. The NTA was formed in 1992 and currently represents more than 3,500 tutors and tutorial administrators across the

United States and internationally."

The monetary benefits of being a tutor vary widely. Entrepreneur mavens Paul and Sarah Edwards say the average rate is $20 to $60 per hour. Other sources cite higher rates in more competitive areas—up to $400 per hour in some Westchester, New York, suburbs. As one New York tutor said, it all depends on how well the tutored student does. He says, "You have to look at outcome and what it's worth to parents."

Vegetarians Everywhere

54 By the end of the 20th century, everyone knew the reasons for eating vegetarian. As detailed in a mid-2004 *Vegetarian Week*, a meat-rich diet is problematic because it is selfish. Western imports of Third World grain to feed western cattle could be better kept in the Third World to feed its citizens.

Also, it is wasteful: The acreage needed to needed to grow corn to feed 24 people produces enough beef to feed two people. It is unhealthy. Commercially grown beef and chicken carry high amounts of antibiotics, hormones, and dioxins. It is painful for the animals.

Over the years, Americans have listened. According to a 1998 Gallup Pool, 31 percent of those questioned said they were positively trying to cut down on meat consumption. In 2002, some 10 million Americans consider themselves to be practicing vegetarians, according to a *Time* poll of 10,000 adults; an additional 20 million have flirted with vegetarianism sometime in their past; and 7 percent of Americans considered themselves as strict vegetarians. Two percent of school-age children, or about 1 million youths, are vegetarians, and eat any vegetarian diet choices at school. Yet three-fourths of people do not eat the required five fruits and vegetables (and certainly not the higher amounts listed in recent government recommendations).

Nonetheless, people are thinking about it. Vegetarian food sales doubled since 1998, hitting $1.6 billion in 2003. The market is forecast to grow another 61 percent by 2008, according to Mintel, a global market research firm. Since the early 2000s, vegetarian cookbooks have constituted one of the fastest-growing cookbook subjects.

There are also entire support systems for raising a vegetarian family. An online magazine, *WebFamily* (*www.webfamily.com*), explains its cause: The goal of *WebFamily* is "to assist parents in raising happy, healthy vegan children by offering tips, expert advice, information, articles, and a connection to other vegan families."

In addition, a small percentage of vegetarians remain so concerned about the loss to wildlife habitat from eating many different cooked fruits and vegetables each day that they are compelled to follow a raw foods diet. As *www.living-foods.com* explains, it is the reasonable choice for anyone concerned about protecting the environment. As the Web site says, "[I]t follows that raw foods diets use less resources and are less cruel (less food used => less wildlife habitat lost to farming) than a cooked vegan diet. So the 'most ethical' vegan diet is a raw food diet!"

Perhaps most telling as a marker of popularity, vegetarianism is promoted in advertisements as a way to maintain youthfulness and sexual allure. Accordingly, People for the Ethical Treatment of Animals (PETA) proclaimed the world's sexiest vegetarians—Tobey Maguire and Joaquin Phoenix for men, Natalie Portman and Pam Anderson for women.

As the decade continues and vegetarianism becomes more commonplace, it also gets redefined. No longer do cooks need to follow the labor-intensive recipes of *The Moosewood Cookbook*, though its creator Mollie Katzen remains a strong voice for the ethics of meatless eating. According to Gourmand Cookbook Awards, research, health and nutrition cookbooks are supplanting strict vegetarian cookbooks as leading cookbook subject areas.

So by hook or by crook, more Westerners count themselves as vegetarian. They do so by redefining what vegetarian means. For example, in Britain (and surely elsewhere), it means eating meat and chicken.

A recent survey of British food habits indicates that 20 percent of Brits consider themselves vegetarians, but that 43 percent of them also eat red meat and chicken.

Ultimately, eating a more vegetarian diet can transform one's politics and world view—that is, taking a more inclusive embrace of the world. In a 2002 *Time* magazine article, Richard Corliss cited the left-wing political dimensions of vegetarianism, noting that vegetarians themselves cite their eating habits as a "nonviolent diet." Corliss adds, "Vegetarianism resolves a conscientious person's inner turf war by providing an edible complex of good-deed-doing: to go veggie is to be more humane. Give up meat, and save lives!" No less than the Mollie Katzen Web site (*www.molliekatzen.com*) professes this thinking in its New Year's greeting. Written by the site's Webmaster, it reads, "Maybe you'll choose to join me in making a resolution to be more compassionate in 2005. This resolution can take many forms: maybe eating more vegetarian, buying more organic, driving less, recycling more, caring about climate change, and working to protect our natural resources and to prevent the extinction of species." Or maybe you'll just eat more salads and stir-fries and call yourself vegetarian.

Wirelessness

55 Only a few years ago, "wired" was the term du jour. To be wired—connected to the Internet—was in; lack of wires was out. Now the reverse is happening. Wires are passé; wirelessness is cutting edge. Teens are text-messaging on their cell phones; executives are working on their Blackberrys. The ideal is to be connected 24/7 to all the necessary devices, data, and people in one's life, but without the cumbersome clutter of physical cables, cords, and modems. This ideal of wirelessness will be shaping society for some time.

At the heart of this new era are wireless networks—telephone or computer networks that carry information via radio waves. Cellular (or cell) phones, pagers, and personal digital assistants (PDAs) such as Blackberrys are all wireless devices. Laptop and desktop computers and assorted gadgets such as printers and digital cameras can be equipped for wirelessness. Even devices that one usually thinks of as requiring a cable, such as the keyboard that links to a computer, can be connected wirelessly. Soon many other consumer electronic devices, from stereos to coffeemakers to wristwatches, could be wirelessly connected. "Everyone is going to be able to tap into this pervasive wireless world," Wade Roush, senior editor of *Technology Review*, told CNN in October 2003.

Wirelessness is big business. According to the Telecommunications Industry Association (TIA), the wireless industry's revenue grew 11.6 percent from 2003 to 2004, reaching $145.1 billion in the latter year. TIA predicted that the market's growth would continue at a 10 percent compound annual rate through 2008, soaring to $212.5 billion. The rise of wirelessness is warming the hearts of investors who remember the collapse of tech stocks and have been waiting for something to revive them.

Wirelessness requires standards so that devices can communicate with one another. For wireless local area networks (LANs), the reigning standard is Wi-Fi, or Wireless Fidelity. This means that any Wi-Fi-enabled computer or peripherals within reach of a base station can connect to the Internet and communicate with other devices in the LAN. Operating in the 2.4 and 5 GHz radio bands, Wi-Fi is widely used now in small businesses, airports, hotels, colleges, and Starbucks coffeehouses. Most urban areas today are dotted with Wi-Fi "hotspots" where the presence of a base station allows any computer user to go online at will. Wi-Fi may become common on cell phones and PDAs as well.

Another increasingly popular standard is Bluetooth, a specification for a shorter range kind of network, wireless personal area networks (PANs). Using a short-range radio frequency (2.45 GHz), it enables connection and communication among devices such as PCs, laptops,

PDAs, and cell phones, as long as the devices are within 10 meters (32 feet) of each other.

Consumer applications of Bluetooth are limited only by the imagination of manufacturers. Several automakers (including BMW, Toyota, and Lexus) are now offering hands-free Bluetooth technology so that drivers can make calls while their cell phones are sitting in the backseat or locked in a suitcase in the trunk. Bluetooth may also become useful in connection with voice over Internet protocol (VoIP), a system for making telephone calls over the Internet. If VoIP becomes more common, Bluetooth might be used for communication between a cordless phone and a computer.

Wirelessness is likely to revolutionize many facets of life. Hospitals will increasingly use it so that a physician, equipped with a portable electronic device, can update the central medical files and send a prescription to the pharmacy from the patient's bedside. The judicial system will see the rise of witnesses backing up testimony with cameras in their cell phones. Mobile phones that are essentially portable computers may make the desktop PC obsolete. Cars will be equipped with up-to-the-minute traffic alerts warning of tie-ups ahead. Emerging improvements will probably embed wirelessness even more into daily life. Intel, for example, is working on building wireless capability into every chip, a plan it calls "Radio Free Intel."

With more data whipping wirelessly through the air, there are opportunities for trouble. The data can move too slowly, which has already prompted upgrading of mobile networks to speed transmissions, notably the mobile network upgrade known as Third Generation (3G). There are security concerns about keeping unwanted eyes from prying into the data passing through the airwaves and keeping out viruses. And some people will react with alarm at yet greater invasions of their privacy and quiet time. Still, wirelessness is going to increase, making communication and computing even more inescapable. "We'll start to think of computing as a natural part of our environment in the same way we might think about heating and air conditioning now," Roush said. "It's just always there."

VI

Marketing

Comfort Brands

56 As change comes even more quickly in the 21st century, some Americans will seek solace in the familiar. Especially for aging consumers (baby boomers and generation X), this means products that were well known in their youth. Because some of these brands have already died a natural death, savvy businesspeople have and will continue to resuscitate the brands. In some cases, the relaunched products are reimagined as they once were; in other cases, they are repackaged in new forms that match current preferences. But the taste, texture, or original label are left unchanged. These elements distinguish the products and allow consumers to recall an unfettered youth.

The brand-revival process has been going on for over a decade, as baby boomers saw their youth slipping away. Brands that were reborn in the 1990s included the Volkswagen Beetle and Burma-Shave shaving cream; resurrected icons included Starkist Tuna's Charlie the Tuna and the hourglass-shaped Coca Cola bottle (but in plastic rather than glass). Similarly, General Motors's Buick line of automobiles has been reimagined for the 21st century (but the Oldsmobile, the nation's oldest car, has been discontinued). Says futurist Watts Wacker, coauthor of *The 500-Year Delta*, "We . . . don't know what's going to happen. So we need some warm fuzzies from our past."

One entrepreneur, Jeffrey Himmel, has resurrected several lost brands with great success. He has saturated the market with inexpensive advertisements that bring back memories and has reintroduced products including Gold Bond medicated powder, Ovaltine chocolate drink mix, the antacid Bromo-Seltzer, and Breck shampoo. Cincinnati-based Redox Brands specializes in acquiring and relaunching name-brand consumer cleaning products on their way to being phased out, such as the laundry detergent Oxydol and Biz bleach. Sometimes that takes some repositioning of the product: for example, the firm decided to market Oxydol to younger women with the slogan "Get Dirty. We Dare You."

Rescuing old brands extends further than lunch-box food and beauty aids. It extends to alcoholic beverages. Some long-established beers have been revived by entirely new demographic groups than the ones that made them famous. Old Milwaukee, Pabst Blue Ribbon, and Falls City Beer were once low-cost, blue-collar choices in their cities or regions. Now they are embraced by young adults who view them as unpretentious and anticommercial. Like their fellow frugal drinkers of past decades, the hip crowd who rediscovered the beers now drink them because they are cheap.

Retro-based toys will continue to have appeal, particularly for adults. For example, in 2002, over 25 percent of holiday sales of *Star Wars* toys were for adults. Similarly, high percentages of adult sales are common for some types of Barbie dolls and the Magic-8 ball. And once-familiar regional brands like Moxie, Bubble Up, and Nehi are available to adults through specialized Web sites like *www.realsoda. com*. At high-toned but cozy retro-candy stores in shopping malls and big cities, familiar candies such as Pixy Stix and bubble gum cigarettes are taking a growing portion of the multimillion-dollar candy market: "It brings back memories of being a kid," said one Midwestern candy store customer. Toy retailer Toys 'R' Us, which brought back its classic jingle for its Christmas 2003 ad campaign, banks on nostalgia. "One of the reasons we brought back the Toys 'R' Us jingle is that it really is one of those memories from childhood for today's parents that they want to replicate for their kids too," CEO John Eyler told National Public Radio.

But all is not well on Memory Lane. Says James Lileks, syndicated columnist and author of *The Gallery of Regrettable Food*, Americans may run through their memorable brands faster than they can relive them: "If contemporary pop culture becomes so saturated with retro references that they become the dominant cultural signifier today, what will we be nostalgic about in 20 years?" Look to the Brand Lab, a University of Illinois think tank that specializes in the study of resuscitating old brands. It says that there are five criteria that designate whether a product is ready for revival, including uniqueness, reputation, and strong brand equity. Then it takes the right entrepreneur to take it under the wing and a public that still wants to relive its happy past.

Gay-Friendly Marketing

57 In the past few years, many initiatives for single-sex marriage and medical coverage were roundly defeated across the country. But gays and lesbians have been embraced by the world of capitalism. Health and beauty conglomerates, travel planners, real estate companies, and other lifestyle providers are courting gays as never before. The reason is simple. As bank robber Willie Sutton is attributed to have said about why he robbed banks, "because that's where the money is." Not only do gays have everyday financial needs, they, more than heterosexual families with need-directed finances, have more discretionary income to spend. And, more than young single heterosexuals, gays and lesbians are more established in their careers and have set up deeper financial reserves. In short, gays are a golden, largely untapped market—but not for long.

Everyday needs are a central area of interest for marketers to gays. For example, manufacturers and service providers reportedly welcome an upcoming gay-and-lesbian television network. It means another source of money. According to demographers, the channel will attract an audience with deeper pockets than the average heterosexual American. In a 2000 study, Kalorama Information market research firm estimated a total gay and lesbian purchasing power in the United States of $340 billion. A recent consumer online survey found the median combined household income of gay couples to be $65,000, nearly 60 percent higher than the 1999 U.S. median income of $40,800. That translates into huge sales for gay toothpaste and soap, not to mention financial services and name-brand prescription drugs. "Over the last 10 years we've seen a dramatic increase in the desire of advertisers to market to this audience," said Howard Buford, founder and CEO of Prime Access Inc., an advertising and marketing company specializing in gay and lesbian and other defined audiences.

Automobiles are a prime big-ticket item now sold energetically to gays. The reason: their spending power. More than one third own a car less than three years old, and respondents between 25 and 34 are the group mostly likely to purchase a new car within a year.

Travel is another bonanza for those serving gays, because 10 percent of the U.S. travel industry is composed of gays. They have helped international destinations such as Toronto and Copenhagen, and U.S. cities such as Philadelphia to become gay meccas. Hotels and sites in the area have become sensitive to the presence of gays. Their services are not only for gays, but rather that the services welcome gays. As reported in the *New York Times*, one customer cited the phenomenon as being treated like just an average customer. Said one gay traveler, "We are completely mainstream as gay and lesbian travelers." For the concierge, that means not laughing at a request for two women seeking a double bed and no additional single beds; for sightseeing crews it means offering details on gay events and sites. In short, it means establishing a relationship of trust among gay customers. It's an investment that pays off in hotels and sites gaining a portion of the twice-as-high per diem expenditures that gays make when they travel.

Joining all consumer needs are the newly developing gay towns. Rather than known gay-favored vacation sites like Provincetown, Massachusetts, are unflashy suburban and exurban communities that are simply stable places to live. One such town, Wilton Manors, Florida, was resurrected from its crime-ridden, downtrodden state by gays in the late 1990s seeking community and more affordable housing than that in South Beach. Now comprising 35 percent of the community, gay residents have revitalized the town, introducing new businesses such as coffee shops and health clubs, raising property values, and spurring real estate development. Just as important are the changing attitudes. The mixture of gays and straights are cohabitating peaceably. A straight Republican Roman Catholic supports a gay Congressional candidate. Gays and straights invite one another to neighborhood parties. As one straight longtime resident remarked in the *New York Times*, "Living in Wilton Manors, you have to change. You can't be so conservative and stuffed-shirt." A transplanted gay resident countered, also for the *New York Times* about the comfortableness of the community, "[Gayness is] a non-issue here, and that's what I like about it."

Good Buying

58 Americans are generous. As individuals, they donated over $179 billion in 2003 and gave even more in 2004. But they are also time-strapped and take a variety of shortcuts to manage their finances. They deposit electronically, bank, and pay online, and save for college by joining a program of corporate donation linked to consumer spending. Recently, Americans have even found ways to streamline their beneficence. Giving but busy Americans multitask their donations by buying from companies that support their causes.

The avenues for donation by consumption are as varied as the Americans using them and the causes they serve. Many are tied only to easing the act of donation, not to a specific charity. The site *www.iGive.com* is one of the most broad-based donation servers, in terms of participating companies and charities. "Help your favorite cause with every purchase," announces *www.iGive.com*, noting that when an iGive.com member buys from one of its nearly 600 participating charities (such as Expedia.com and QVC), it donates up to 26 percent of purchases to the buyer's chosen charity. The site calls the process Virtuous Shopping, which translates into Virtual Karma. It seems to be working: In the past year, iGive.com has raised over $375,000 for over 1,000 charities.

Other charity-consumer organizations are geared to specific cause. The Web community EyesOnThePrize.org was developed on Mother's Day 2000 by 10 gynecologic cancer survivors to support other women with similar cancers. One of its forms of support is generating donations by deciding to "Shop EOTP!" That form of shopping can range from buying EOTP flowers (the iris is its signature bloom), books, tapes, EOTP T-shirts, sweatshirts, mugs, and mouse pads, all through iGive.com.

Some companies develop products that support major causes. For example, breast cancer research and treatment is supported by dozens of companies including Target and Kellogg that sell signature pink items from scarves to pens. Shoes from major companies are sold on QVC for breast cancer research in a program sponsored by the Fashion Designers of America. And don't forget the millions of dollars for cancer research raised by the sales of the $1 LIVESTRONG plastic bracelets.

While health-related charities dominate those linked to consumer spending, there are many non-health-related alliances. For example, the VH1 Save the Music Foundation helps support music education in the U.S. public school system through the sales of a music video made for the cause called "For the Kids." For years, Save the Children has sold specially designed ties, colorfully festooned with children. Even PETA, People for the Ethical Treatment of Animals, offers a specially produced recording of *Liberation Songs to Benefit PETA*.

Many causes offer a collection of products from various sources, the sales of which go in whole or part to the organization. Among the best known is UNICEF. One of its books, *Children Just Like Me*, is published by Dorling Kindersley, which donates part of the royalties to the UNICEF cause.

Other charity-consumer links are local and as individual as the solitary contributor. For example, Ginny's Charity offers a Florence Nightingale Doll made by the Vogue Doll Company; sales of the doll support the Oak Valley Hospital Foundation, a rural hospital in Oakdale, California. The hospital is in Ginny's California hometown Oakdale, California.

In essence, these various charity-consumer links are much like grade-school chocolate bar or Girl Scout cookie sales. The difference is that now the process is much more sophisticated and nearly ubiquitous.

Marketing to Grandma

59 Aging Americans now consider 67 the new 57, and they have buying habits to show it. More than their predecessors, today's senior citizens think of themselves as being younger than their actual years and as a result, are active members of society, with all that it means. Many do not follow the traditional retirement path and instead still work, full- or part-time. Most important for marketers, they are active consumers who have and still spend money. They use credit cards, buy new cars, and get new mortgages. Seniors also hold three-fourths of the nation's wealth and control two-thirds of spending funds. In *The U.S. Market for 55+ Consumers*, a report by market research publisher Packaged Facts, seniors are "64 million strong" and [have] $2.4 trillion in buying power. But they buy differently than they did when they were half their age, and marketers are learning how they want to be heard.

For example, the Packaged Facts report notes, Americans age 55-

plus spend a higher percentage of their food budget on food to eat at home, with total home food expenditures totaling $101 billion annually. Senior citizens in the 65- to 74-year-old age group allocate 8.9 percent of their total budget to food for home and those 75 years old and over, 9.2 percent. This is significantly higher than the average of 7.6 percent for all age groups. Marketers reach them with single-serve or smaller-sized portions of easy-to-prepare healthful foods. Prepackaged vegetables like foolproof Idaho or sweet potatoes, cut up and ready to turn into soups or side dishes are examples. High-fat super-sized boxed mixes are out; nutrient-rich dishes are in.

The report also found that the work, rather than age, is a defining factor among the 55+ crowd. Working makes them think, act, and spend like someone about 10 years younger. They buy safe, smaller cars and take out car loans.

They may also choose to live differently. Just as they once moved to towns with good school systems and young families, they now spend money to move to communities with people of their age and areas of interest. "Fewer and fewer people will retire the old-fashioned way," said Don Montuori, acquisitions editor for Packaged Facts. "[W]hen they do retire, people are seeking new models for retirement (for example, living among 'like-minded neighbors')." To that end, developers of niche mature residences have prospered, with developments in the Northwest, for example, that are designed for the active and sports-minded, with residences surrounded by hiking and climbing trails, as well as traditional exercise facilities.

Seniors are also educating themselves more. Many are returning to college or graduate school, often to audit classes. According to the *Wall Street Journal Online*, colleges report the programs are a tool to boost the school's image in the community. State schools also say that when they ask for money from the state legislature, it helps a lot to show that the school offers its resources to the wider community. Other colleges say their audit programs break even or turn a small profit. The University of Washington, for instance, makes thousands of dollars a year from audit fees, which are put into the operating budget for the school. Boston University's Evergreen program brings in about $35,000 to $40,000 in revenue a year, which the university says covers three part-time administrators as well as instructors for some seniors-only classes. Schools add that the auditing programs can also bring in financial donations and even serve as marketing tools.

In addition to learning, seniors also shop electronically. Already, two thirds of online buyers are older than 40, a National Retail Federation survey indicates. Further, while they use the Internet for health research and entertainment, they also buy. Almost 80 percent of computer owners older than 50 have made a purchase on the Internet, says AgeLight, a consulting firm in Clyde Hill, Wash.

Not only are seniors the fastest-growing group of Internet users, they also appear to be the most resistant to spam and scams. According to *DM News*, only one in five retirement-age people online reported having responded to a spam offer, whereas about one in three people between the ages of 18 and 64 reported the same. That wisdom-borne wariness also carried through to responses to email scams as well, turning on its head the great tradition of telemarketing and direct mail scams, which often target the elderly.

Still, according to Clickz, it is not difficult to reach the senior market. It just requires simplicity and truth. Clickz marketing expert Paul Soltoff suggests the following:

- Clearly state the savings opportunity as a primary benefit.
- Keep copy brief and concise.
- Avoid misleading and misdirected statements and claims.

These marketing ideas and others will be useful for current seniors and the larger group to come—the baby boomers. Today, there are 35 million senior citizens in the United States. By 2020, when most baby boomers have reached retirement age, those numbers will soar to 54 million. They will all need and want to continue buying.

Personal Advertising, or Mass Customization

60 As technological advances allow American consumers to control how they get their goods and culture, advertisers try to stay a step ahead. On the Internet and on television, advertisers will tailor their ads to match their target audiences, much as some cable TV outlets do already. Soon Internet and television outlets will be able to amass enough information to individualize their pitches to each subscriber. For consumers, these electronic advertisers will do the grunt work; they consult a client's list of needs and offer customized items. A personalized advertiser can look over a client's shoulder and shop for him or her. Personalized advertising represents a new way to build a business. One home-furnishings executive called the amassing of personal information a way to create a "customer relationship management system . . . a set of policies and procedures that guides all the interactions between the store staff and the customers or the prospects."

Each form of electronic communication uses a different approach to reach consumers, and much of it is in use in some form already. For example, advertisers on cable TV access customers through the set-top box or the video-on-demand server. Their software is placed in the server and collects information on the income and composition of the household subscriber. Using this information, advertisers can adjust the images and message of an advertisement to match the subscriber's level of interest in a product.

On the Internet, companies will use a variety of one-to-one Web applications to reach desired customers. One software technology allows cable and satellite operators to profile and deliver individually targeted commercial advertisements. The software will identify individuals the advertisers want to reach based on specific demographic, psychographic, and purchasing habits that the advertiser wants to capitalize on. It will then organize the viewers into groups that will get certain commercials according to the desires of the advertiser.

Google has become an Internet giant by developing technology that allows search words entered by a user to call up relevant ads from sponsors. The ads are clearly separated from the search results, so as not to compromise the purity of the search, but they still draw a great deal of business to sponsors from customers who are searching for exactly what the company is selling. In 2004, Google went further, launching an e-mail service, Gmail, that would display targeted ads based on the content of the e-mail displayed. Gmail sparked an outcry from privacy and civil liberties organizations objecting to Google software reading people's e-mail, but it was a logical outgrowth of an already established trend.

Through software applications, companies will be able to build personalized communities online to which they can send specialized content and advertisements. Some companies, such as Amazon.com, already use individualized audience targeting to increase sales. Banks and other financial institutions are introducing a new sales medium to automatic teller machines (ATMs). This medium collects data on the user's holdings and navigation practices on the Web to offer product recommendations during the screen time once marked "Please wait . . ." Another e-mail personalization application uses a rules-based "personalization engine" and the company's Web content management system to target individuals and assess the content of e-mail messages. This procedure helps marketers and advertisers create e-mail newsletters and promotions. Technology to deliver personalized advertisements over wireless telephones also exists.

While these technological changes redefine marketing, consumer groups and the government will counter with measures to protect consumers' privacy. But even as laws may be implemented, the consumer world is likely to be besotted with personalized electronic advertisements and entreaties. That's e-novation. It's the personalized marketing that Rob Carscadden, president and chief operating officer of the marketing technology company Zaq Interactive Solutions, Inc., calls a shift in advertising away from mass media toward "a personalized direct marketing model."

Teleshopping for Everything

61 First it was catalog ordering by phone. Then it was buying online. Shopping outside the box (be it a mall or department store) has become mainstream. And it is growing. According to Forrester Research, some 63 million U.S. households will buy online by 2008, which is double the 34 million households buying online in 2002. Global Internet shopping has grown massively as well. According to a Drexel University study, it has doubled annually, from $35 billion in 1998 to over $3 trillion in 2003. The trend is so deep and transformative that Internet experts and authors of *The Age of E-Tail: Conquering the New World of Electronic Shopping*, Philipp Gerbet, Dick Schneider, and Alex Birch, call the age of Web retailing a golden period of exploration comparable to the Age of Discovery in the 15th century.

Reasons for the popularity of Internet shopping and the behaviors it generates are ongoing subjects of interest. According to a study by the London Business School and the University of California, Irvine, working women are likely to turn to electronic shopping as a way to make more time for maintenance and discretionary activities—activities they can't or don't want to do online. For while electronic shoppers may order food and other necessities online, they are likely to continue to travel outside the home for maintenance activities such as children's school-related programs or medical visits. The overall rate of shopping is also likely to increase, says the report, despite the time-saving electronic shopping. People will still shop for escape and for entertainment, which is how people traditionally viewed the act of shopping.

Still, Internet stores shouldn't consider the deal closed. According to Forrester Research, the majority of all online consumers (65 percent in 2004) are "cross-channel shoppers" who research online but buy offline. These shoppers are Internet-savvy but want to kick the tires physically before buying the item. Their numbers are growing: the number of new cross-channel shoppers in the past year was 30 percent.

In the future, grocery buying on the Internet will become commonplace, say researchers. Currently, it is more of a novelty than a standard practice, with delivery systems and lack of availability getting in the way. But according to a study by the Institute for Horticultural Development in Victoria, Australia, the baby boomers' hectic family schedule, followed by an isolated senior lifetstyle, will result in higher home food deliveries.

Some attempts at online "shopping" have been aimed at the improvement of society. For example, at the turn of the century, Santa Monica, California, leaders attempted to increase voter participation with an interactive computer terminal system that allowed citizens to discuss public affairs online with each other and with elected officials. Over the first few years, the system has not been widely used, yet those who did use it may have had an effect on city policy on homelessness.

Public and private Internet shopping sources are faced with the same concern: how to reach the audience. This need will prompt Internet marketing improvements that make the experience similar to an in-store encounter with a knowledgeable salesperson. To that end, various software are available to companies to create online stores, with product displays and demonstrations. An increasing number of sites even offer real-time human assistance. To do that, online sites have had to develop varieties of customer models, from inexperienced to savvy; fast downloading of information; and forms of interaction that reflect the customers' interests. According to the Drexel University study, such refinements in the shopping experience will allow online shopping to overtake traditional on-site shopping. "[T]he dominance of electronic purchasing is inevitable," the study says, and retailers have to change to fit it. "Internet marketing," it says, "must be like a smart-missile that can anticipate and intercept the consumer's product searches."

In the age of at-home Internet shopping, one product that has been a perennial flop might finally take off. It is the videophone, which allows the receiving and transmitting of either live or recorded audio and video signals. With it, you and the Lands' End operator, for example, can look at each other while placing an order, thus restoring the social interaction that at-home Internet shopping might have taken away.

VII

Politics

Asymmetrical Warfare

62 At the height of the Cold War, Americans had no problem picturing what a direct attack on the United States would look like. A roughly comparable superpower—the Soviet Union—would strike us with intercontinental ballistic missiles similar to ours. This would have been symmetrical warfare, in which the enemy would have been essentially a mirror image of us. But when a direct attack on the United States finally came on September 11, 2001, the enemy turned out to be radically asymmetrical: nineteen hijackers armed with knives and box cutters. With such low-tech instruments our own technology (passenger airplanes) was turned against us, killing 3,000 individuals on American soil in a single day. Americans had entered the Age of Asymmetrical Warfare.

In one sense, asymmetrical warfare is as ancient as history. It has been at work anytime a force of insurgents or raiders has used crude weapons and guerrilla tactics to harass and undermine a more numerous and better-equipped enemy. What is different now about the Age of Asymmetrical Warfare is that unconventional tactics, whose effectiveness was once limited to regional or civil conflicts, are now being used by foreign enemies to challenge the world's greatest powers on their own turf. Those enemies range from "rogue" states such as North Korea and Iran, who refuse to play by the rules of the present-day international system, to shadowy nonstate organizations such as Al Qaeda, which launch terrorist attacks against civilian and military targets. Despite being far weaker in population, wealth, and technology than their First World adversaries, they inspire fear and influence policy by being determined, ruthless, inventive, and hard to destroy. Asymmetrical warfare is also known as fourth-generation warfare, or 4GW, according to a theory of how it has succeeded three previous stages of combat: classical, industrial, and maneuver warfare.

Present-day asymmetrical forces are hard to counter for a variety of reasons. Some leaders of rogue states, because of their insularity and peculiar ideologies, seem bizarrely deaf to the appeals to rational self-interest that deter other regimes—for example, promises of aid and threats of sanctions. Even when invaded, such regimes have proven capable of surviving in insurgent form to make life miserable for the invading armies—as Saddam Hussein loyalists did after the United States invaded Iraq. Some asymmetrical forces, such as Al Qaeda, might be organizations that have no single homeland and are thus able to hide effectively from the military or police forces pursuing them. And some are fanatics, like the suicidal 9/11 hijackers associated with Al Qaeda, who actively seek death in service to their cause.

Whatever the reasons, asymmetrical forces are hard to wipe out and are increasingly more dangerous. Every technological advance the developed world creates—from nuclear weapons to shoulder-launched missiles to poison gas to weaponized anthrax—is one more weapon that asymmetrical forces can turn against it. Even the fast-moving circuits of the Internet may become a terrorist weapon, if hackers succeed in sabotaging vital systems. The damage from such a "cyberwar" or "e-jihad" may range from a day's inconvenience to global apocalypse.

The Age of Asymmetrical Warfare is driving government policy worldwide, and nowhere more than in the United States. It has already sparked two U.S. wars: the 2001 invasion of Afghanistan in search of Osama bin Laden and other perpetrators of 9/11; and the 2003 invasion of Iraq to overthrow Saddam's regime on the theory that it might be developing weapons of mass destruction and might have links to Al Qaeda. The military itself is changing in response to the Asymmetrical Age. Los Alamos National Laboratory's *Research Quarterly* reports that asymmetrical warfare has fueled a transition to a "lighter, more-flexible military, one that relies less on overwhelming numbers . . . and more on stealth, rapid response, and precision weaponry."

With asymmetrical warfare has come a new emphasis for military planners on urban warfare. An annual forum called Urban Warfare puts military and industry together to discuss the challenges of urban operations, which are increasingly the most difficult missions facing U.S. forces. Electronic communication, traditionally a strength of the U.S. military, becomes difficult as infantrymen move through buildings and alleys. Dealing with such problems was critical in the 2004 battle for Fallujah in Iraq.

Asymmetrical warfare has also shaped foreign policy, driving the formulation of the Bush Doctrine, with its proviso permitting the United States to launch pre-emptive wars. It has also led to stronger links with Britain and weaker ones with France and Germany, on account of their respective stances toward the Iraq war. At home, the Age of Asymmetrical Warfare gave birth to a new cabinet department of Homeland Security and the Patriot Act, with its controversial curbs on civil liberties.

For the most part, the United States is conducting asymmetrical warfare the way a big power might be expected to, by using all the advantages of its size and wealth. But even big powers can benefit from fielding their own asymmetrical forces. In Afghanistan and Iraq, U.S. Special Forces crept in small numbers behind enemy lines to play important roles: advising and supporting indigenous rebels; gathering intelligence; capturing or killing enemy leaders; and calling in surgical air strikes to take out targets.

Of course, many voices have been critical of how the United States is adapting to the Age of Asymmetrical Warfare. According to some of these schools of thought, the United States should combat terrorism through means such as international police investigations and being a good global neighbor rather than full-scale war. This kind of debate is likely to continue for some time—as will the Age of Asymmetrical Warfare that sparked the debate.

Delocalized Politics

63 Former Speaker of the House Thomas "Tip" O'Neill's dictum of "All politics are local" is not necessarily true. Increasingly, local elections deemed politically crucial to a political party, are funded by the national party committee and special interest organizations. Most important, they are designed and run from the national level as well, often by a leader of the ruling party that wants to tighten its grasp on the country. This differs from the old-time neighborhood party deputies, who worked a district and delivered its votes. And it is hardly the storied campaign built on grassroots support. This is management from the top down.

One 2004 campaign that worked and won from the top down blocked the reelection of Democratic South Dakota Senator Tom Daschle. A long-time senator and minority leader of the Senate, Daschle was effective in countering some of Republican President George W. Bush's objectives, and thus was targeted for removal. In a campaign supported by national political party operatives, conservative members of the national media, Republican former U.S. Rep. John Thune, defeated Daschle by about 4,500 votes.

As if to underscore the national movement to unseat the Democrat, a Daschle organizer reported to the Associated Press that many of the people who called Daschle's office to reel in the senator's defeat were not from Daschle's state. Many out-of-state callers have said they are happy the Senate minority leader will be out of work, she said. "He lost the election, what else do they want?" the organizer said, adding that those dismayed at Daschle's defeat locally far outnumber such calls.

In part, the nationalization of local politics has to do with the increasing power of big money from national sources. By the 1990s, candidates and observers found that the hard and soft money from national businesses and political organizations was corrupting the campaign process. Candidates found they were losing control of their campaigns to outside groups with national agendas, as political money has outpaced the law. Attempts at campaign reform have thus far been rebuffed.

China Rising

64 The rise of China is "perhaps the most important long-term trend in the world," *New York Times* columnist Nicholas D. Kristof wrote in 2002. It has been a trend long in coming: Twenty years earlier, John Naisbitt in *Megatrends* (1982) noted "the recent emergence of China as a new contender in manufacturing." Today, China is the world's sixth largest economy, the scheduled host of the 2008 Olympics, and, after a long campaign, a member of the World Trade Organization. China, although not yet a superpower, is rapidly advancing in the wealth, capabilities, and prestige that make for elite status.

China's strength stems partly from its population, which, at 1.3 billion, is the world's largest. It also stems from a dedication to free enterprise that has been growing for a quarter-century, ever since Deng Xiaoping came to power in the late 1970s. Although China's leadership is nominally Communist, its commitment to market reforms has helped put the nation's economy in overdrive. China's annual output is growing at a double-digit pace, faster than any other major economy. Foreign investors are flocking in. The profits from all that growth are distributed unequally, with the urban coastal areas reaping the most from the boom, yet the standard of living is rising even in the rural interior.

China's newfound power is also rooted in a commitment to science and technology that is evident in the background of its president, Hu Jintao, trained as a hydrologist. China has had nuclear weapons for nearly four decades and also has satellites and intercontinental ballistic missiles. But it is growing scientifically in other ways. Its space program, which launched a man into space in 2003, is valued for its military and industrial potential as well as scientific aspects. In addition, China is developing a biotechnology sector, partly thanks to its willingness to permit experiments forbidden by U.S. regulation.

Despite all its progress, China does not yet rank as a global behemoth on the level of the United States, which has been the world's sole superpower since the collapse of the Soviet Union. It is a regional power, jockeying with Japan for influence in East Asia. But it has one major weakness: the mismatch between its authoritarian system of government, inherited from Communism, and the freedom and openness associated with Western-style economic growth.

As the standard of living rises in China and people grow used to competing on the global market, the Chinese people are increasingly prone to be frustrated with the pace of political change and to view their Communist leaders as irrelevant. The gap between rich and poor is growing, and social services are woefully inadequate, increasing the potential for unrest. The government still has a tendency to revive statist economic policies: in 2004, to brake what is considered economic overheating, it re-regulated numerous industries. In addition, the government tends to be secretive and slow to respond to popular needs, as notable in its handling of both the AIDS and SARS epidemics.

Despite popular frustration, full-scale democratization remains elusive. China's leadership showed in the Tiananmen Square massacre of 1989 that it would crack down when faced with the possibility of overthrow, and it has remained ruthless with dissidents ever since. China is also as ready as ever to restrict the flow of information. In 2004, news broke that Google's recently launched news service in China was programmed not to display search results from Web sites banned by the Chinese government.

However, in many ways, the opening of China's society is already underway. A poll in 2002 revealed that 80 percent of Chinese want to elect their officials directly. Faced with growing discontent, in 2003 the Communist Party pledged more help for the poor and further market reforms.

Provided that political instability does not derail China's economic growth, it will continue to climb in global stature. As China becomes more powerful, it will increasingly come into conflict with the world's only superpower, the United States. China will increasingly try to increase its influence in East Asia not only commercially, but militarily as well—for example, by developing a modern navy with regional and global reach.

There have been numerous moments of tension between the United States and China in recent years: the accidental NATO bombing of the Chinese embassy in Belgrade, Yugoslavia; the alleged Chinese stealing of U.S. nuclear secrets; the forcing down of a U.S. spy plane in China. Yet, hot war between China and the United States is unlikely: both have nuclear weapons and would stand to lose too much in a nuclear exchange. A prolonged cold war, like the one that prevailed for decades between the United States and the Soviet Union, is a possibility, but unlikely given the integration of both countries into the global market. There will be mutual suspicion, jockeying for power, perhaps even saber rattling. But in the end, the desire to make money from each other is likely to keep China and the United States at peace with each other—especially if China's government succeeds in becoming more open and responsive to its people.

Europe as Immigration Center

65 In some ways, Europe is the new America. Politically stable and offering promise for security, it has attracted millions of immigrants over the past 10 years. In classic immigrant style, they hail from and end up in many places: from Tunisia to Turkey; Morocco and Tunisia to Spain; Turkey to Sarajevo. Other routes include Belarus to Poland, Hungary, and the Czech Republic; from Istanbul to Sarajevo, and still others.

This immigration into Europe is welcomed by government and business on some level, as it offers a labor force that will replenish aging European workers. But it also fuels worry about how the European nations will provide the social safety net of pension and other work benefits to their new compatriots. Some politicians and citizens are also worried about how the new immigrant demographic mix will alter the look and sensibilities of long-established nations. As immigrants continue to press into Europe, supporters and detractors may press for new laws and attitudes.

During the 1990s, Europe experienced a slight annual decrease in legal immigration and a high number of 500,000 irregular immigrants. During the same period, the number of countries from which immigrants came expanded greatly, with 50 percent of immigrants in 1997 coming into European Union countries hailing from Central and East European countries (particularly Yugoslavia, the former Soviet Union, and Turkey); and then the Maghreb countries (Morocco, Algeria, Tunisia). Thus far in the workforce, they are heavily represented in the service industries and in self-employment.

Despite the immigrants' employment in relatively low-paying work, there is concern among Europeans about the economic effects of immigrants on European workers. With 15 million Europeans unemployed, there is fear in some regions that immigrants will steal jobs by agreeing to a lower pay scale.

However, for the most part, European governments and businesses see the need to recruit a non-European work force, particularly those with certain skills. To fill spots for highly technical computer and operational positions, businesses are actively seeking trained non-European workers. Barbara Roche, the UK's immigration minister, has made it easier for non-British students to stay. "In the past we have thought purely about immigration control," she said. "Now we need to think about immigration management. Some regions lacking blue-collar workers are calling for laborers. In Spain, where the indigenous population is declining, North Africans pick oranges and grapes; Poles and Romanians work on construction sites. Projecting into the future, Jean-Pierre Chevenement, the former French interior minister, said that during the next half-century, Europe will need 50 million to 75 million immigrants to fill jobs.

Some groups are mounting political resistance to further immigration. In response to growing numbers of non-Europeans on the continent, several nationalist right-wing parties have gained strength. Parties including Jorg Haider in Austria, Pia Kjaersgaard in Denmark, and Filip Dewinter in Belgium are defining themselves on platforms promoting immigration reform and unified national identity.

Meanwhile, immigrants are seeking ways to become more settled in their new European homes. For example, Muslim immigrants to France and elsewhere have requested ways to practice their cultural beliefs in the communities where they live. In October 2004, the symposium on The Multi-cultural Society, held at the Centre Culturel Irlandais in Paris, heard how Muslims in France have petitioned for permits to build mosques, Muslim cemeteries, and gain the right to slaughter animals in accordance with *halal* rules. They have also spoken out for the right of female students to wear traditional Muslim headgear.

The European Union (EU) recognizes the potential for growing conflict with immigration laws that vary among nations. For that reason, at an EU summit in October 2004, EU leaders decided to develop "common policies on asylum and immigration." In the meantime, the people keep coming.

Exurban Voters

66 On the suburban frontier lie the exurban voters, and they are changing the country. Not only are they exploding the population in once rural, lightly populated areas like Frederick County, Maryland, and Douglas County, Colorado, they have also established new voting allegiances and are determining elections. As of the early 21st century, they and the Republican Party are singing the same song. Both are calling, "Cut taxes, and don't mess with my SUV."

The exurbs have been growing since the 1980s, after international businesses began moving some of their offices outside the city. Before the 1980s, reports Robert Lang, a demographer at Virginia Tech, only one-fourth of businesses were established away from the city. But in the 1990s, it became commonplace to see office parks and other business headquarters being built in suburban areas far out of the city. As companies built the exurban work sites, their employees followed and set up shop in nearby towns.

Exurbanites are distinguished, says demographer Lang (in the *New York Times*), by a populace that does not have to commute to, live in, or visit the city. Because they work in an office park in New Jersey, Maryland, or Colorado, they don't have the exposure to the usual urban concerns (crime, need to maintain old infrastructure, constant demand for social services) that city dwellers or even commuters do.

Instead, their concerns revolve around comfort and space and how to maintain them. Generally, exurbanites want to keep their towns from becoming too crowded, as they have seen happen in suburbs closer to the city, but they don't mind the benefits that strip-mall development (especially with national brand-stores) can bring. One government expenditure they approve of is roads so they can travel to work faster. But they don't want higher taxes to get it.

In the 21st century, these middle-class desires for maintenance rather than change have been answered by the Republican Party. The effects of exurban voters to swing close elections to Republicans in 2002 is proof of the Republicans' appeal. In Maryland, Democratic candidate for governor, Kathleen Kennedy Townsend, lost to Republican Bob Ehrlich largely due to his command of the outlying exurban Harford and Frederick counties. Similarly, in Georgia, incumbent Democrat Max Cleland lost to Republican Saxby Chambliss for the Senate seat in Georgia when Chambliss swept the exurban Forsyth and Gwinnett counties. Rural and exurban voters were also key to the Republican victory in the presidential election of 2004.

Because of demographic shifts, an increase in population, and the forcing of the suburban limit ever outward, exurban voters are sure to build their power base. But, according to some prognosticators, eventually the Democratic Party will overrun the Republican Party in these geographic areas. In their book, *The Emerging Democratic Majority*, Ruy Teixeira and John B. Judis claim that social and demographic changes over the next few years will shift voters toward the Democratic Party. The new Democratic Party, according to Teixeira, will be more heterogeneous than the old and more in tune with the needs of the service economy. It will be "the party of the post-industrial future."

The Democratic Party will draw its support from workers in what Teixeira calls "ideopolises," which are the cities and suburbs "organized around the production of ideas and services." These areas are peopled by lawyers, other professional workers, low-level service and information workers, nurses, teachers, and union members, as opposed to the urban wage and assembly-line workers of the 20th century industrial era. Demographically, the party will contain high numbers of women, minorities, and immigrants. But much of the Democratic Party's constituency also will be comprised of exurban voters, who will place domestic issues above that of national security and will want progressive political leadership to effect change.

Though it may be hard to believe given the Republican dominance in the White House and Capitol Hill, Teixeira believes the shift to the Democratic Party will come soon. Indeed, in 2004, Republican Bush beat Democrat Kerry by just five points among newly registered rural and exurban voters in the key swing state of Ohio. In an article for *www.TomPaine.com*, Teixeira says, "Before the decade is over, the Democrats are likely to complete this journey, and the country will move from a conservative Republican majority to a progressive Democrat one."

Independence Day (from Political Parties)

67 The historic Democratic lead in party affiliation over the Republicans has been eroding for decades, and according to a 2003 Harris Poll is now at a five-point margin: 33 percent of American adults consider themselves Democrats, 28 percent Republicans. Yet, in recent national and local elections, the majority of party-affiliated voters split their votes. In so doing, they were demonstrating a greater voting trend: the growing disassociation from strict party affiliation and turn toward independent voting.

According to the Harris Poll, 24 percent of Americans call themselves political independents. This and other findings suggest that independents are the fastest-growing political constituency in the United States. For various reasons, U.S. voters do not want to be affiliated with either of the two major political parties; yet, because independents by their nature have not banded together in a party affiliation, they lack power as a group to influence public policy on a large scale. As a result, they are pursued by Democrats and Republicans according to individual issues, such as campaign reform, environmentalism, or tax cuts.

Still, the power of unaffiliated voters remains strong, particularly in affecting national elections. In 2000, self-proclaimed independents split their votes between Democrat Al Gore and Republican George Bush: each got 44 percent of independents' vote. But the 3 percent national showing by Ralph Nader may have tilted the outcome of the election toward Bush. And in 1992, Ross Perot won 14 percent of the vote for president as a member of the United We Stand Party, which may have helped to elect Democratic candidate Bill Clinton.

To solidify the power of independents, various interest groups want to build consensus and define independents as a political and social force. Activists for the cause believe that independents would carry more weight to promote independent-minded candidates of any party and to shape policy. One group, the Committee for a Unified Independent Party, states its goal as "building the independent movement" in order to "take on the corruption of the two parties" and "end political corruption and the influence of special interests." This independent action group calls for political reform from both parties that will make the democratic process more open to ordinary people.

Despite gathering together under the name of "independent," there is little as yet in the early 21st century to mark them as a political power. One characteristic of independents, reports surveys by ABC, the Henry J. Kaiser Family Foundation, and Harvard University, is that voters who call themselves independent often lean toward established party policy. "You scratch independent leaners and you will find closet partisans," says political scientist David Magleby, dean at Brigham Young University. Added Magleby, "One of the reasons people resonate to the term 'independent' is because of their hostility to parties and institutions. They want to be more neutral and they don't want to be tainted by a negative term that makes it seem you are captured by a party."

For example, *Washington Post*–ABC News polls on 2002 elections indicated that 85 percent of the Democratic-leaning voters would vote for the Democrat, and 68 percent of Republican-leaning independents would vote for the Republican candidate. As for the small percentage (less than 10 percent) of independents who are truly independent, often they decide not to vote, says Magleby. "Pure independents do march to their own beat. They are volatile. They have the lowest rates of turnout." There are signs that independents may think differently from the general public. According to a 2005 Westhill Partners poll, President Bush's plan to privatize Social Security received 59 percent disapproval from independents—a stronger reaction than the 52 percent disapproval rating among the public at large.

India Prospering

68 "India" and "poverty" have long been words that go together. But on the world business front, India is becoming known as something else—a thriving place for investment and opportunity. India's economy is now the second fastest growing in the world, after China. In years to come, it will probably prosper as never before.

India's economic renaissance began in 1991, when the government started liberalizing an economy that had been heavily subject to state planning. Since then, India has dismantled numerous regulations, lifted restrictions on foreign investment, and generally cut red tape. New industries, such as software development companies and service centers for financial institutions, have been allowed the freedom to grow with minimal state controls. They have been so successful at persuading U.S. companies to "outsource" software and services work that a political backlash developed in America about the export of jobs to India. Bangalore and Hyderabad have become particularly prosperous as a result of these high-tech industries.

Just as important to India's prospering has been a cultural change away from a traditional antipathy to materialism and spending, and toward a Western-style consumer society. As prosperity fuels the growth of India's middle class, more of them look for material treats that go with that status. Demographically, India is a young country—half its people are under age 25—and its youths are increasingly likely to enjoy buying stuff. "Consumerism as a term is no longer seen as a bad word," Yogesh Samat, head of the growing Indian coffee-bar chain Barista Coffee, told the *New York Times*. Although there were no shopping malls in 1998,

India now has 150 of them. A taste for mobile phones has helped make India the world's fastest-growing telecommunications market.

There are also thorns in this rosy picture. Twenty-six percent of the Indian population is still living in poverty. India's neighbor and rival China is enjoying even greater growth. Bureaucracy and poor infrastructure (bad roads, unreliable electricity) continue to hamper growth in many places. With 70 percent of the work force employed in agriculture, the Indian economy can still be severely hurt by a bad monsoon season. However, despite the tragic loss of life, the tsunami of 2004 resulted in relatively little damage to the Indian economy, and India's government has refused foreign aid in rebuilding.

There is also the perennial danger of war with neighbor Pakistan, which, like India, is nuclear equipped. Indeed, among the people most interested in selling to India are arms merchants, vying with each other to sell fighter jets and radar systems to the booming Indian defense market. In the coming decade, India is expected to be the world's largest importer of arms.

Will India remain true to free-market principles? Leftists gained greater influence in India's 2004 elections, rousing fears among many investors of a return to statist policies. But those fears have been mostly allayed: Edward Pulling, manager of JP Morgan Fleming Indian Investment Trust, told *IFAOnline* in 2005 that India's progress toward a free-market economy had not been halted by the elections. As long as it doesn't destroy itself through war, India is likely to survive its other problems to become one of the economic success stories of this century.

Islamic Flashpoints

69 The terror attacks of September 11, 2001, brought more global attention to the Islamic world than it had received in years. Now the question is, where next? What Islamic countries might be the next flashpoints for terrorism, war, or revolutionary change? What trends might affect the Islamic world at large?

It is difficult to generalize about the Islamic world, which comprises 1.5 billion people in many different parts of the globe. Still, one notable trend is an increased suspicion and hostility toward the United States as a result of the war in Iraq. Polls in 2003 showed that majorities in seven of eight predominantly Muslim nations said they were worried that the United States might threaten their countries. The occupation of Iraq by American troops has revived feelings of humiliation that still rankle from the colonial past. This has aided the recruitment efforts of Al Qaeda and other Islamist terrorist groups; even the buildup to the war aided recruitment. In March 2003, on the eve of the war, one American official told the *New York Times* that Iraq had already become "a battle cry" for Al Qaeda recruiters.

On the other hand, the holding of elections in Iraq in 2005 was a promising sign that peaceful democratic change might provide a counterforce against war in the Islamic world. News from other Islamic countries supported the trend. About 58 percent of Iraq's registered voters participated, despite violence from insurgents that killed more than people. Afghanistan held its first ever direct election for president in 2004, and Saudi Arabia held its first regular election in 2005, though only males were allowed to vote. Also in 2005, Palestinian Authority President Mahmoud Abbas announced a cease-fire with Israel, restarting a peace process that had been stalled.

Against these pointers toward peace are signs that Islamism, a political ideology rooted in Islam, is continuing to spread. However, here too the picture is complex. Though the best-known brand of Islamism (the brand of Al Qaeda and the Taliban) is an anti-Western theocratic fundamentalism, it exists in varied forms. In all cases, it is a studied response to the modern world, and often a postmodern blending of elements. It may have Marxist echoes in its critique of Western economic imperialism. It may be prone to conspiracy theories, including anti-Semitic ones. The radical or militant versions of Islamism advocate using violence and terrorism to establish a totalitarian theocratic regime. But there are also liberal versions of Islamism, which seek to synthesize religious and liberal principles. These kinds of Islamism may be conducive to peace between the West and the Islamic world.

Another complication is the role of women. Islamic women in some parts of the world are beginning to seek the kind of equality before the law that prevails in Western societies. In India in 2005, for example, a group of Shiite Muslim women announced the formation of an All-India Muslim Women Personal Law Board. Formed in response to a lack of interest by the religious leadership of the community in women's concerns, the board hoped to increase awareness among Muslim women of their rights.

However one tries to understand the Islamic world, it is important to realize that the term *Islamic world* can be misleading, suggesting a homogeneity that does not exist. Each country with a Muslim majority has a different history and a different set of problems. Turkey is predominantly Muslim but has a strong pro-Western, secular tradition. Even so, its Parliament voted against the Bush administration's request to use Turkey as a staging ground for the Iraq war. Ironically, the fight in favor of Bush's request was led by a devout Muslim from an Islamist background, Prime Minister Recep Tayyip Erdogan. Whether in the Islamic world or outside it, politics makes strange bedfellows.

One closely watched potential Islamic flashpoint is Pakistan. Even though the country is an American ally that aided the U.S. war in Afghanistan, it is believed to be harboring terrorists and is politically unstable, with the potential of becoming an Islamic theocracy. Its current leader, Pervez Musharraf, took power in a coup, and the country has no strong democratic tradition. Of greatest concern internationally is the fact that it has nuclear weapons. In January 2004, some tension was abated when Pakistan and India agreed to resume formal peace talks, easing fears of a nuclear war between the two powers. But in December 2003, Musharraf barely dodged two assassination attempts by Islamist groups.

Crises with international repercussions may erupt anywhere in the Islamic world. In Saudi Arabia, for example, Islamist militants late in

2003 tried to assassinate security officials, perhaps in an effort to desta-bilize the pro-American government. For the foreseeable future, the only constant in the world of Islamic flashpoints will be flux.

The "L" Word—Liberal

70 According to polls in the 1950s, a large segment of Ameri-cans called themselves "liberal." Why not? Liberals had a strong his-tory of progressive reform and of looking out for the average guy. They had experienced financial panics and the Depression, and the result was progressive political policy. Social security, civil rights, child labor laws, and more—liberals could claim these ideas as theirs, just as they could, to various extents, FDR, TR, HST, and JFK. Fifty years later, the word liberal has come to mean something so corrupted that it is an epi-thet. When in early 2005, former Republican mayor and moviemaker Clint Eastwood was denounced as a "liberal ideologue" because of the characters in his movie *Million Dollar Baby*, it's clear the word liberal has lost its original meaning. Whether the word and the liberal tradi-tion will rise—and how it will change—is for the next few decades to decide.

There are suggestions from many quarters:

First, say critics, they should reproduce more of themselves by hav-ing more children. According to research reported in conservative Web site *www.realitycheck.com*, abortions since Roe v. Wade in 1973 have accounted for more than 5 million more deaths of potential Democrats than potential Republicans. James Taranto of the *Wall Street Journal* has referred to these trends as the Roe Effect. "Abortion is making America more conservative than it otherwise would be," he says. Because "chil-dren's political views tend to reflect those of their parents—not exactly, of course, and not in every case, but on average[,] . . . abortion depletes the next generation of liberals and eventually makes the population more conservative."

Other critics say that anyone who will counter conservatives must become comfortable talking about their faith. Says Steven Waldman in *Slate* during the 2004 election, findings at the time reveal that 92 percent of Americans believe in God. Most of them want a candidate who is comfortable with his or her religion. Says Waldman, "Americans believe that one of the most important sources of inner strength is faith. During the darkest hours of the country, when the president is wandering the halls alone . . . voters are going to be more comfortable with the commander in chief who has serious resources, and I don't mean financial ones."

Liberals also have to make clear to themselves and others their moral strengths. As cognitive scientist George Lakoff reports in his book *Moral Politics: How Liberals and Conservatives Think,* both liberals and conservatives form what he calls their "worldviews" around family, but the Republicans have made their allegiances better known. He says, "Conservatives talk constantly about the centrality of morality and the family in their politics, while liberals did not talk about these things until conservatives started winning elections by doing so. My findings indicate that the family and morality are central to both worldviews. But where conservatives are relatively aware of how their politics relates to their views of family life and morality, liberals are less aware of the implicit view of morality and the family that organizes their own political beliefs. This lack of conscious awareness of their own political worldview has been devastating to the liberal cause." Understanding this basic tenet of liberal belief as well as others is central to liberals understanding their strengths and thus gaining more support among voters.

As liberal thinking is reimagined, there are signs that all the lights in the liberal household have not gone out. As reported in the magazine for Stanford Business School, one is the success of racial redistricting in increasing the presence of liberals and minority voices in Congress, particularly those from Southern states. Work by Kenneth Shotts, associate professor of political economy at the Stanford Graduate School of

Business, indicates that the recent legislation allowing for the creation of majority minority districts has increased legislative liberal presence. In a paper published in *The Journal of Politics* in February 2003, Shotts wrote, "The fraction of southern representatives to the left . . . increased after racial redistricting in the 1990s, a pattern that contrasts starkly with the well-known fact that the number of southern Democrats decreased during this period. My finding implies that racial redistricting promotes liberal policy outcomes."

And, as of 2005, liberal Al Franken's *Air America* radio programming is still going strong. He has even beaten TV and radio star Bill O'Reilly at the ratings game and, according to reports, at man-to-man combat.

Remembering the Forgotten Continent

71 Africa has long been known as the forgotten continent. North America and Europe shine on the world stage because of their rich and powerful nations. In Asia, Japan has long been prominent, and other countries, such as China and India, are rising as economic and political powers. South America has had its troubles, but it is increasingly part of an integrated and prosperous Western Hemisphere. Africa alone has been left out of world affairs. Only now is Africa beginning to be remembered.

Africa's woes began with the indignity of colonization by Europe in the 19th century. Nationalist movements won independence in the 1950s and 1960s, but the new countries were unstable, with disputed boundaries, leaders who were often corrupt or incompetent, and factions that plunged African nations time and again into civil war. Famines periodically wracked the continent. During the Cold War, the two superpowers, the United States and the Soviet Union, poured foreign aid into Africa, chiefly to fund their own client states and entice them from switching to the other side. But after the Cold War was over, there was no more Soviet Union, and the United States was much more reluctant to extend foreign aid. The continent was left more or less on its own. Some of the results have been calamitous, others promising.

The worst calamity has been AIDS. In sub-Saharan Africa, 28.5 million people were infected with the HIV virus as of 2001, the highest incidence in the world. In addition, many countries have continued to suffer from brutal dictators, while civil wars and regional wars have continued to ravage the continent. In the Democratic Republic of Congo, the death toll from a prolonged civil war and related causes was 3.3 million from 1998 to 2002. Sudan has been another trouble spot. In 2004, the U.S. Congress unanimously passed a resolution giving the name genocide to the atrocities happening in Darfur, Sudan, and urging the White House to intervene.

The promising developments have come about precisely because Africa is no longer the plaything of rival superpowers. Rather, Africa now has to compete, like all other regions, for the attention of global investors and multinational firms looking to make a profit. The bad news is that it has a long way to go before it can build the infrastructure of a first-world power, or even of a developing one such as Thailand or Singapore. The good news is that if it develops the habits that investors like—stable government, low government spending, low inflation, privatized economy—it has the potential to attract the investment capital that can drive development.

Africa has the resources to be attractive to investors, if African countries would only stay stable enough to make ongoing business possible. The oil reserves in Nigeria's Niger Delta attracted several multinational oil companies, but they had to shut down operations temporarily in 2003 on account of ethnic fighting. The diversity of conditions across the continent makes for a great deal of economic diversity. In 2005, according to the Economist Intelligence Unit, two African countries were expected to have the world's fastest growth—Equatorial Guinea at 19.4 percent and Liberia at 15 percent—while two will have the world's slowest growth—Zimbabwe at -3.1 percent and Côte d'Ivoire at -1.2 percent.

Several African countries have been striving to show themselves worthy of investment. Even Libya, once a global pariah, renounced terrorism and weapons of mass destruction in 2003, setting the stage for an end to international sanctions. For other countries, the road to the world's good graces is as short as a balanced budget. According to allAfrica.com, Ugandan president Yoweri Museveni has made his country one of several African nations with balanced budgets and strong protection of property rights.

South Africa is another country that is trying to promote growth. This is a nation that only recently, in the 1990s, emerged from apartheid and built a multiracial democracy. Now, according to Reuters, South Africa is aiming to copy the miracle that built Asia's "tiger" economies by building a combination duty-free industrial development zone and deep-water port. Known as the Coega Industrial Development Zone, it is modeled on similar zones in countries such as Singapore and China.

In addition to stimulating private initiatives, some African countries have been supporting their native industries by demanding fair treatment at world trade conferences. For example, they have sought elimination of agricultural subsidies in the developed world that block their farmers from competing.

All this African activity has been jogging the memories of the developed world, enticing world leaders and deep-pocketed businesspeople to visit Africa. According to the International Monetary Fund, since 1994 the economies of the sub-Saharan African countries have been growing an average of 5 percent a year. Still, there are skeptics about Africa's reliance on the capitalist bandwagon. In Cairo's *Al-Ahram Weekly On-Line,* scholars Rita Abrahamsen and Ray Bush wrote, "The manner of Africa's integration into the world economy serves primarily to ensure the further extraction of profit by Northern countries." On the other hand, Africans seem to be ready to have some profit extracted by northern countries so long as some hope for a reasonable livelihood is left for the southern ones. For the time being, Africans are no longer willing to remain forgotten.

States in Trouble

72 Recent federal tax cuts have been among the largest in history. But recent federal mandates on state educational testing and the Medicare and Medicaid demands soon to come from aging baby boomers are hitting state budgets hard. These mandates affect two major state budget elements—education and health care. Paying for implementing mandated educational tests and for part-federally supported but also federally mandated health care is already putting states into financial distress. In January 2005, the president and president-elect of the bipartisan National Council of State Legislators implored the U.S. Senate and House Budget Committee members "to be mindful of the effects that federal budget decisions have on state budgets and to avoid exporting the federal deficit to the states through unfunded mandates and other cost shifts."

As early as the mid-1990s, governors and mayors predicted deficits if the federal government imposed state mandates but not federal monies to implement them. Said Colorado Governor Roy Romer, "[T]he Governors are concerned that attempts to balance the Federal budget will come at the cost of states and localities. . . . [We will have] to pick up the cost of programs, such as child care, mass transit and education, that were previously supported with Federal funds."

But some conservative thinkers note that some policies that are popularly considered unfunded mandates are either not unfunded or not mandates, or both. For example, the conservative think tank, The Heritage Foundation, notes that the No Child Left Behind Act is not a mandate, and that states can opt out of it if they wish. So far, none has.

Part of the discrepancy arises from the various ways people define mandate. To the government, a mandate is "any provision in legislation, statute, or regulation that would impose an enforceable duty on state, local, or tribal governments." States view mandates more broadly, and among other elements, flat out reject the idea that mandates can be offered without adequate support to implement them.

According to the *Harvard Political Review*, "Unfunded mandates occur when the federal government places new legal requirements on states and localities without providing funding to finance the additional responsibilities. To uphold its fiscal responsibilities, and help ease mounting budget deficits, the federal government must provide state and local governments with financial aid to pay for unfunded mandates."

"Alleviating the burden of unfunded mandates should be a bipartisan cause," the *Review* says. But the National Council of State Legislators, which met at the start of the 2005 congressional session, is not expecting national cooperation. It is expecting a battle.

VIII

Religion and Spirituality

Christian Cool

73 Alternative churches located in coffee bars. Christian rock music climbing up Billboard's Top 200 chart. Bibles in teen-magazine format. T-shirts that say "Jesus Is My Homeboy" and rings that say "WTW" for "Willing to Wait"—a promise of sexual abstinence. It is all part of Christian cool, the trend toward greater acceptance of Christianity in youth culture. Christianity "is becoming a more cool thing to do," high school sophomore Marci Fluhr told Louisville, Kentucky's, *Courier-Journal.* "God is saying I am an exciting God," high school senior Lena Womack, a fan of alternative Christian music, told *Nugget Newspaper* in Sisters, Oregon. "I can provide you with fun and exciting songs."

The phrase "Christian cool" was popularized in a *New York Times Magazine* article by John Leland in May 2004, but the association of Christianity with coolness precedes the article. One Christian organization for college students calls itself C.O.O.L. on Campus, for Christ Over Our Life. Christian cool is edgy, stylish, committed. Its practitioners, sometimes called alt-evangelicals, may connect more with subcultures such as extreme sports, punk, and body piercing than with established denominations. The Christian Tattoo Association alone has more than 100 member shops. Alt-evangelicals connect readily with the Christian tradition of being outsiders. "It's a counter-cultural thing," New Jersey pastor Tim Lucas told Leland. His congregation identifies "with being an underground movement, which is what Christianity was in the beginning."

One alt-evangelical profiled by Leland is Cameron Strang, founder of Relevant Media, a Christian cool publisher. Strang has two earrings, a beard, and a shaved head. His *Relevant* magazine, a bimonthly that reaches 70,000 people, covers subjects such as body piercing, extreme prayer, and punk rock. Alt-evangelicals want a version of Christianity that speaks to them. "My generation is discontent with dead religion," Strang told Leland. "Our generation wants a tangible experience of God who is there."

Alternative or "emerging" churches may have unusual names like Threads or Liquid and use multimedia clips from movies to supplement their sermons. Alt-evangelicals can read their New Testament in teen-magazine format, available under the titles *Revolve* and *Refuel*. Young female Christians can attend Girls of Grace, two-day conferences hosted by the Christian pop group Point of Grace. The conferences combine concerts, fashion shows, Bible study, and makeovers. The emphasis on fashion and makeup is important in helping girls feel they can be both Christian and fashionable. "For so long, girls thought to be religious you had to wear non-stylish clothes and have your hair in braids," college freshman Christina Morreale told the *Courier-Journal*. "Now you don't have to be that different, but at the same time you can still be your own person."

Not everyone thinks that Christian cool is cool. Some evangelical Christians, such as Pastor David L. Brown of Logos Ministries, think Christian rock is the "devil's music." Ever since Elvis, says Brown, it was the music of "sex and rebellion," and adding references to Christ has not improved it. "I pray that the devastating results of rock music will be realized in the Church before it steals anymore of the souls of our youth," says a 16-year-old student from Indiana quoted by Dial-the-Truth Ministries. Some traditional Christians suspect that Christian teens are wandering close to heresy as they stretch their religion's boundaries. According to the Rev. Josh McDowell in an opinion piece by Dale Buss in the *Wall Street Journal*, a majority of professing Christian teens say the bodily resurrection of Jesus Christ never happened. Their morality is not that different from non-Christians: According to a Barna survey, only 10 percent of Christian teens say that music piracy is morally wrong, a similar figure to the 6 percent found among non-Christian teens. "In fact," says Buss, "some leaders believe that mushy doctrine among the younger generation ranks as the No. 1 crisis facing American Christendom today."

While Christian cool sometimes gets chastised from the right, it also has its critics on the left. Some think that movements like Girls of Grace reinforce conservative social values. "'Traditional values' is a way of talking about women basically knowing their place," Stephen Ray, associate professor of theology and philosophy at Louisville Presbyterian Theological Seminary, told the *Courier-Journal*.

Despite the controversy, Christian cool has been a boon to retailers, providing a new way to sell products to the youth market. Christian or not, young people like to buy things that identify them as part of a group, and Christian cool is the latest niche. Hence the proliferation of rings, records, T-shirts, and other merchandise. Christian cool is likely to continue to grow and evolve, providing many opportunities for both spiritual and commercial advancement.

Christianity: Decline and Rise

74 An old story about Christianity is that it is on the wane, in decline, soon to be defunct. There is some evidence to back up this claim, but not enough to tell the whole story. The real future of Christianity looks more complicated.

In Europe, cradle of Christian civilization, Christian belief and church attendance have reached relatively low levels. According to the Gallup International Millennium Survey, only 48 percent of European respondents say that God is very important to them, and 48 percent of Western Europeans almost never go to church at all. The European Union made a conspicuous point in 2003 of not including mention of Christianity in its charter, despite the urging of the Pope. A survey by Opinion Research Business in Britain in 1999 reported that only 45 percent believed Jesus was the son of God.

The United States has a reputation among developed countries for being relatively more religious than Europe. According to the Gallup poll, the percentage of Americans who believe in God or a universal spirit has stayed stable in the 90 percent range for years. But specifically Christian belief is another story. According to the American Religious Identification Survey, the proportion of Christians in the United States declined from 86 percent in 1990 to 77 percent in 2001. And even among avowed Christians, there is much disagreement with certain traditional Christian doctrines. A Barna Research Group study found that among mainline Protestant denominations such as Lutherans, Episcopalians, Methodists, and Presbyterians, only 27 percent accepted the traditional Christian view that man does not earn his way to heaven by good works. Among both Catholic and mainline Protestant Church members, only 17 and 20 percent respectively think Satan is real.

Evidence like this has led to predictions that Christianity as we once knew it has had its day. Episcopal bishop John Shelby Spong, an advocate of liberalized doctrine, even wrote a book with the title *Why Christianity Must Change or Die*. And it is true that in the developed world, Christianity increasingly must compete with other forms of religious belief and nonbelief, both new and old—everything from neoagnosticism to Islam.

Yet, it is unlikely that traditional Christianity will simply wither away any time soon. Setting aside the question of whether there are divine guarantees that Christianity will prevail, there are three factors that probably ensure its continuing strength: the mission fields of the developing world, the renewed popularity of orthodoxy, and the attractiveness of fundamentalism.

Christianity is the world's largest religion, counting 1.9 billion members, or roughly a third of the global population, according to *Time Almanac 2005*. Its nearest rival is Islam, with 1.1 billion members. In Africa and Asia, the number of Christians has risen dramatically in recent years, to about 360 million in Africa and 313 million in Asia in 2000, according to the *Encyclopedia Britannica Book of the Year*. Of those, 9 million were added in Africa and 23 million in Asia in just the three years from 1997 to 2000. Christianity is flourishing in, of all places, China, despite lack of a historical link to Christianity and despite years of persecution and suppression by its atheistic communist rulers. The global spread of Christianity is likely to continue, driven in part by the same forces that are making English a global language and pushing sales of Western products and popular culture throughout the world: namely, the starting advantages possessed by Western businesses (and churches) in an increasingly borderless world market.

Even within the developing world, orthodoxy shows no signs of yielding quietly to critics like Bishop Spong. Instead, a pro-orthodoxy movement is developing in many denominations. Mel Gibson's 2004 film *The Passion of the Christ* became a runaway hit with a highly literal depiction of the suffering and crucifixion of Jesus. Methodist theologian Thomas Oden, a former advocate of liberal doctrine who has turned into a defender of orthodoxy, argues in *The Rebirth of Orthodoxy: Signs of New Life in Christianity* that the era we have entered is not post-Christian but post-secular. Says Oden, "God is at work in grass-roots Christianity, awakening a ground swell of longing for classical ecumenical teaching in all communions." Orthodox belief has proven resistant to change in several high-profile cases. The Catholic Church maintained its ban on clerical marriage and ordination of women despite the opposition campaigns that arose in the wake of the church's pedophilia scandal.

Supporting the groundswell of orthodoxy is the growth of fundamentalism. An increasing number of Christians are Evangelicals,

Pentecostals, or members of other groups whose faith tends toward the conservative, fervent, and evangelizing. Sociological factors that might help account for this trend include a yearning for simple explanations in a complex world—the same yearning that is driving the spread of Islamic fundamentalism. The adherence of Evangelicals/Pentecostals to traditional Christian doctrine is markedly stronger than for mainline Protestant groups: for example, according to Barna, 55 to 73 percent of Evangelical and Pentecostal groups accept that Christ was without sin, as compared to 28 to 33 percent of mainline Protestant groups.

Another Barna study shows that people who evangelize or share their faith with others are more likely than non-evangelizers to hold traditional Christian views such as that Christ was without sin and that every word of the Bible is true. Since these are the people who are spreading the Christian message, the Christianity of converts now and for the foreseeable future is likely to be traditional in character. In many companies, for example, a movement is now afoot to pray and pros-elytize openly through "workplace ministries"—and the faith of these ministries tends to be traditional. That will add ballast to the long-term persistence of Christianity despite the persistent rumors of its imminent demise.

Homosexuality and the Churches

75 Churches across America will continue to accept, reject, or try to moderate the presence of homosexuals in their pews. Although many homosexual churchgoers will continue to attend services without notice, others make enough clamor and call for involvement that churches will need to figure out solutions. Churches are not built to keep people out; they have wide doors and tall spires to bring people in. How American churches encounter gay and lesbian worshipers will show in one way or another how serious the churches are in maintaining themselves in the 21st century.

Recently, churches have faced internal conflict when some of their hierarchy declare themselves gay. The Episcopal Church was set into turmoil in 2003 when an openly gay clergyman, the Rev. Canon V. Gene Robinson, was elected and ratified as bishop of the diocese of New Hampshire. At the time, several leading Anglican archbishops in Southeast Asia, Africa, and South America have served notice that they would retaliate if the American church confirmed Robinson's election or moved toward official blessings of same-sex unions. Conservative bishops in the United States and overseas have warned that either decision could force "a dramatic realignment," if not actual schism, within one of the nation's oldest denominations.

Other Protestant churches have faced similar debate. The United Methodist Church has, however, made some public statements against accepting the homosexual lifestyle. At the 2004 General Conference a resolution passed providing that "no annual conference board, agency, committee, commission, or council shall give United Methodist funds to any gay caucus or group, or otherwise use such funds to promote the acceptance of homosexuality."

Some Christian Web sites advocate rejection of the "learned" and "willful" homosexual lifestyle. On *www.ChristianAnswers.net*, the question of how Christians should approach homosexuals, the answer is, "To 'straight' Christians in the church, however, the familiar old admonition to 'hate the sin, but love the sinner' surely applies in such cases. Homosexuals, long accustomed to being looked upon with disgust by most people, are understandably anxious for acceptance by society. Nevertheless, they must not be encouraged to continue in their wickedness, for it may well cost them their eternal souls. Instead, they need to be 'loved into the kingdom,' being delivered first of all from their rebellion against God, then to Christ for salvation and cleansing."

The Catholic Church has also made decisions about the presence of homosexuals in its clergy. About the admission of gay members to the priesthood, Dr. Joaquin Navarro-Valls, spokesman for Pope John

Paul II, questioned whether ordinations of homosexuals were even valid. "People with these inclinations just cannot be ordained," said Navarro-Valls. "That does not imply a final judgment on people with homosexuality. But you cannot be in this field."

Nonetheless, anecdotal data about homosexuality in seminaries is ongoing, and homosexuality stands as one of the reasons behind the priest-youth sexual encounters reported over the past several years. Yet as reported in *USA Today*, there is no definite link between homosexuality and sexual abuse. "He points to several small studies, which find homosexuals are no more likely than heterosexuals to molest kids," says San Diego psychologist Robert Geffner, editor of *The Journal of Child Sexual Abuse*, a professional research journal.

A more extensive study, says A. W. Richard Sipe, a retired La Jolla, California, psychotherapist and ex-priest, reiterates that position and uncovers other findings. In what is believed to be the longest term, largest study on priests' sexuality, Sipe followed 1,000 priests for up to 25 years. He found that about 6 percent of priests have sex with minors, choosing boys over girls by a 3:1 ratio. But he discovered no tie between sexual abuse and homosexuality, and says gay priests were no more likely than straight priests to break vows of celibacy.

But about not accepting the homosexual way of life, the Catholic Church is clear. As its catechism says about homosexuality, "Its psychological genesis remains largely unexplained . . . tradition has always declared that 'homosexual acts are intrinsically disordered.' They are contrary to the natural law. They close the sexual act to the gift of life. They do not proceed from a genuine affective and sexual complementarity. Under no circumstances can they be approved. . . . [Yet t]he number of men and women who have deep-seated homosexual tendencies is not negligible. They do not choose their homosexual condition; for most of them it is a trial. They must be accepted with respect, compassion and sensitivity. Every sign of unjust discrimination in their regard should be avoided."

For gays to gain acceptance in the church is difficult and uncertain. As Rev. Gene Robinson said, "The process of coming out to yourself is far more difficult than other people's dealing with your coming out," he said. "People forget that gay and lesbian folks have swallowed all the negative messages that the rest of the culture has. You have to undo that." But as the Concerned Clergy and Laity of the Episcopal Church says, "Today, there are two religions in the Episcopal Church. One remains faithful to the biblical truth and received teachings of the Church, while the other rejects them."

Islam Evolving

76 Islam is in the news nearly every day, what with terrorist attacks by Islamist militants and war in Muslim countries. But less publicized is the change that is occurring within the religion of Islam as a result of its peaceful contacts with the modern world. What is currently playing out is no less than the evolution of liberal Islam.

Playing a large role in this evolution are the millions of Muslims who now live not in Islamic countries but in the secular democracies of the developed world. In the United States alone, there are about 5 to 6 million Muslims, and more are coming, through immigration, birth, or conversion. In Europe, there are now more Muslims (32 million) than there are Anglicans (27 million). By some estimates, early in the 21st century Islam will surpass Judaism as the second largest religion in the United States, after Christianity.

There are signs already that the new generation of Western Muslims is different from their forebears. Asma Gull Hasan, as she describes herself in *American Muslims: The New Generation* (2000), is hip, twenty-something, feminist, and Muslim. The American-born daughter of Pakistani immigrants, she feels her generation is at the vanguard of a "de facto Reform Islam." Far from corrupting Islam, she considers American Islam to be more religiously pure than Islam in other countries precisely because it lacks the cultural baggage found elsewhere: it is "a return to the Qur'an without the influence of pre-Islamic Arab culture."

The new generation of Muslims is, of course, Internet-savvy, and they are giving birth to a whole world of CyberIslam. This includes Liberal Islam Web sites, even one *(www.liberalislam.net)* whose sources of wisdom encompass that great desert philosopher Ben Kenobi in the *Star Wars* films.

As social change takes place, scholars are making their own contributions by identifying theological justifications for liberal Islam. M. A. Muqtedar Khan, in *American Muslims: Bridging Faith and Freedom* (2002), defends the compatibility of Islam and democracy. Charles Kurzman, in *Liberal Islam: A Source-Book* (1998), argues that liberal Islam is a thriving tradition currently undergoing a revival and that it includes such concerns as democracy, separation of church and state, women's rights, and freedom of thought. According to law professor Aziza Al-Hibri, Thomas Jefferson himself once used the Koran as a source for his statement, "There is no coercion in religion."

Some liberal reformers are taking their case directly to the governments of the Islamic world. Mansour al-Nogaidan, for example, is one of a circle of reformers in Saudi Arabia who are denouncing the Wahhabist ideology of the country's rulers and calling for more democracy.

The emergence of a new kind of Muslim is perhaps seen best in Shazia Mirza, a British-born child of Pakistani immigrants who has gotten international attention as a standup comic. A devout Muslim, she wears the hijab, the Muslim female head covering, but is incongruously modern in her style and references—incongruous only because of her audience's preconceptions of what a Muslim is like. After 9/11, she broke the ice with audiences by saying, "My name is Shazia Mirza. At least that's what it says on my pilot's license." Some might find Mirza's humor offensive. But the huge laughs that followed that joke were a sign that the convergence of Islam and the modern world might be not only possible, but entertaining as well.

Neoagnosticism

77 Agnosticism has always been the middle ground between belief and disbelief in God. Where theism affirms that God exists, and atheism denies it, agnosticism says, "I don't know." However, in practice, agnostics since Thomas Huxley (the English biologist who coined the term in the 19th century) have usually allied themselves with the atheists. The traditional agnostic says, "I don't know if God exists, so I will withhold belief in him and carry on as if there were no such thing"—making such a person a de facto atheist. This tradition is now breaking down. At least some contemporary agnostics most definitely carry on as if there were such a thing as God—even if it is not exactly God. These are the neoagnostics.

Winifred Gallagher, who numbers herself in this group and coined this term in her 1999 book *Working on God*, defines neoagnostics as "well-educated skeptics who have inexplicable metaphysical feelings." They are not sure there is a God, but they hunger for higher meaning and search for it by trying out different forms of religious belief and practice. They distrust what they call "organized religion," that is, any spiritual institution that requires its members to believe and do certain things, such as go to church on Sunday. In keeping with their advanced education, neoagnostics are disproportionately upscale; as Gallagher says, "They are everywhere, especially at the top." They are also disproportionately young and hip. "Now it's becoming the in thing to be spiritual," Buddhist teacher Jagad Guru Paramahamsa told *Christianity Today* in 1999. "It's more cool, modern, and progressive to be spiritual. But without God," says Paramahamsa.

Neoagnostics tend to agree with remarks such as "I believe in spirituality, not religion" or "I don't believe in a personal God, but I do think there is a sacred or transcendent dimension to life." The link between advanced education and this kind of spirituality without a traditional God is supported by a number of studies. For example, the 1998

General Social Survey found that people with more than four years of college are more than twice as likely (17.2 percent) as people with only a high school education (7.4 percent) to believe in a "higher power but not a personal God."

The personal spiritual quest Gallagher describes in *Working on God* is a good example of the neoagnostic's eclectic search for meaning through the world's numerous religions, mythologies, and mystical traditions. Gallagher sampled Zen Buddhism, Judaism, and Christianity, trying out their practices, asking skeptical questions, and ultimately stirring together her own personal spiritual brew.

As neoagnostics struggle to construct their personal spiritualities, a booming industry has sprung up to cater to them: books, religious goods (everything from candles to kachina dolls to Wiccan pentagrams), retreats, and lecture series. Some traditional religions are more adept than others at attracting neoagnostics. Tibetan Buddhism, for example, is a highly organized and dogmatic tradition, but its leader, the Dalai Lama, is a master at presenting its more accessible teachings to nonbelievers in a genial and nondemanding way. Many neoagnostics are interested in the movement broadly known as New Age, which emphasizes occult and paranormal phenomena and the teachings of the East (as transmitted by way of California), but neoagnostics tend to sift New Age claims as skeptically as any other claims. The Internet, with its computerized search engines, has proven, so to speak, a godsend to neoagnostic spiritual searchers. At this writing, Google responds to the phrase "spiritual search" with 10.8 million results (up from 4.35 million results about one year earlier).

Many neoagnostics are scientific materialists at heart, tending to believe that the natural world, produced through evolutionary processes, is all there is: no afterlife, no choirs of angels. But, buoyed by research findings showing that medical benefits accrue to those who meditate and pray, and by brain studies showing neurological changes during meditation and prayer, they believe that something good is going on when one feels spiritual, even if there are no spirits as such. Perhaps they are simply being driven by their gene for spirituality, described by

Dean Hamer in his book *The God Gene*. Biologist Ursula Goodenough, in her book *The Sacred Depths of Nature*, writes: "As a non-theist, I find I can only think about these [mystical] experiences as wondrous mental phenomena. But in the end it doesn't matter: All of us are transformed by their power."

Other neoagnostics are not committed to absolute materialism, and are willing to accept the possibility that there is something spiritual or transcendent over and above nature. They don't know what it is, and suspect they can't know what it is, but want to tap into its power just the same.

Neoagnosticism has its critics: religious people who say that it shows a dilettantish unwillingness to commit to one tradition; atheists who say that it shows a muddle-headed refusal to accept the consequences of there being no God. Nevertheless, neoagnosticism is likely to remain an important movement because of its balance between two conflicting factors in 21st-century society: the hegemony of modern scientific culture, with its denial of the supernatural, versus the persistent human hunger for the supernatural. It will probably flourish as long as democratic capitalism flourishes, because of its optimal use of what democratic capitalism provides: religious liberty and a marketplace to provide for every need, including spiritual ones.

Pray Your Way to Health

78 Without announcing it, many Americans link religion and health. In a 2003 *Newsweek* poll, 70 percent of Americans asked said they prayed often for the health of a family member—which was substantially less than the 27 percent who pray for their own financial or career success. The impact of religious belief on health and the place of faith in the practice of medicine are becoming an area of intense research and controversy among medical practitioners.

Interest in the link between religion and health has been spurred by dozens of recent studies on the subject. A survey of about 150 investigations on religion and health pointed in some cases to the positive effects of religion. The strongest link was a study offering persuasive evidence that church or service attendance promotes longer life. This study also provided moderate evidence to support the hypotheses that religion or spirituality can protect against cardiovascular disease and that being prayed for improves one's physical recovery from an acute illness.

In a 2003 *American Psychologist* finding reported in *Vibrant Life*, 40 studies revealed that over the time the studies covered, regular attendees of public religious services had a 29 percent lower death rate than those who did not or rarely practiced. This study also took into account other factors aligned with church attendance that could improve health. For instance, the study considered the idea that attending religious services promotes the building of social support systems, and that actively religious people tend to take better care of themselves than those who do not attend services regularly.

Other studies have documented the health benefits of Eastern-style meditation, particularly in relieving stress, anxiety, and depression. Some studies have focused on the power of intercessory prayer to heal people who are being prayed for by others. Results have been conflicting. In one study of nearly 1,000 heart patients, those who were being prayed for without their knowledge experienced 10 percent fewer complications. Another study, however, found no evidence that prayer affected the numbers of people dying from leukemia or heart disease.

The studies of prayer and meditation have spurred many medical schools to understand and acknowledge the force of religion in patients' lives. More than half of U.S. medical schools offer courses in spirituality and medicine. The courses, far from teaching faith healing, focus on understanding the importance of religion and spirituality to patients and how it may affect a patient's state of health. Some doctors today even pray with their patients. Gynecologist John Guarneri told WESH NewsChannel 2 in Florida, "I think you have to look at what we are as human beings. We're body, mind, and spirit, and I think as physicians we, at times when it's appropriate, should be addressing all three of those things."

A leading researcher in the link between faith and health, Dr. Harold Koenig, M.D., MHSc, founding director of the Center for the Study of Religion/Spirituality and Health at Duke University Medical Center, believes that the studies validate the claims for religion and health. Speaking at a conference on Spirituality and Healing in Medicine, Dr. Koenig said, "Religious beliefs and activities [correlate] with better mental and physical health in the vast majority of the studies."

Some researchers, such as Dean Hamer in his book *The God Gene*, even point to the possibility of a gene or group of genes linked with belief. In support of this possibility, researchers quoted in the *Telegraph* point to the usefulness of a moralizing God to effect social cohesiveness and perpetuate life, particularly among larger societies. Says John Burn, medical director of the Institute of Human Genetics at the University of Newcastle (England), "A willingness to live, and if necessary, die, for a belief is a powerful selective advantage. I think there is a genetic propensity for us to believe."

Countering research on the health benefits of religious belief is research published in the *Lancet*. Researchers at the College of Physicians and Surgeons at Columbia University found little empirical support for the claim that good physical health is promoted by religious or spiritual belief. Lead author Richard P. Sloan, Ph.D., professor of behavioral medicine at Columbia University, noted that the research did not identify other variables that could account for a link between health and religion and did not refine their definitions of religious activity.

Further, the researchers suggest that even if a rigorous study identified causal links between religion and health, medical practitioners should not attempt to integrate religion into medical treatment. Dr. Sloan said, "[W]e would never expect a doctor to say, 'There is compelling evidence that marriage is beneficial to health. My advice is to get married.' That would be regarded as an outrageous intrusion. It is even more so for religion than marriage."

Whether gaining an awareness of a patient's spirituality becomes standard operating procedure for physicians, it is likely that Americans will continue to access their God during health crises. As Dr. Koenig said in *Newsweek*, "[O]lder adults in America today are a very religious population."

The Religion Shopping Mall

79 Say what you will about consumer culture, it is not closed-minded. Americans are always open to shopping around, considering alternative brands, and trying out the new-and-improved. This is just as true if the commodity in question is not detergent or jeans but religion. Americans are open-minded about religion, and America has turned into one big religion shopping mall.

True, there are some Americans who view their religious convictions as immovable, and would not ever consider altering them. But in our consumer society, such a stance is itself a choice, like unstinting loyalty to Maytags. Many other Americans, even if raised in a certain religion, are likely to shop around once they are let loose from the home, looking for the best possible fit for their own spiritual style. Some Americans are not raised in any religion, and are even more likely to consider a multitude of faiths should they feel a spiritual quest coming on.

Two broader trends feed this tendency. One is the omnipresence of consumer culture, which tends to color everything in its own free-market hue. Another motivating factor is the likelihood that each of us will come into contact on a daily basis with people of different faiths. Gone are the days when everyone the average Methodist met was another Methodist. Now cable and satellite television transmits a variety of religious talking heads into our homes, from Buddhist monks to Catholic nuns to Protestant televangelists. Recent news events rooted in the Islamic world have driven high sales of books about Islam. Immigration is constantly complicating the religious demographics of America. At one time, a book on American religion was published with the title *Protestant-Catholic-Jew*. Now it would have to include the country's 5 to 6 million Muslims, 2 to 3 million Buddhists, 1 million Hindus, and 250,000 Sikhs. The subtitle of Diana Eck's *A New Religious America* (2002) says it all: *How a "Christian Country" Has Become the World's Most Religiously Diverse Nation.*

There is not literally a religion shopping mall—a brick-and-mortar mall with each religion occupying a separate storefront. But the Internet comes close. Many denominations and even individual houses of worship have Web sites inviting people to join. In addition, there are multifaith Web sites such as *www.Belief.net* and *www.Faith.com*, which cater to every spiritual need and provide information on virtually every religion.

The religion sections of bookstores are also versions of the religion shopping mall. Even in the Bible Belt, bookstores offer not only Bibles but books by the Dalai Lama, works on the occult, and tomes on "earth-based religion," such as Wicca and paganism. There are also books about the religion shopping mall itself—the intertwining of the consumer mentality with religion—such as *Spiritual Marketplace* (2001) by Wade Clark Roof and *Shopping for Faith* (2002) by Richard Cimino and Don Lattin.

Just as consumer culture has changed the way believers act in searching for religion, it has also changed the way religions or houses of worship act in trying to attract believers. Houses of worship are more apt to be image-conscious and consumer-friendly—whether by literally setting up shop in a shopping strip, offering swank vacations at retreat centers, or packing in believers in giant megachurches. Megachurches may themselves resemble shopping malls, providing one-stop shopping in the form of multiple Sunday services, cafes, baptism pools, picnic spots, and parties. Denominations may mount professional PR or advertising campaigns. Some religions may alter their doctrine, or at least their presentation of doctrine, to make it more palatable to consumers—playing down the dogma of hell, for example, to keep churchgoers from leaving.

Indeed, one characteristic of the religion shopping mall is consumer mobility. Believers who feel free to shop among religions feel free to go back and forth among different religions, and to mix and match. They may accessorize an underlying Episcopalianism, for example, with a dash of tai chi energy training and a few prayers from the Upanishads. They may thoroughly mix traditions to form what Cimino and Lattin, in *Shopping for Faith*, call hybrid religions. They may adopt the practices of a certain faith while de-emphasizing belief in its doctrines—a position similar to that of Elaine Pagels in *Beyond Belief* (2003). They may even be neoagnostics, who are not sure there is a God but nevertheless want to build their own personal spirituality.

There are still stick-in-the-mud believers who insist the important question is not whether a religion caters to one's "spiritual needs" but whether it teaches the truth. As C. S. Lewis wrote in *Mere Christianity*, "the question should never be: 'Do I like that kind of service?' but 'Are these doctrines true?'" Such an austere position will probably always attract some people, but it does not change the existence of the religion shopping mall; rather, it is one of the options available in the mall.

The Union of Church and State

80 The First Amendment to the Constitution declared that "Congress shall make no law respecting an establishment of religion, or prohibiting the free exercise thereof." With this amendment, the Founding Fathers erected what Thomas Jefferson called a "wall of separation between church and state." That wall has stood more or less secure for over two centuries, but lately it has been showing signs of wear. An increasing number of Americans seem committed to tearing it down and are beginning to get their way.

The presidency of George W. Bush has been a field day for attempts to unite church and state. A devout Christian, he created an Office of Faith Based Initiatives that gave public financing to religious groups for social welfare purposes. He later proposed to Congress that financing for federal job training programs be given to religious groups even if they discriminated in hiring based on religion. Bush supported Congress's passage of a ban on partial birth abortions in November 2003, which earned him further support from religious conservatives, also known as the religious right. He appointed conservative Christian judges. His reelection campaign relied heavily on Christians who held rallies for him, spoke out on the radio, and supported him behind church walls. "Bush's victory not only establishes the power of the American Christian right in this candidacy, but in fact established its power to elect the next Republican president," Republican adviser Arthur Finkelstein told Israeli daily *M'ariv*. Come Election Day, 64 percent of voters who attended church once a week voted for Bush; so did 79 percent of evangelicals.

Many of the Christians supporting Bush in the 2004 election were Protestant, but some were Catholic. Conservative Catholics lobbied strongly for Bush, including twelve bishops who declared that voting for Democratic candidate John Kerry (a Catholic but a supporter of abortion rights and gay civil unions) was a "mortal sin." Bishop Michael Sheridan of Colorado Springs, Colorado, went so far as to proclaim that Catholics who voted for a candidate like Kerry were placing themselves "outside full communion with the Church" and jeopardizing their "salvation."

Since his reelection, Bush has continued to seal his bond with Christian groups. He has pushed for a Constitutional amendment to ban gay marriage, a favorite issue of Christian organizations such as Focus on the Family, led by Rev. James Dobson. Dobson was a major supporter of Bush in his reelection campaign. It is likely that Christian conservatives will continue to shape the policies of Bush and many in Congress, persuading them to unite church and state closer than ever.

At the same time, those trying to preserve the wall between church and state will fight back, intensifying the struggle.

In other parts of the country besides Washington, D.C., the battle over the wall between church and state has also been escalating. A case in point has been the teaching of evolution, a perennial hot-button issue for some Christians because of its apparent conflict with the Biblical account of creation. In Cobb County, Georgia, the school board added stickers to biology textbooks cautioning students that "evolution is a theory, not a fact." Several parents sued the board to remove the stickers. In January 2005 a federal judge ruled in the parents' favor and ordered the stickers removed, saying the stickers were a de facto "endorsement of religion," and so unconstitutional.

Meanwhile, in Dover, Pennsylvania, the school board voted to inform students of an alternative to evolution known as intelligent design, which infers the existence of an intelligent designer behind the universe. Aided by civil liberties groups, several families are challenging the decision in court.

According to the *New Yorker's* Hendrik Hertzberg in June 2004, "The salient division in American political life where religion is concerned . . . is between traditional supporters of a secular state . . . on the one hand, and, on the other hand—well, theocrats might be too strong a term." That division is likely to get wider—and, for a while at least, the quasi-theocratic side will be ever more prominent.

9

Science and Technology

A Better Light Bulb: LEDs

81 Build a better light bulb, and the world will beat a path to your door. A better light bulb is now here—the light-emitting diode (LED).

Once restricted to such homely functions as calculators and digital watches, the LED is now bursting into a host of new applications. At the Jefferson Memorial in Washington, D.C., 17,000 LEDs illuminate the monument's interior. Traffic signals are increasingly being replaced by LEDs. Surgical lamps, giant video screens, mobile phones, and automobile brake lights are all using LEDs. LEDs are being used in signboards at stores and displays at stadiums. In the coming years, as new technology makes them cheaper, brighter, and more versatile, LEDs will become even more pervasive, replacing conventional light sources, such as incandescent bulbs and fluorescent tubes, in the home and office.

The heart of an LED is an LED chip, a semiconductor that emits light when energized by an electric current. The chip is often made from gallium arsenide or another semiconductor compound. The word "diode" in "light-emitting diode" refers to a type of component that allows current to flow in only one direction. The most familiar LEDs emit visible light—such as red, yellow, green, and blue—but some emit light in the infrared part of the spectrum. These are used in such places as TV remote controls and the bill validators of vending machines.

LEDs have several advantages over conventional light sources. For one thing, they are extremely reliable and durable, providing more than 40,000 hours of operational life, about 20 times that of bulbs. Vibration or minor shocks rarely damage LEDs. Since regular replacements are unnecessary, LEDs are especially useful for applications such as traffic signals and signboards, where maintenance work is hard. LEDs are also energy-efficient. They achieve direct conversion of electric energy into light, consuming less power and generating less heat than other sources of light. They present less of an environmental burden than fluorescent tubes, which must be filled with mercury vapor to produce light. Finally, LEDs save space, because they are smaller and thinner than bulbs. For these reasons, LEDs have become common in portable devices such as digital cameras and cell phones, where the small size of the device limits battery capacity, and in cars, where conservation of power is a concern.

An advantage important to makers of signs and signals is that LEDs offer more clarity than conventional lights. Conventional bulb-based traffic lights, for example, transmit their signals through lenses that are tinted red, yellow, or green. But on bright afternoons, those tinted lenses reflect sunlight, making it hard to tell whether the light is on or off. The LED light in a traffic signal is itself colored, eliminating the need for tinted lenses and the confusion arising from reflected sunlight. LEDs are also contributing to greater clarity in train platform signboards.

LEDs are becoming more prominent wherever video images are displayed on large screens. Economics is driving the change. Conventional projector lamps have to be replaced frequently and become too hot as they are forced to become brighter to compete with ambient light. LEDs, by contrast, are bright and have lower maintenance costs. Even churches are using these systems; Willow Creek Community Church in South Barrington, Illinois, installed one in its 7,300-seat auditorium.

The big breakthrough will come if LEDs are generally adopted for indoor home and office use. That day has not come yet, but it is on its way. Engineers have developed white LEDs suitable for general lighting, achieved by combining blue LEDs and phosphors. As of yet, their light is less intense than that of fluorescent lamps, but more so than incandescent lamps. Further research is needed to be able to produce sufficiently bright LEDs for widespread indoor use at a commercially viable price. But with the LED market expanding, that is expected to happen. Already, some companies are marketing LED tube lights, rope lights, beam lights, and floor lights for a variety of home uses.

A type of LED known as organic light-emitting diodes (OLEDs) may become an important component of television screens, laptop displays, and mobile phones. Made from polymers rather than the semiconductors that characterize other LEDs, OLEDs are able to do the job of liquid crystal displays (LCDs) in displaying images, but with considerable savings in energy. In a laptop, that might translate into less battery power and weight.

Hitachi Cable News calls the LED "the new 'light' of the 21st century," and this may not be an exaggeration. It may be especially important in parts of the Third World where supplies of electricity are scarce. Because the power requirements of LEDs are low, they can be powered by solar batteries, bringing light to once-dark areas. This technology is likely to become widespread not only in many parts of the infrastructure, such as traffic lights, but as close to home as the headlights of one's car and the lighting in one's living room.

The Decline of the Web Browser

82 Once upon a time, Netscape and Internet Explorer waged a battle to see which would control the Internet. Both were Web browsers, computer-based software applications that allow people to view Web documents, follow their links, and transfer files back and forth. But browsers alone are no longer the whole story. Today the Internet is routinely accessed without browsers—and even without computers. As the Internet penetrates everywhere, the decline of the Web browsers has begun.

In December 2003, Nielsen//Net Ratings reported that three out of every four home and work Internet users, or 76 percent of active Web surfers, access the Web using an Internet application that is not browser-based. The most popular applications were the media players Windows Media Player and Real One/RealPlayer and the instant messengers AOL Instant Messenger, MSN Instant Messenger, and Yahoo! Messenger. File-sharing applications were also popular.

"With 76 percent of Web surfers using Internet applications, functionality has grown beyond the browser to become a fundamental piece of the overall desktop," said Abha Bhagat, senior analyst, Nielsen//NetRatings. "It's become harder to distinguish when you're on the Internet, blurring the lines between what's sitting on the desktop and what's coming from the World Wide Web."

Google Deskbar is doing its best to blur the lines. Launched in November 2003, the free software allows users to run a Google search on the Web right from their Windows taskbar. There is no need to switch applications or launch a Web browser. The search box is usually visible in the Windows toolbar; after the search words are entered, a mini-viewer pops up with the results—and users can jump to a site within the mini-viewer. There's even a shortcut (Ctrl-Alt-G) to move the cursor to the search box without moving the mouse. Robin Good at *www.masternewmedia.org* calls the Google Deskbar a "mini-browser under disguise."

The decline of the browser is being furthered by the number of devices through which people can now access the Internet. No longer is a desktop or laptop computer the only way to get online. Camera phones and other cell phones frequently connect to the Internet. In November 2004, Vodafone launched a mobile phone music download service across Europe—betting that customers would want to use a cell phone to buy and listen to music as if it were an iPod. Home appliances, from refrigerators to televisions, are increasingly "Internet-enabled," as are smaller devices, such as radio frequency identification (RFID) chips. The information being accessed by the appliance may be truly invisible—such as a refrigerator hooked to a power management system that tells it to lower its power consumption during peak electrical usage. The refrigerator needs no browser for this.

Broadband connections, always "on" in the background at home or office, are also making it harder to know when one is accessing the Internet. In the early days of the Web, when dial-up networking was virtually the only way to get online, the dialing noises and authentication ritual made it easy to know when one was linking to the Web. Now, said Susan Kuchinskas of *www.internetnews.com* in December 2003, "connectivity is such a given that many people may not realize when they're 'on' the Internet and when they're working within the desktop."

"In terms of our perceptions, the Internet in all its various incarnations will soon become as ubiquitous in our modern, everyday life as, say, electric power, running water or written words," Jack Lyness, senior vice president for Internet marketing firm e-agency of Oakland, California, told Kuchinskas. "The Internet is fast becoming part of every tool and toy we use, to the point that eventually, we won't think about it."

The proliferation of ways to connect to the Internet poses a problem for those trying to keep it viable. Computer scientist Roger Clarke, in a presentation at Internet MasterClass '04 at the University of Queensland in December 2004, said, "The Internet was conceived for moderate numbers of stationary devices." As more devices connect to the Internet, he said, the augmentation or replacement of the existing Internet protocol might be required to support those developments.

Web browsers are not going to disappear entirely anytime soon; with their familiar and useful "Back" and "Home" buttons, they are too much a part of everyday Internet life. But like the big three networks once cable came along, they will increasingly be only one slice of a broader spectrum, one part of how we access an Internet that is always "on." "As the Internet becomes more widespread, it becomes more a part of the infrastructure, like an electrical grid, that allows others things to be plugged into it," Michael Ponzo, Marketing Director, Motorola's DSP Standard Products Division, told *Home Toys* in February 2002. Since he made that comment, more things than ever have been plugged into the Internet.

Gaming the Search Engines

83 In today's world, searching is the second biggest activity on the Internet, next to e-mailing. Millions of people use computer search engines every day to lead them to the information or products for which they are looking. They routinely expect that the search engines will be honest—that they will turn up the most relevant results at the top. But an entire industry has arisen to try to skew those results in favor of companies and individuals who pay the right price. Meet the people whose job is gaming the search engines.

There are innocent and not-so-innocent ways of gaming search engines. The most innocent way is known as Google bombing, a term coined by Weblogger Adam Mathes in 2001. Google is the most popular search engine and so highly valued that it rose to a market capitalization of $27.2 billion by the close of the day it went public. It is popular because of its great success at ranking the most relevant results at the top of the search, a success it achieves in part by taking into account the number of times other Web sites link to a given site—the more links, the more important the Web judges the site to be. Mathes figured out that if he could persuade enough Web site owners to use a certain phrase to link to a certain site—a process he called Google bombing—he could influence Google to raise that site's rank. The first Google bomb came when he persuaded his blog readers to link the phrase "talentless hack" to his friend Andy Pressman's site. The result: for a time, if you Googled "talentless hack," the first result that came up was the hapless Pressman's site.

This was a good joke—a humor bomb—but Google bombing soon spread to other uses. As categorized by John Hiler in *Microcontent News* in March 2002, later Google bombs also included ego bombs, which were devoted to publicizing someone's name, as well as justice bombs, which were intended to remedy some political or personal grievance. As of this writing, because of one justice bomb, if you type "miserable failure" into Google, the top result will be the official White House biography of George W. Bush.

Whatever the justification, Google bombing tends to be short-lived in its effectiveness, as pages evolve and links go dead. Even now, if you search "talentless hack," the top result will not be the Web site of Pressman, the friend Mathes meant to satirize, but that of Mathes himself—because of all the people linking to his original article on Google bombing. This kind of friendly gaming of Google has a way of expiring naturally.

Then there is the less friendly kind of gaming, that of the industry known as search optimization—a for-profit business dedicated to helping Web sites lift their search engine rankings. There is a lot of money to be made in this business, because companies want their Web sites to come up in the first 10 or 20 results. As an ad for SearchEngineWeb-Promotion.com, a search optimization firm, puts it: "[I]f your Web site appears after the 2nd page, even if it's just the 3rd or 4th page, forget it. You're nowhere. Who looks past the first 20 web sites listed, anyway?" The tactics of the search optimization industry include fairly benign ones, such as assisting companies in attractive presentation of their content, but also more nefarious efforts to trick search engines into ranking them highly.

One of these tactics is spamdexing or index spamming—also known as keyword stuffing. This is the practice of improperly loading Web pages with words that will probably be used as search terms and thereby increase the chance of being found and accessed. (Spamdexing can also refer more generally to all illegitimate attempts to skew a search engine.) Index terms can be incorporated into the metadata, or HTML structural code, in the document head or put in parts of the document body that the user does not usually see. Even if the site has little or nothing to do with a topic, spamdexers will stuff it with keywords relevant to that topic, so long as it is popular. According to *www.searchengineguide.com*, in February 2005 the top 10 search engine keywords included "paris hilton," "iraq election," "ebay," and "eminem." Spamdexers might load their Web sites with these keywords, later exchanging them for whatever keywords become popular later. Search engines have fought back against spamdexing with various safeguards and may block sites that practice it.

There are other techniques for gaming search engines. In what is called cloaking, search optimizers disguise the content of their sites so that search engines are fooled into thinking it is relevant to popular queries when it is not. They may also resort to a version of Google bombing—what Hiler would call money bombing. In this technique, they set up "link farms," a multitude of interconnected Web sites that exist mainly to link to each other. They may also pay other sites to link to their site. Either way, Google will tend to boost their site's ranking because of all the links it is receiving.

Those who run search engines are working hard to combat all the spamdexing, Google bombing, and other methods of fooling their search algorithms. In the most extreme case, Google has resorted to banning deceitful Web sites from appearing in its search results: for example, in 2004, Google banned a company called WhenU for its cloaking activity. However, by early 2005, WhenU was back in those results, and the gaming of the search engines was continuing.

Globally Warmer

84 Despite record cold and snow in some parts of the country, global warming has not gone away. Even President Bush's skepticism about the issue—a skepticism not shared by most climate scientists—has not made it go away. Here is a weather report on what we can expect on this issue in the next few years.

We can expect continued accumulation of evidence that global warming is occurring, and that it is being caused by rising levels of greenhouse gases. These are substances such as carbon dioxide that are known as greenhouse gases because of their heat-trapping properties. These gases are emitted by the world's factories, automobiles, and other fossil fuel-burning machines. Evidence for global warming and the greenhouse effect comes from many quarters, and it will continue to pile up. For example, the Greenland ice sheet melted more in the summer of 2002 than at any time in the 24 years in which its status was tracked. In 2005, scientists announced that the west Antarctic ice sheet, previously believed stable, is beginning to collapse. The level of carbon dioxide in Earth's atmosphere is 100 parts per million higher than it has been for at least 400,000 years. Polar bear numbers are falling because the sea ice where they hunt for seals is melting. Global temperatures are rising faster than they have in the past thousand years. The UN-sponsored Intergovernmental Panel on Climate Change (IPCC) predicts that the planet's average surface temperature will rise by 2.5 to 10°F (1.4 to 5.8°C) by the year 2100.

Despite the evidence, we can also expect simple-minded disbelief in global warming based on local conditions—the "How can they say there's global warming when it's snowing again?" response. This ignores the fact that global warming has to do with average global temperatures over sustained periods, not fleeting weather in one place or another. Indeed, one prediction of global warming is that the Eastern seaboard may become colder in winter, not warmer. This is because thawing sea ice and heavier rainfall in the North Atlantic may contribute to the formation of cold fronts in this region. So Easterners shouldn't expect global warming to deliver a windfall of balmy January weather any time soon. In fact, scientists and environmentalists are shifting to talking about human-induced climate change rather than global warming to avoid the misconception that all parts of the globe are getting warmer.

Some scientists, who are presumably better informed than the average Joe or Jane, still insist that they don't know how much influence humans have on climate, and whether global warming is occurring at all. But these scientists are increasingly in the minority, even if their views are attractive to some industrial leaders and policymakers. Still, they have some friends in the popular media, including Michael Crichton, whose 2004 novel *State of Fear* attacked global warming as a myth.

The one thing that might make human-induced climate change slow down is if humankind cuts back on our burning of fossil fuels. Most industrial nations, including Japan and the countries of the European Union, agreed to do just this in the Kyoto Protocol, but in 2001 President Bush refused to accept that treaty. At issue was the Kyoto position in favor of mandatory greenhouse gas restrictions versus Bush's refusal to accept anything but voluntary measures. In 2004, even the Bush White House admitted in a report that human activity had contributed to global warming. But it remained unclear what, if anything, the administration would do about it.

Even if the developed world moves to implement mandatory greenhouse gas restrictions, the developing world may not be quick to sign on. With globalization encouraging even the poorest countries to compete as industrial nations, smokestacks and car exhausts are churning in many more places than before. In China, for example, coal use is rising faster than almost anywhere else in the world—a serious matter because coal, when burned to generate electricity, releases more greenhouse pollution than oil or natural gas. India, another country rising in industrialization, is also escalating its emissions of greenhouse gases.

As the world tries to balance its hunger for energy with the need to curb greenhouse gas emissions, alternative sources of energy may begin to look appealing. Nuclear power may come back into vogue, after its long period in the wilderness because of public safety concerns. Solar and wind power, long dismissed as "sunshine and breezes," may begin to look more serious. Ideas that once sounded science-fictiony may be seriously developed, such as space-based solar power.

If, despite everyone's best efforts, global warming does not slow down, Band-Aid measures may start to proliferate. In a *New York Times* op-ed piece, Oliver Morton recommended dropping a giant tarp on the summit of Africa's Mount Kilimanjaro to protect the mountain's retreating snowcap. Unless such a measure is taken, Morton argues, the snows of Kilimanjaro may become a thing of the past.

Band-Aid measures won't help solve the most dire predictions of global warming: hurricanes more ferocious than any before seen; the Dust Bowl returning to the Great Plains; New York City flooded as a result of melting polar caps. Before things reach that point, it is possible that humanity will notice with more soberness that the globe is getting warmer, and do something about it.

The Incredible Shrinking Science

85

The idea of nanotechnology, the industrial application of science on a very small scale, dates back to the 1950s, but the term itself was coined more recently by K. Eric Drexler and popularized in his 1986 book *Engines of Creation*. It is now one of the hottest fields in science. If all goes as hoped, sophisticated technology invisible to the naked eye will soon be used for everything from medical treatments to quantum computers to microprecise crime scene investigation to self-cleaning kitchens.

The term *nanotechnology* shares the prefix *nano-* (extremely small) with the nanometer, which is 1 billionth of a meter, or 100,000 times as thin as a human hair. Nanotechnology takes place on a scale of 100 nanometers or less—a scale that is home to viruses, individual molecules, and the tiniest features of microchips. For most of history, the nanoscale was off-limits to human tinkering. People could chop down trees and thread needles, but not until recent decades could they directly manipulate molecules, even atoms, to produce working machines on a nanoscale. The aim of nanotechnology is to arrange atoms in a specified order to do useful work, and to do so cost-effectively. Cost-effectiveness is easier to achieve if molecular machines themselves do the task—nanomachines that can self-replicate and mechanically position atoms to make useful products.

In recent years, science has been making progress toward the dreamed-of nanofuture. Carbon nanotubes were invented, cylindrical molecules of carbon that are stronger than steel and can conduct more current than silicon. Scientists developed nanowires, virtual strings of atoms only a few nanometers thick, and a nanothermometer that can measure temperature changes at the molecular level. IBM developed the Millipede, a data storage device that uses nanoprobes to store one terabit of data per square inch. New York University scientist Nadrian Seeman is conducting research into building complex, atomically precise structures using DNA. In 2003, Israeli scientists for the first time used biological self-assembly to create a functional electronic nanodevice. With a toolkit of DNA, carbon nanotubes, bacterial proteins, antibodies, silver, and gold, they produced a self-assembling nanotransistor. In 2005, Australian scientists reported on their work developing nanoscale polymer capsules that could one day be used to deliver chemotherapy directly to tumors while leaving adjoining tissue unharmed.

As nanotechnology, backed by taxpayer dollars, gains momentum in the laboratory, the business world is signing on to reap the potential profits. Some nanotech materials are already on the market: nanoscale clay particles to strengthen car bodies; carbon nanotubes contributing greater stiffness to Babolat tennis rackets. The National Science Foundation projects that sales of nanotech products will reach $1 trillion by 2015. With all the hoopla, venture capital has been flowing steadily into nanotech companies, and the few publicly traded startups, such as Nanogen, have been attracting investors. Investors are especially hungry to put money in companies such as IBM that have strong portfolios of intellectual property—valuable nanotechnology patents that other companies will need to license to get their work done.

Still, there are reasons to be wary of the nanotech bandwagon. One is the danger that the sector is being overhyped; all one has to say is "dot-com" to remind investors of how easily tech stocks can generate bubbles that burst. The fancy molecular machines that all the fuss is about are not yet here, and no one knows for sure which companies will be the winners and losers once they do arrive.

Another problem is that the health and environmental hazards of nanotechnology are as yet little explored. DuPont researchers discovered in 2002 that when they injected carbon nanotubes into the lungs of rats, 15 percent of the animals died—not an encouraging sign as nanotubes proliferate in industry. A study commissioned by the British government recommended in 2004 that new regulatory controls be implemented for "free" nanoparticles that could come in contact with humans. No doubt there will be increasing regulation and controversy as the nanotechnology field develops, just as there has been for biotechnology. But just as biotechnology has continued to develop with great speed in the last few decades, nanotechnology will probably do so as well in the years to come.

Newgenics

86 The idea of "designer babies"—children bred or bioengineered for superiority—has been a staple of science fiction for years, from the scenery-chewing Khan of *Star Trek* fame to the 1997 Ethan Hawke movie *Gattaca*. This idea has usually been associated with eugenics, the discredited, state-administered 20th-century efforts (by Nazis and others) to weed out genetic undesirables. Yet, the customizing of embryos is no longer science fiction but fact, and a new, privately driven kind of eugenics is afoot. Call it newgenics: not a coordinated effort to build a master race, but a decentralized trend in which parents try to give their kids a genetic edge by any available means.

Even setting aside the wonders of genetic engineering, the kids'-competitive-edge business is a huge industry. It spans everything from Kaplan SAT prep courses to orthodontia to infant formulas that are supplemented with fatty acids supposed to bolster your baby's intellect. Short kids can get growth hormone to enhance their height; fidgety kids can get Ritalin to improve their concentration. Add present-day knowledge of the human genome and gene manipulation, and the possibilities become even greater. For parents willing to plunk down big bucks to spruce up their already-born children, why not go the extra step and have the children born to order?

This brave new commercial world has been brewing since the 1970s, when production of human embryos in a test tube—in vitro fertilization (IVF)—came into being as a way of helping infertile couples conceive. This was the same decade when genetic engineering first began to be practiced, with genes snipped from one organism and implanted into another. Both of these technologies—IVF and genetic engineering—spawned successful industries, the former providing embryos for implantation in the wombs of formerly barren mothers; the latter yielding a host of new medicines, crops, and genetically engineered lab animals. Together, they created an amazing possibility. If human genes could be spliced at will into bacteria, they could, in theory, be spliced into human embryos, such as those produced by IVF technology. In theory, genetic engineers could endow the human embryo with genes for this or that trait—blue eyes, genius intelligence, a great pitching arm. All that was needed was exact knowledge of which genes did what—knowledge that was mostly lacking back in the 1970s.

Today, knowledge of which genes do what is still very incomplete, but it has been advancing steadily, and it took a major step forward on April 14, 2003. That was the day that the Human Genome Project announced completion of its multiyear effort to sequence all 3 billion DNA letters in the human genetic inheritance or genome. Even now, scientists are using that mammoth genetic roadmap to try to understand specifically how genes figure in diseases and contribute to our various traits. As their knowledge grows, it is increasingly likely that IVF labs will be able to offer parents designer babies or superbabies, with just the traits they've been looking for.

Indeed, through different technologies, parents have already been practicing newgenics (Edward Black's term in his book *War against the Weak*). Back in the late 1970s, a millionaire inventor named Robert Graham founded a sperm bank for the production of "genius babies," with sperm donated by exceptionally bright or athletic individuals. More than 240 children were conceived through the bank; a sampling of 15, surveyed by Slate.com in 2001, turned out to be bright and healthy, though not yet Nobel Prize–winners. This may seem like a fringe case of newgenics, but another example is completely mainstream: genetic screening. This technology, in use since the 1980s, is the basis for amniocentesis, a common procedure in which amniotic fluid from an expectant mother is tested for various genetic markers. Through amniocentesis, older pregnant women throughout the world are informed whether their fetus has an extra copy of chromosome 21, the cause of Down syndrome; if it does, many of these women opt to abort the fetus. Similar choices are being made every day to rule out the birth of children who have other genetic diseases, or are simply the wrong sex: in China and India, for example, parents regularly use prenatal testing to ensure that their child will be a boy.

The latest twist is to combine IVF and genetic screening so that parents can select the optimal embryo among several conceived for them in the lab. Through preimplantation genetic diagnosis (PGD), couples who have a history of genetic diseases, such as cystic fibrosis or hemophilia, can rule out any embryos with genes for those diseases, allowing only a healthy one to be implanted in the mother's womb. In one case, that of the Nash family in Colorado in 2000, it was used to ensure the birth of a child who had the same tissue type as his already-born sister and could therefore provide her a stem cell transplant she needed.

If you think PGD is only being used in extreme situations such as this, think again. In some U.S. fertility clinics, PGD is already being used to ensure that only an embryo of the right sex is implanted. In the United Kingdom, the Human Fertilization and Embryology Authority (HFEA) permits parents to select embryos so that the resulting baby can be a tissue donor to a sick sibling. According to *Washington Monthly*, fertility specialists are receiving requests to screen embryos for homosexuality and hyperactivity, whenever, and if ever, that becomes possible.

Intentional genetic engineering of human embryos—the deliberate splicing in of desired genes or removing of undesired ones—is still not being practiced. But it has happened as a side effect. Babies conceived in the 1990s through a process called cytoplasmic transfer have altered mitochondrial DNA, resulting from the injection of cytoplasm from the eggs of a fertile donor into the eggs of an infertile patient. That altered genetic material will be passed on to those children's descendants, if any—making this possibly the first example of germline (or inheritable) genetic engineering in humans.

With the market for newgenics as large as it is, and with genetic knowledge and rapidly advancing technology, it seems inevitable that parents will soon be customizing their babies to an even greater degree than they are already doing. Human cloning is fraught with both technical and legal obstacles, but should these be resolved, parents may even be able to clone little genetic replicas of themselves.

The only brake will probably come from legislators convinced that newgenics is a bad idea. The case against newgenics is already being made from many directions: conservative Christians arguing that it entails aborting or distorting of embryos; left-wing opponents seeing a divide coming between rich people who can afford superbabies and poor people who can't. One critic, Francis Fukuyama, argues in his book *Our Post-human Future* that our basic ethical principles and political rights (such as equality) are based on judgments about human nature. Therefore, he says, alterations to human nature, such as those that might arise from the creation of a race of designer babies, threaten those principles and rights and should be avoided through state regulation.

To a greater or lesser degree, state regulation will be imposed, but it is unlikely to stop the forward rush of newgenics. Unlike the old state-sponsored eugenics, newgenics is fundamentally a matter of individual parents wanting the best for their children, and paying whatever they can afford to bring it about. That drive is rooted in old-fashioned human nature, and mere laws and regulations are unlikely to stop it. If legislators crack down too hard, irate voters (influenced by the fertility industry lobby) will probably vote them out. Newgenics, in one form or another, is here to stay.

Opening Up the Internet

87 The Internet appears to be a wide-open place: get online and go anywhere you want. There are no limits to your searches, research, shopping, game-playing, chatting, match-making, or freedom to click. Yet to some people, this freedom is only apparent. The freedom of the Internet, in their view, is in danger unless more is done to preserve and expand it—in terms of opening up software (open source) and opening up scholarly knowledge (open access). It is their mission to open up the Internet.

The open source movement seeks to liberate all the places where software is used, from personal computers to servers, on the Internet and off. The movement promotes software that is free to download, install, copy, and redistribute. An open source program includes source code and permits others to modify that code to create improved versions or derived products, as long as those too are free. The rationale is that open source software will improve faster because people can pass it around and revise it freely. In the words of the Open Source Initiative (OSI), a nonprofit corporation, "When programmers can read, redistribute, and modify the source code for a piece of software, the software evolves. People improve it, people adapt it, people fix bugs. . . . We in the open source community have learned that this rapid evolutionary process produces better software than the traditional closed model."

Open source may be an idea whose time has come. Its products are spreading quickly in many venues. These products include the tremendously successful Linux, which is the world's most used Unix-like operating system. Apache, which runs most of the planet's Web servers, is open source. Mozilla, the open source redesign of the Netscape browser, is becoming increasingly popular. OpenSSL provides secure communication through strong encryption over the Internet. Other open source software ranges from the arcane, such as GNU compilers and tools, to consumer-friendly items such as music players designed for Linux, such as XMMS and Zinf.

As open source has become a growing trend, large technology corporations are joining the bandwagon. IBM, Hewlett Packard, Sun, and Apple have all made investments in open source, with Apple incorporating an open source operating system called Darwin into its Mac OS X. Big businesses are starting to use open source software more widely in their IT departments.

Microsoft Windows—a decidedly closed-source product—is still the most popular operating system, but Linux is the second most popular and gaining ground. Other countries are even more receptive to it than the United States. The European Union, the United Kingdom, Israel, and Brazil are all indicating a preference for Linux. The city of Munich recently switched from Windows to Linux.

Even as the open source movement seeks to open up software, the open access movement aims for freer circulation of knowledge. In the words of Peter Suber, Open Access project director, open access literature is "digital, online, free of charge, and free of most copyright and licensing restrictions." The aim is to permit scientists and scholars to exchange information freely, the better to critique and build on each other's findings. The open access movement focuses especially on peer-reviewed scientific and scholarly articles, but has also been extended to novels, music, images, and software (where it overlaps with open source). The publishers of open access literature do not charge readers for reading these works, but they may be able to make a profit with priced add-ons.

Open access has attracted many eminent universities and scholarly groups and has been gaining steam. In September 2004, the International Committee of Medical Journal Editors called for an open-access registry and database of drug trial data. In December 2004, Google announced a project to digitize and index millions of books from five libraries. Numerous Web sites are part of the movement, from Project Gutenberg, which offers full-text books in the public domain free of charge, to the Berkeley Electronic Press, a publisher of free online scholarly journals.

The open access movement also aims to liberate the deep Internet or invisible Internet, the part of the Internet stored in online databases that are not searched by standard search engines. In the deep Internet are many scholarly archives that should be made more available, according to the open access movement.

Even as some forces push for greater access to software and knowledge, other Internet forces are pushing in the opposite direction. As the commercial presence grows stronger on the Web, it will find more creative and pricey ways to charge for its data and entertainment. As more people shift from dial-up to broadband Internet access, the number of Internet service providers could dwindle to just two or three in any given location—the regional phone company, the local cable company, and perhaps satellite Internet. If that happens, they may restrict the options people have to explore the Internet, offering packages that require a premium price for access to more sites. "The open, pluralistic, free-for-all character of today's Internet could soon come to resemble something much more like cable TV, with rising prices, limited access, and a monotonous diet of mostly corporate content," said Arthur Stamoulis in *Dollars and Sense* (September/October 2002).

Standing against the forces closing the Internet are people like those in the open source and open access movements. Nobody should expect them to close their mouths anytime soon.

The Privatizing of Space

88 The old song said "Fly Me to the Moon," and Richard Branson, founder of Virgin Airlines, is nearly ready to answer that call. At least he promises to get you into space. In 2004, he announced that a new venture, Virgin Galactic, would be offering suborbital flights into space within three years for a starting price of about $200,000 per ticket. It is a major step forward in a growing trend, the privatizing of space.

Since its beginnings, space exploration has been a government-run enterprise. The launching of rockets into orbit originated in Cold War rivalry between the U.S. and Soviet governments, and for a long time it seemed that only nation-states could muster the will and afford the huge budgets necessary for space travel. But as the private sector has grown in prominence in economies throughout the world, and as national governments have cut back their spending, the idea of entre-preneurial colonization of space has started to sound good.

The technology for such ventures is coming into shape. Virgin Galactic's spaceships will be modeled on SpaceShipOne, a privately built rocket plane that soared more than 62 miles above the Earth and returned twice in five days in September through October 2004. In so doing, it won the $10 million Ansari X Prize, which set the challenge of two rapid-succession suborbital trips in the hope of spurring a private spaceflight industry with ships that could make frequent roundtrips like a spaceliner. SpaceShipOne was designed by Burt Rutan and financed by Microsoft cofounder Paul Allen, who said after the achievement, "Hopefully we'll all be in space before you know it."

That may be an exaggeration, given that even Virgin Galactic, using SpaceShipOne technology, plans to charge $200,000 per ticket. But to put it in perspective, the only previous space tourism has been by ultra-rich people who sign up for flights with the Russian space program for $20 million a pop. Virgin's new venture represents a 99 percent price cut—practically a steal. And presumably the price will drop further as more companies compete for space tourism dollars and technology costs fall.

It is already clear that SpaceShipOne is only the beginning. Many of the teams that had competed in the Ansari X Prize competition are now planning to try for privately funded orbital flight—not just up and down into space for a few minutes, but around the world for hours or days. Numerous firms are involved in other space-related enterprises besides tourism, from unmanned launch vehicles to space burial services to systems for tracking satellites.

The government itself is looking to increase the involvement of private companies in space. To implement President Bush's ambitious long-range vision of manned missions to the moon and Mars, the President's Commission on Implementation of U.S. Space Exploration Policy called in its final report in 2004 for commercialization of space. "Today an independent space industry does not really exist," the report said. "Instead, we have various government funded space programs and their vendors. Over the next several decades . . . an entirely new set of businesses can emerge that will seek profit in space." Among other things, the report calls for NASA to turn over its unmanned, low-earth orbit space launches to private companies.

The International Space Station (ISS) is one potential hub for commercial space activity. NASA is actively seeking commercial participants on the ISS, in the hope of "stimulating business investment in the development of new markets and industries in low Earth orbit." The development of private launch firms is another growth area. The Alaska Aerospace Development Corporation contracted with the U.S. Missile Defense Agency to provide space launch services for tests of the nation's missile defense system, with the first launch taking place on

December 14, 2004. The corporation's Kodiak Launch Complex is the country's first non-federally owned commercial spaceport.

Other states are looking into building spaceports of their own, though there are plenty of obstacles. If safety concerns are an issue with airports, spaceports pose even bigger worries, such as the falling of spent stages from multistage rockets onto populated areas. Some states may decide to support only re-usable launch vehicles. Speaking to Space.com in 2000, Robert Triplett, chairman of the Oklahoma Aeronautics and Space Commission, was confident that the problems would be worked out. "This industry will change greatly in the next five to 10 years."

Commercialization may aid in reviving public interest in space, which has declined greatly since the highs it reached around the time of the first moon landing in 1969. True, the sight of corporate logos on rockets may make them seem more mundane. On the other hand, the chance to fly above the atmosphere as a tourist may be just the thing to restore the excitement of space.

RFID: Bigger than Bar Codes

89 Bar codes are now ubiquitous. On nearly every supermarket product, library book, and even hospital medication are those black-and-white striped labels that UPC scanners can scan, registering price and product information. Bar codes will probably be around for some time, but they are beginning to have competition. The day of radio frequency identification (RFID) tags has begun.

An RFID system uses radio waves to identify items or people. It consists of two basic parts: a tag or transponder equipped with a microchip and a tiny antenna that enables it to receive and respond to radio frequency queries; and a reader or transceiver that sends out the queries and receives the responses. The information stored in the tag's microchip usually includes a serial number that uniquely identifies the item or person. The reader is able to convert the radio waves from the tag into digital information that can be sent to and used by computers.

RFID technology has a number of advantages over bar codes. In a bar code system, the bar-coded item must be in the line of sight of the scanner for the bar code to be scanned. In RFID, line of sight is not necessary for reading: the tag need only be within about 20 feet of the reader. This makes it capable of tracking moving objects, as long as the RFID tag passes within range of a network of readers. Another advantage is that in a standard commercial bar code system, the bar code identifies only the product line, while RFID can also identify the unique item. Bar codes must be on the exterior of the product, while RFID tags can be embedded in packaging or encased in plastic for greater durability. On the other hand, bar codes are much cheaper than RFID and good enough for many uses. A supermarket typically doesn't need to keep track of every individual can of peas, just of how its overall canned pea stock is doing.

So what is RFID good for? It is already widely in use at toll plazas across the country, speeding cars past tollbooths and automatically charging their accounts, thanks to the information transmitted from the RFID transponders on their windshields. Manufacturers use them to track items on production lines within their factories and some retail chains (such as Benetton) for tracking inventory within their stores. RFID tags are used to expedite payment (for example, Mobil Speedpass at Mobil gas stations), to control access to institutions (through RFID badges), and to track containers, pallets, and trucks. They are small enough to be embedded safely into organisms, so livestock and pets can be tracked. The Toyota Prius and some Lexus models offer "smart keys" equipped with RFID so that the car unlocks and can be started while the key remains in the owner's pocket.

Controversy sets in when use of RFID identification is contemplated with humans. There are many applications already in play: tracking prison inmates with wristwatch-sized transmitters; using implanted transmitters to guard police in Mexico City against kidnapping; tracking hospital patients and guarding against medication error. Some of these applications have brought protests about privacy concerns. In early 2005, grade school students in Sutter, California, were required to wear RFID badges so the school could simplify attendance-taking and improve security. Angry parents rebelled at having the school monitor their children's every move and got the American Civil Liberties Union (ACLU) involved. "There is a way to make kids safer without making them feel like a piece of inventory," parent Michael Cantrall told the Associated Press.

The potential secrecy of RFID is another concern. RFID tags can be made so small that people may not know when they are being tracked by chips hidden in their clothes or property. A group called Consumers against Supermarket Privacy Invasion and Numbering (CASPIAN) is proposing federal labeling legislation to require complete disclosures on any consumer products containing RFID devices.

At the moment, the more widespread use of RFID is still deterred by cost. A tag runs 20 cents or more right now, but the Holy Grail is a tag that costs about 5 cents, which may not be available for some time. Still, RFID is clearly spreading, and despite protests, is likely to continue spreading rapidly in the next few years.

Rosie the Robot Redux

90 Where are all the robots we were supposed to have? Why don't any of us have a mechanical maid like the Jetsons' Rosie the Robot, or a rolling buddy like Will Robinson's friend Robot in *Lost in Space,* or even a killer cyborg like the Terminator? The fact is, the robots are already here, but not in the shape we expected them. Welcome to the age of robo-gadgets.

After decades of research in the fields of artificial intelligence (AI) and robotics, scientists no longer expect that they will manufacture a genuine "Rosie the Robot" anytime soon: an artificial person that seems virtually human as it bickers with human masters, irons their clothes, cooks their meals, and flirts with other robots. The complexity of such a virtual human is beyond present-day science. But by concentrating on smaller modules of human behavior, such as navigating around obstacles or smiling, AI and robotics researchers have been remarkably successful at creating machines that perform certain particular human tasks or mimic particular human traits. Some of these machines have been around for decades—industrial robots assembling cars; animatronic presidents at Disney World—but until recently, they required a technically trained service crew and were affordable only to corporate budgets. Now, with advances in basic science at places like the MIT Artificial Intelligence Laboratory (in operation in some form since at least 1959); faster, cheaper microprocessors; and burgeoning commercial interest, robots with advanced AI are beginning to penetrate the consumer market. Though technologically sophisticated, these robo-gadgets are designed for ease of use and middle-class pocketbooks.

First there were toys, like My Real Baby, an animatronic infant doll from Hasbro that responded expressively to a child's handling (laughing when tickled; crying when not fed) and AIBO, Sony's doglike entertainment robot. These just-for-fun robo-gadgets began appearing early this century, and their sales have depended on the vagaries of children's tastes. They have been followed by utilitarian robo-gadgets, such as the Roomba, a robotic vacuum cleaner from iRobot, a company whose origins lie in the MIT AI Lab and that previously developed My Real Baby in collaboration with Hasbro. The debut of the Roomba in December 2002 received a big publicity blitz, with spots on *The Today Show* and *Live with Regis and Kelly*. Adorned with a *Good Housekeeping* seal, the saucer-shaped device vacuums automatically, intelligently avoids stairs, and even cleans under beds while you do other things.

Other utilitarian robo-gadgets are starting to appear, including Robomower, a robotic lawn-mower from Friendly Robotics. The coming years will see a profusion of robo-gadgets, each automating some area of household drudgery. Which robo-gadgets succeed will depend on price and ease of use. Initial sales will be driven by the coolness factor (one Amazon.com customer called the Roomba "the coolest thing I ever bought"), but sales will peter out quickly unless the robo-snowblower, robo-garbage-carrier, or robo-dishwasher is affordable and does its job without much fuss.

Some robo-gadgets will be barely recognizable as robots. The Segway Human Transporter looks like a two-wheeled scooter, but underlying its uncanny ability to maintain balance is some seriously high-tech computer wizardry. A company called Yobotics is using its expertise in walking robotics to develop the RoboWalker, a powered device that disabled people can wear like mechanized braces to augment or replace their leg functioning.

Robo-gadgets are increasingly being used for activities that require extreme delicacy, such as surgery, or that are dangerous for humans, such as searching rubble for survivors. Combat is a major growth area for robotics. Flying Predator drones—airborne robots operated by humans from afar—attacked Iraqi antiaircraft batteries in the Iraq war in 2003. On the ground, the U.S. Army used an unmanned robot vehicle called PackBot to conduct search and surveillance in Afghanistan. An armed bomb-disposal robot is scheduled for deployment in Baghdad. The Pentagon has budgeted $127 billion for a military robotics project called Future Combat Systems.

Other devices might be called virtual robo-gadgets: software programs that make use of AI advances, such as fuzzy logic, which allows computers to deal with imprecise assessments, and neural networks, which learn through experience on the analogy of human brains. When you visit Amazon.com and are greeted with a list of personalized book or CD recommendations, you are meeting a virtual robo-gadget: a recommender system that analyzes patterns in your previous choices to predict what else you might like. (Ironically, e-retailers have found that these recommender systems work better when human editors regularly tweak them.) AI programs will increasingly be used in banking, police surveillance, stock-picking, medical diagnosis, mechanics' shops—even such humble activities as gambling. In December 2002, an Australian researcher unveiled MAIT, an automated sports tipster that reportedly outperformed the best human tipsters at predicting the results of Australian Rugby League matches.

A full-service robot maid is still a far-future dream, but robo-gadgets in the near future will be able to do multiple tasks—not just vacuum but also detect money on the floor, for example. That will fit with the current trend of smart hybrid devices, gadgets that offer more value to customers by doing more than one thing. Some robots will be designed as "basebots," versatile platforms to which useful functions can be added as the technology develops, just as a home PC gains new functions as new software is added. Indeed, future robo-gadgets may be integrated with the home computer, accessing its processing power through a wireless connection. Off in the distance, the dream of the robotic servant will continue to drive innovation. *New Scientist* reported in 2001 that a company called Probotics was developing a robot named Cye who could fetch you a beer from the refrigerator. "That's something I know I can build," said Henry Thorne of Probotics. "In 15 years I want it to be able to fix your toilet."

The Science of Happiness

91 A generation ago, hardheaded scientists couldn't be bothered with a concept like "happiness." Liquid oxygen and protons—that was science. "Happiness" was a vague concept fit for wedding speeches and greeting cards. But increasingly scientists have become interested in the nature of happiness and whether they can use rigorous research to increase the total stock of it. Psychologists such as Ed Diener define and study happiness as subjective well-being, a person's own judgment of how well his or her life is going. As the scientific discoveries proliferate, look for new drugs, techniques, and science-based advice on how to become more cheerful, content, and serene—in a word, happier.

As scientists study happiness, they seek to define it in a rigorous way. One important discovery of recent years is that happiness has a genetic component. Through studies of identical twins reared apart, psychologist David Lykken has found evidence for a gene-based "Happiness Set Point"—a basic level of contentment that an individual tends to have no matter what fortunes or misfortunes life throws at that person. According to *New York Times* columnist Richard A. Friedman, M.D., some people appear to be born with a "joyous temperament," known as hyperthymia, which makes them cheerful and optimistic in both good times and bad. Their mirror opposites are people with dysthymia, a chronic, mild depression that makes them incorrigibly gloomy, something like the donkey Eeyore in the Winnie-the-Pooh stories.

Researchers are now hard at work trying to pinpoint the genes that have an impact on happiness. In 2003, scientists discovered one candidate: a gene involved in the brain's use of serotonin, a chemical messenger, or neurotransmitter, believed to influence mood. In a study of 800 adults, people with a certain form of this serotonin-transporter gene were at higher risk of depression than people with a different form. At the moment, such studies are in their infancy, but in time, they may lead to new treatments to remedy depression and boost happiness.

Genetic research is linked to studies of the biochemistry of happiness: that is, what happens in the brain as neurons swap neurotransmitters to communicate with one another and how that affects mood. Beginning in the 1980s, biochemical research yielded an important new class of antidepressants, the selective serotonin reuptake inhibitors, or SSRIs. The most famous member of that class was Prozac (fluoxetine), but many others have arisen, including Luvox (fluvoxamine), Paxil (paroxetine), Zoloft (sertraline), and Celexa (citalopram). They are now commonly prescribed for depression, along with older treatments such as heterocyclics (tricyclics) and newer ones such as Wellbutrin (buproprion).

Many of the 19 million Americans estimated to be clinically depressed have benefited from one or more antidepressant pharmaceuticals, and new drugs are constantly in development, whether to minimize side effects or improve effectiveness. Current avenues for research include trying to boost the growth of new nerve cells in a region of the brain called the hippocampus and attempting to block release of the stress hormone cortisol.

As pharmacological remedies improve and become more widespread, some people worry that the country will become a nation of happiness zombies, induced by drugs to feel blissful instead of going out and achieving satisfaction through hard work. "[A] fraudulent happiness is just what the pharmacological management of our mental lives threatens to confer upon us," wrote the President's Council on Bioethics in a recent report. This concern seems to be based on a misunderstanding of what antidepressants do. Unlike cocaine or heroin, SSRIs are not addictive and do not produce a euphoric high. They don't tend to reduce the desire to do hard work, but enable it in people who might otherwise be too depressed to work. A study at the University of California at San Francisco showed that nondepressed volunteers were not made any happier by taking the SSRI Paxil.

Happiness is a complex phenomenon, and no reputable scientist thinks that a single gene or chemical makes or breaks happiness. Research by Diener indicates that environmental factors play a large role in happiness, and he has found that the happiest people always have two things: good mental health and good social relationships. Lykken, in his book *Happiness: The Nature and Nurture of Joy and Contentment* (2000), proposes that there are many actions we can take to make the most of our Happiness Set Point, such as focusing on the things that give us pleasure and counteracting negative emotions. Cognitive-behavioral therapy, which focuses on teaching people to change negative patterns of thought, has shown some effectiveness in treating depression. In *Destructive Emotions: A Scientific Dialogue with the Dalai Lama* (2003), Daniel Goleman offers scientific evidence that compassion, as stimulated by Buddhist meditation techniques, can induce a state of joy—and, conversely, that emotions such as hatred and craving can make for misery. Goleman's evidence comes from a conference attended by psychologists, neuroscientists, philosophers, and Buddhist monks. Its eclectic roster is itself a sign of how far scientists today are willing to go in their quest to understand happiness.

Smart Devices

92 Once a phone could only place a call. Now phones can also maintain a calendar and receive television broadcasts. Devices of all kinds, from refrigerators to cars, are getting smarter everyday—and they will be getting smarter still in years to come.

Several factors are driving the increase toward smarter devices. One is Moore's law, which states that the amount of data an electronic chip can contain will double about every 18 months. That trend has held for decades, making it possible to give computing power to devices that never had room for it before or to increase their power if they did. Another factor is the development of practical and affordable wireless connections, which makes it easier for devices to communicate with one another, forming smart networks. Still another factor is convergence, the trend toward integration of different devices. Already some personal digital assistants (PDAs) have converged with cell phones to provide both functions in one unit—a smart phone. Finally, consumer demand is pushing companies to offer smarter devices. The trend toward smart phones has been growing as sales of stand-alone PDAs have been falling.

Numerous smart devices are already on the market. The Ceiva Digital Photo Receiver, for example, is a smart photo frame: an electronic digital device that can store up to 20 photos at a time, displaying them in a continuous slide show. The Amana Messenger Refrigerator has several smart features, including a digital voice messaging system allowing users to leave messages for other household members, and electronics that can monitor such conditions as the need to change the air filter. The LG Internet Family is a system of four appliances that connect and communicate via a power line communication (PLC) and can be accessed remotely through the Internet: a fridge/freezer, microwave, washing machine, and air conditioner.

Radio frequency identification (RFID) technology is responsible for other kinds of smart devices. Toll plazas equipped with RFID technology, for example, are smart enough to speed RFID-tagged cars past tollbooths and charge their accounts. RFID is part of a larger trend toward smart networked objects, smart devices operating in a network.

Even smarter devices await us in the near future. Smart dust, for example, consists of tiny wireless microelectromechanical sensors (MEMS) that can detect anything from light to vibrations. Researchers are trying to get each chip as small as possible, about the size of a grain of sand. Their commercial applications are many: factories might use smart dust to catch manufacturing defects by sensing out-of-range vibrations; hospitals might use it to track patient movements. Sensing traffic conditions and monitoring household power consumption are two other applications. The U.S. government sees military potential in smart dust and has begun experimenting with it. As it falls from a high altitude, smart dust could send back signals of what it senses on the ground, including enemy military hardware.

Wearable computers are another smart device that may soon emerge on the market. The ideal is to have a computer built within ordinary clothing supplemented by ordinary eyeglasses. Acting as a seamless extension of body and mind, it would replace everything from the computer and PDA to the cell phone and personal music system.

Cars have slowly been getting smarter, using computers for both mechanical functions and dashboard extras. But even brainier cars are in development, including the ultimate dream—self-driving cars. Also in development are smart homes, such as the MavHome Smart Home project at the University of Texas at Arlington. As envisioned by that project, a smart home is not just four walls and a roof but an intelligent agent that perceives its environment through sensors and can act upon it through actuators. The home's goals include minimizing cost and maximizing comfort.

As smart devices get more mobile and independent, they overlap with robo-gadgets, consumer-friendly robots that can do everything from vacuum to fetch a beer from the fridge. Eventually, everything that is not alive may be smart in some way, from smart rocks (equipped with solar cells to gather the sun's energy) to smart rain (equipped with sensors to place precipitation in the right spot). Such science-fiction speculations may be a long way off, but humbler smart devices are here now, already starting to change the way we live.

To Catch a Thief, Better DNA Tests

93 Technology is always improving, and that includes forensic technology, tools used to link criminals to a crime through scientific analysis of evidence. DNA testing is now more sensitive than ever, and other forensic science techniques are improving too. The drive to improve them has come partly from the ordinary necessities of police work—matching suspects to crime scenes—and partly from the terrorist attacks of September 11, 2001. They left forensic scientists with 30,000 biological specimens, many barely recognizable as human, and a massive problem of identification. Speaking to Indystar.com in 2005, John S. Morgan of the National Institute of Justice called the breakthrough in forensic identification techniques arising from September 11 "a real revolution."

DNA testing is the principal focus of the revolution. Once forensic scientists had only the crude implements of fingerprints and blood type to link suspects to a crime scene, but since the 1980s they have been able to analyze the DNA in blood, hair, saliva, or semen found on the scene and attain near-certainty about a suspect. Many criminals have been convicted and innocent people cleared by DNA analysis, a procedure that now takes only about two days, compared to the weeks or months it used to take. Yet there have long been limits to this technique. For one thing, the DNA samples found at crime scenes have often been too minute for analysis. A method called polymerase chain reaction (PCR) has been used since the 1980s to amplify tiny amounts of DNA—from, for example, less than one drop of blood—into volumes large enough for testing. But sometimes the DNA traces at crime scenes were even smaller than this, so there was room for an even more sensitive test.

Beginning in Britain in 1999, such a technique, called low copy number DNA analysis (LCN DNA), came into use. High-sensitivity labs using LCN DNA can get a DNA profile from just 6 cells, compared to the 150 cells needed for conventional DNA testing. LCN DNA takes longer than routine DNA profiling techniques—usually several weeks—but the results have been worth it. The trace evidence that LCN DNA can analyze may not even be visible: a few skin cells, perhaps, left in a fingerprint or a ski mask. LCN DNA targets areas where a perpetrator may have transferred DNA through touch, as in residue from skin or sweat. Profiles have been generated from abandoned tools, weapon handles, and even matchsticks. Once a profile is obtained, it can be matched against databases of known felons, suspects, and other crime scenes.

LCN DNA is especially useful for investigating crimes where other profiling techniques have been exhausted or when there are few options for forensic evidence. In New York City, the *New York Times* reported in May 2004 that LCN DNA is beginning to open up a category of crimes that had previously seemed hopeless: burglaries. These and other property crimes usually left behind so little evidence that more than 80 percent of them were never solved. But LCN DNA has made it feasible to analyze the crime scenes of burglarized homes and stolen cars, and the chief medical examiner's office planned to open a new lab to take advantage of that tool. LCN DNA is also useful in cold cases, crimes from the past that have remained unsolved, sometimes because

DNA tests in the past have either failed or been rejected as impossible.

Methods for collecting DNA evidence have been advancing along-side methods of analysis. The College of Criminal Justice, Sam Houston State University, and the Department of Forensic Science, University of New Haven, recently developed a DNA collection method that uses adhesive tape for collecting DNA samples. The technique not only lifts skin cells from the crime scene but preserves them from air, moisture, and other contaminants.

There have been other advances in forensic science. Evidence from a sexual assault used to have to be recovered immediately afterward to be analyzable. Now analysis can take place from evidence recovered up to five days after the incident. DNA testing equipment is becoming more portable. Emerging methods will allow investigators to run DNA analysis at the crime scene rather than in the lab. Data mining of criminal databases—including DNA profiles—assists in solving cases. Advances in miniaturization and microchip technologies may bring important changes to DNA typing.

Nothing is perfect in police work. The emphasis on DNA testing is causing a storage crunch in police evidence rooms as potentially analyzable material piles up. Prosecutors are having a harder time obtaining convictions because the bar has been raised by advances in forensic techniques. And, as the O.J. Simpson case proved, a smart defense attorney can always cast even the best DNA evidence into doubt. Still, better DNA analysis, and better forensic techniques generally, will do what they can to protect the public.

The War on Germs

94 In the old days, it seemed that germs were on the run. Vaccines and antibiotics effectively protected people from ancient microbial scourges such as polio, diphtheria, and pneumonia. Smallpox, in 1980, became the first disease to be completely eradicated by vaccination. Germs were spoken of lightly in advertising campaigns: Americans counted on their Listerine to kill millions of germs on contact.

Then AIDS emerged, killing more than 100,000 Americans by 1990. Tuberculosis, a disease believed to be a thing of the past, began recurring in epidemic form. Antibiotics, once surefire treatments for bacterial respiratory infections, frequently failed to do the trick because bacteria were developing antibiotic resistance. In 2003, scientists scrambled worldwide to do battle with yet another new disease, severe acute respiratory syndrome (SARS). Today, no one assumes germs are on the run.

Complicating the war on germs is the danger of deliberate infection by terrorists. In fall 2001, anthrax attacks on the eastern seaboard killed five people and sickened fourteen. Experts say that the country is still unprepared for another bioterrorist attack. Asked about this issue by *National Geographic News* in April 2003, Laurie Garrett, author of *The Coming Plague* (1994), said "[A]nybody . . . who is on the ground in public health in this country will tell you we are a far cry from being ready for such a thing."

Even without terrorism, public health officials have their hands full dealing with the germs nature delivers. The outbreak in Asia of avian influenza A (H5N1), a virulent new strain of bird flu, has been challenging infectious disease experts around the world. As of February 2005, there have been 55 human cases of the strain in Vietnam, Thailand, and Cambodia, resulting in 42 deaths.

One consolation in this case is that, for the most part, avian influenza A (H5N1) has so far not achieved sustained person-to-person transmission, which would make containment harder than bird-to-person transmission. Another consolation is that contemporary science affords weapons for dealing with such a new strain. For example, scientists in the World Health Organization's influenza network used a new method called reverse genetics to develop a vaccine and diagnostic test for A (H5N1). The technique involves replacing the genes that make the virus harmful to birds with genes that are harmless.

Avian influenza demonstrates one of the ways that new diseases emerge: by incubation in an animal reservoir, then transmission from animals to humans, sometimes as a result of a new mutation. Paradoxically, another cause of new epidemics can be better hygiene and less exposure to microbes as children. A recent Australian study shows that test subjects who had the greatest number of younger siblings and who were least separated from them in age were the least likely to develop multiple sclerosis (MS). The infections they caught from the younger children seem to have helped train their immune system not to attack their own nerves, like it does in MS. This finding echoes the history of polio, which became epidemic only when modern hygiene led people away from being exposed to it harmlessly in early childhood.

One risk factor for the spread of disease is government incompetence. The Chinese government initially denied the seriousness of the SARS outbreak, which contributed to its spread. Another risk factor is the same modern transportation that permits medicines and epidemiological teams to be transported rapidly around the world. Speaking about the devastating 1918–1919 Spanish influenza pandemic, Jeffrey Taubenberger of the Armed Forces Institute of Pathology in Washington told ABCNews.com: "In 1918, the flu spread at the speed of ships and trains. Now we have jumbo jets crossing the oceans on a routine basis. In many ways a virus might be more dangerous now than back then."

Whatever happens with this or that disease, complacency is a bad idea. For the foreseeable future, the struggle of humans against germs is likely to resemble not so much a victory lap as persistent urban warfare.

What a Tangled Web: Network Theory

95 In the 1980s chaos theory (or complexity theory) was the emerging science that spawned journal articles, attracted research dollars, generated popular books, and had everyone excited. In the 2000s the emerging science du jour is network theory.

To a network theorist or network scientist, a network is any set of individual nodes connected by links—your high school graduating class; the Internet; Al Qaeda; the stock market; airports; power grids; epidemics; brain cells; the entire human population. Since the mid-1990s, network scientists have been analyzing such real-world networks, looking for the principles that govern them. They draw on a tradition of network (or graph) mathematics that reaches back to the 18th-century Swiss mathematician Leonhard Euler, but they have dramatically advanced the field by using sophisticated computers to do the heavy number-crunching. Like the earlier chaos theory, which centered on chaotic or complex systems, including networks, network theory has begun to attract big research dollars, stir academic debate, and penetrate popular consciousness.

One way to understand network theory is through the John Guare play *Six Degrees of Separation*. This play drew on a 1967 experiment by psychologist Stanley Milgram that tried to show that anyone in the United States could reach anyone else through a chain of fewer than six people. Another way is through the game Six Degrees of Kevin Bacon, which draws on the same source. The "six degrees" phenomenon points to the existence of what are called "small-world" networks: networks in which the path of links between any two nodes tends to be short. The phenomenon also provided the title for a 2003 book on network theory by Duncan J. Watts, *Six Degrees: The Science of a Connected Age*.

The findings of network theory are now being applied in many fields, including sociology, computer science, economics, disease, and war. For example, network theorists have shown that many small-world networks are characterized by hubs; a hub is a node with many links, in contrast to ordinary nodes, which have relatively few links. In network theory jargon, hub-laden networks are called "scale-free." The destruction of hubs can devastate a scale-free network, even though the destruction of several randomly selected nodes might not. As network theorist Albert-László Barabási explains in his book *Linked: The*

New Science of Networks (2002), this principle has vast implications; for example, security personnel should realize that the apparently indestructible Internet could be crippled by destroying some of its hubs; and epidemiologists might try to stop disease outbreaks by identifying and treating hubs (e.g., Typhoid Mary) in the transmission network.

For a fun use of network theory, users of AOL Instant Messenger can consult *http://buddyzoo.com*, which analyzes their buddy lists to see the degrees of separation between different screennames, find out which buddies they have in common with friends, measure their popularity, detect cliques, and so on. For a more serious purpose, the U.S. military is working with network theorists to fight terrorism, and with good reason: 9/11 and its aftermath showed the resilience of two prominent networks, Wall Street and Al Qaeda. The destruction of the World Trade Center failed to shut down Wall Street for more than a few days, because the U.S. business world is not a simple hierarchy in which all functions depend on one center; it can't be shut down simply by destroying one of its prominent edifices. The same holds true for Al Qaeda, which despite the invasion of Afghanistan and the removal of some of its top leaders was not destroyed. To understand how to defeat Al Qaeda and protect the United States from future attacks, network theory is needed.

Network theory is now rippling through the publishing world, underpinning books from Malcolm Gladwell's *The Tipping Point* (2000) to Ed Keller and Jon Berry's *The Influentials* (2003), which profiles local leaders "who come from every city and town and who shape the opinions and trends in our country." Other books set out to explain network theory to the uninitiated, including those mentioned previously by Watts and Barabási, and Mark Buchanan's *Nexus: Small Worlds and the Groundbreaking Science of Networks* (2002).

Network theory intersects with a variety of other fruitful notions, including networked business, a business model based on linkages with partners; smart mobs, leaderless groups of people using technology; and emergence, the spontaneous self-organization and adaptive behavior that emerges from networks of simpler entities, such as cells, ants, and Web users. Books such as *Sync: The Emerging Science of Spontaneous Order* (2003) by Steven Strogatz not only talk about a great many emergent phenomena, but are themselves examples of such a phenomenon—the network of books that are now talking about networks, and will probably be doing so for some time.

10

The Sexes

Blondes Forever

96 In September 2002, major international news outlets reported that in 200 years natural blondes would become extinct. More precisely, news reports said that research by the World Health Organization (WHO) found that there would be too few people with recessive blonde genes in the grandparents' generation to continue the blonde trait beyond 2202. The last natural blondes, they said, would be in Finland, the country with the highest concentration of natural blondes.

Within days, the report was found to be untrue. CNN, ABC, and the BBC Web site retracted their statements. The World Health Organization said in a statement that it "has no knowledge of how these news reports originated but would like to stress that we have no opinion on the future existence of blonds." Ultimately, according to the *Washington Post*, the erroneous information was traced to an article in a German magazine that cited a WHO source who could not be verified. So the blonde will go on.

While natural blondes are not an endangered species, their numbers may decrease in the future, says Jonathan Rees, professor of

Dermatology at the University of Edinburgh. According to Rees, "The frequency of blondes may drop but they won't disappear." In remarks for *BBC Online*, he says, "The only reason blondes would disappear is if having the gene was a disadvantage and I do not think that is the case."

Truth be told, only 0.001 percent of adults are naturally blonde, but thanks to effective, inexpensive hair dyes and increased popularity of light hair across the continents, the number of blondes will increase. They'll just be bottle blondes. Since the early 20th century, people have been able to buy chemically activated blonde hair dye, and now, reports *USA Today*, 40 percent of all hair color sold is blonde. In the United States alone, one in three American women dye their hair blonde (while 1 in 20 American women are natural blondes), reports Joanna Pitman's book *On Blondes*. Of these women, many, such as singer Beyonce Knowles and athlete Serena Williams, are African-American. Others, like singer Eminem, are male (and men account for over $200 million of the hair care market). Reasons for becoming blonde include the desire to look younger, feel sexier, be cool. Since the 1970s, when L'Oreal enticed people to try blonde hair color with the words, "Because I'm worth it!", being blonde has also become a statement of self-affirmation.

In fashion-conscious Japan, sales of blonde hair coloring have increased dramatically; for one major hair color company, blonde coloring accounts for one-fourth of its sales in Japan. There, a head of rich black hair that was traditionally called a "woman's life" is now just as likely to be a lighter shade, sometimes blonde. Sales of blonde coloring continue to be strong throughout Europe, where women have been lightening their hair for generations. For example, both of Prince Charles's wives, Diana and Camilla, have been bottle blondes.

The fact that a minor report predicting the demise of blondes would raise international interest points to the ongoing fascination with blondes. For over 2,000 years, people have been drawn to the blonde as a symbol of youth, power, and sexuality. So it continues. As a hairstyling mogul said in *USA Today*, "Blond hair is a global fashion." The $1.4

billion hair care market backs him up, as does research indicating that bottle-blonde women are more attractive to men than natural blondes.

Father Goose

97 If you could get in a time machine to visit a playground 30 years ago and compare it to a playground today, the children cavorting on the swings and slides would look about the same. But if you took a good look at the adults kissing scraped knees and breaking out snacks, you would notice a difference: Thirty years ago, practically all the adults would have been women, whereas today at least a few of them are likely to be men. Move over, Mother Goose; Father Goose has arrived.

The feminist movement scored big inroads in getting women into the workplace and teaching them they did not have to be stay-at-home moms. As a windfall for fathers, it made it possible for men to get out of the workplace and be stay-at-home dads. At first, the standard model for a stay-at-home dad, as in the 1983 movie *Mr. Mom*, was one who lost his job and was forced into the humiliating and awkward position of changing diapers all day while his wife brought home the bacon.

But increasingly, fathers are choosing to stay home with their children because they like their children and enjoy spending time with them. In some cases, an additional factor is that the mother cares more about her career than the father cares about his. In other cases, financial sense is the deciding factor—if the mother earns more at her job than the father earns at his, that might be reason enough to make the father the stay-at-home parent. Usually, couples where the father stays home with the kids have a strong commitment to handling child care personally, rather than leaving it to a nanny or day care program. The only question on the table is which parent will do the job.

Fathers will probably never be 50 percent of the nation's stay-at-home parents. Mothers will likely predominate in this business for the foreseeable future. At the moment, about one in three U.S. children under 15 has a mother at home full-time, while the proportion with a father at home full-time is less than 1 percent. Even so, the number of stay-at-home dads has been growing and will probably continue to grow. According to Census data, the number of stay-at-home dads in the United States rose 18 percent since 1994; 336,000 children under 15 were being cared for by a stay-at-home dad by 2003.

As this trend continues, a variation on the full-time dad is likely to gain prominence: the family in which both parents work half-time jobs and each watches the kids half-time. Sometimes economic considerations drive this model, but often it is a simple matter of sharing the wealth: both parents want to work and both want to enjoy their children. Blue-collar men have led this trend, splitting shifts with their wives so both can work and raise the kids. A policeman or fireman, for example, may work the overnight shift, sleep during the day while the kids are at school, then take care of the kids when they come home from school. After dinner, his wife, who has worked during the day, takes charge of the kids and the cycle begins again.

This model is ideal for freelancers, telecommuters, and other people who work from home. The authors of this book, for example, have collaborated on writing it while splitting shifts of caring for their daughter. The shift-system of child care is more unusual for couples with a full-time, white-collar job outside the home, but even here where there's a will, there's a way. In November 2003, *New York Times* columnist Lisa Belkin reported on several couples who each share a single high-level position—neonatologist, astrophysicist, pastor—with each parent in the couple doing the job half-time and taking care of the children the rest of the time.

Another unusual but growing model is that of two fathers—members of a gay couple—in which one father stays home with the children while the other works. There are 60,000 male couple households with children in the United States, and 26 percent of them include a stay-at-home parent.

Becoming a stay-at-home dad has its drawbacks. Some are the same ones faced by stay-at-home moms: boredom with making peanut-butter sandwiches and engaging in playground chitchat about children's snow gear; the feeling that one's career aspirations are dying on the vine; the sense that one's contribution to society is not really valued. Fathers may face an additional sense of isolation and anxiety that comes from being surrounded by mommies and suspected of not being fully a man. A 1996 study by Robert A. Frank, Ph.D., showed that 63 percent of at-home fathers felt somewhat isolated, compared to 37 percent of at-home mothers.

The benefits? Several studies indicate that children benefit from having a full-time, stay-at-home parent, and that they receive particular advantages if that parent is the father. According to a fall 2000 article in *Christianity Today*, a study from the Center for Successful Fathering in Austin, Texas, says that when a father is actively involved in parenting, children benefit with higher grades, fewer anxiety disorders, greater ambition, and lower risk of delinquency or teen pregnancy. Another study found that such children scored higher on verbal skills and academic achievement. Not measured in such studies are the benefits to the father—relearning how to play; living at a slower, saner pace for a few years; and not missing a moment of that most fleeting of joys, the growing up of one's children.

Life after Feminism

98 Four decades after Betty Friedan published *The Feminine Mystique* in 1963 and the postwar wave of feminism began, American women seem to live with more power and comfort than they once did. Some of the battles have already been fought or at least launched. Women make up at least half of college undergraduates and nearly half the work force. There is also more social freedom. They can cohabit, live alone, or marry. Again, statistics bear this out. They show that cohabitation and living alone are on the rise for women. Marriage rates remain fairly constant, though those who want to marry do so earlier than they did a generation ago.

In these ways, one of the main points of feminism has come to pass—feminism of the post–World War II era is a part of everyday life. But in the 21st century, feminism has also taken on new forms. There is no longer (if there ever was) a unified goal, like "Sisterhood is Powerful." From postfeminism to libertarian feminism, various causes take the feminist mantle, and each serves a different goal. Some versions of feminism are broadly social in outlook, some targeted and political. Some are championed by women, some by men. All involve how women can and should live.

The new millennium began with talk of a third wave of feminism. One book about it, *Manifesta: Young Women, Feminism, and the Future* by Jennifer Baumgardner and Amy Richards, posits this feminism as a mix of personal liberation and commitment to social justice for all women. They still believe, however, that motherhood and domestic life unavoidably cause entrapment and patriarchal control. Motherhood is "the opposite of liberation," they say.

This limited view of life with the opposite sex and the need to equate independence with solitude is part of what Katie Roiphe criticizes in her book *The Morning After: Sex, Fear, and Feminism*. While supposedly promoting free speech and openness about sexuality, the feminism that she observed during the late 20th century among the highly educated is narrow and unbending.

Others see that postfeminism can mean nothing more than returning to the past. Columnist Maureen Dowd observes a postfeminist return to the supposedly pampered wife of the mid-20th century. She writes that "[m]any women I know, who once disdained their mothers' lifestyles, no longer see those lives as boring and indulgent. Now, they look back with a tad of longing." As statistical backup, she cites a survey by *Cosmopolitan* magazine in which two-thirds of 800 females agreed that, given the chance, they "would rather kick back than climb the corporate ladder."

To social critic Susan J. Douglas, this retrograde form of postfeminism is a right-leaning "engineering process" whose aims are to keep from instituting pro-family social welfare programs and to make money for major corporations. To the author, it is "Postfeminism Inc."

The "individualist feminists" of ifeminism.com see their version of modern feminism as an embrace of personal freedom, choice, and personal responsibility. In short, it is a form of libertarianism. In their online introduction, ifeminism.com states that "ifeminism turns the old stereotype of feminism on its head." Rather than looking to reform government laws on equality, individualist feminists promote libertarian ideals to remove government involvement in people's lives. In particular they wish to remove government interference with women's sexual activities. "You cannot create equality with men by embedding gender privilege for women into the law," they say. Individualist feminist heroes include novelist Ayn Rand, founder of the *Catholic Worker* Dorothy Day, and cultural critic Camille Paglia.

Many young women simply seek a way to live with feminism in their everyday life. As former-graduate-student-turned-Web-columnist Melissa Gelula wrote for the online journal *Sexing the Political*, "I sense that many women, who, like me, found the feminism at some point in their lives, and never thought they'd let it go, might secretly wonder about its continued applicability in their personal, parenting, or professional lives, and may struggle to keep it alive in a culture that's still very counter all-things liberatory."

Every once in a while, something happens to remind women of the barriers that feminism arose to confront. Such was the case when Harvard President Lawrence H. Summers provoked controversy by arguing that women's "intrinsic aptitude" might account for their shortage of numbers employed in science and engineering. To feminist and social critic Katha Pollitt, living with modern feminism may require revitalizing it and making it a forceful ideology. To do that, she suggests, it may be necessary to once again make it what it was in the 1970s: "a do-it-yourself, direct-action social movement." Can it really mean going back to "Free to Be You and Me"?

More Free Milk: Cohabitation Abounding

99 Two generations ago, parents cautioned daughters not to move in with a boyfriend because he would never marry them: "Why buy the cow when they can get the milk for free?" they said. According to the 2000 Census, few people are listening. The census reported that the number of unmarried persons living together as partners increased by 72 percent over the past decade. Further, those cohabiting span the demographic and economic spectrum and include all ethnic groups. Marshall Miller of the Alternatives to Marriage Project, a national nonprofit organization for unmarrieds, notes in his organization's statement that society has "seen unmarried cohabitation transformed from something scandalous to something most people do before they marry or instead of marrying." Cohabitation has moved in for good.

In 1970, only 1 of 10 couples lived together without being married. But between 1960 and 2000, the number of cohabiting opposite-sex couples has increased 10 times, from 439,000 to 4.7 million couples. As of 2003, unmarried people account for about 5.5 million households. With about 55 million married couples, married people predominate in the United States, but overall their number is diminishing. In 1990, married couples accounted for 55.1 percent of U.S. households; as of 2000, they account for 52 percent. Both numbers pale at the 1950 figures: 78 percent of U.S. households had married people.

Other census information points to the variety of types and reasons for cohabitating. To begin with, there is no typical age for cohabitating. One-third of all cohabitants are between 25 and 34, 23 percent are over 45, and 4 percent are senior citizens. The average period of cohabitation is two years. Living together as preparation for marriage is now commonplace: about half of women who have married and have reached age 30 have lived with their mates first. Almost half of cohabiting couples have children. In all, there are 3.3 million children living with an unmarried parent who is cohabiting with a person he or she is not married to. Senior citizens who cohabitate but do not marry usually do so to retain their pension, Social Security, and Medicare benefits. People below the poverty level are more likely than other economic groups to live together; according to some estimates, up to one-third of cohabiting couples with children live below the poverty line.

Even as cohabitation increases, conflict continues over its long-term effects on relationships and the family. Studies in the mid-1990s have suggested that cohabiting couples are generally not as committed to their partner or the relationship as married people. Studies in the *Journal of Family Issues* in 1995 and in *Journal of Marriage and the Family* in 1996 report that cohabiting couples are less likely to be satisfied with their relationship and are less likely to be monogamous.

A 2003 study by Penn State University researchers in the *Journal of Marriage and the Family* found that living together before marriage is still linked to higher rates of troubled unions, divorce, and separation. The study compared the marital happiness of couples from 1964 through 1980, when cohabitation was not commonly practiced, to couples during the years 1981 to 1997, when it was. In both cases, cohabitating couples in both groups had a higher incidence of marital unhappiness and a higher than average divorce rate. One reason was increased incidence of infidelity. Married women were five times less likely to have an additional sex partner than do cohabiting women. In part, say researchers, the negative outcomes are linked to the choice of riskier partners that living together encourages.

Yet, studies also find that while the cohabitation rate has gone up over the last 20 years, the divorce rate has not. Since 1980, it has remained at about 50 percent, and in the early 21st century, it has leveled at 43 percent.

Cohabitation is also being legitimized by the various forms of legal recognition it is receiving from governments and businesses. As of 2005, it is estimated that over 3,500 private companies, colleges, universities, and state and local governments offer benefits for domestic partners such as health insurance and family leave. The annual BLR Survey of Employee Benefits shows that the number of employers offering benefits to domestic partners has increased from 13 percent in 2003 to 19 percent in 2005. Ironically, gay and lesbian couples who would like to be married rather than cohabitate find it impossible in most jurisdictions; indeed, President Bush has supported a constitutional amendment to make marriage for them impossible.

Commenting on the changes in the way people live together, Dorian Solot, executive director of the Alternatives to Marriage Project, proclaims, "Getting married isn't the only way to live happily ever after." Millions of unmarried cohabiting Americans are testing that statement now, and millions more are going to try in the next decades. In various forms, they will contribute to the even larger trend of the 21st century—the redefined family. Unmarried couples, stepfamilies, and gay families will join married parents with children as accepted types of the American family, which will live on. Says Robert Schoen, demographer at Johns Hopkins University, "Yes, family forms are changing, but the family does not show any signs of fading away."

The New Teen Facts of Life

100 Adults tend to have a Madonna-and-whore view of teenage sexuality: the teens are either innocent about life, promiscuous as rabbits, or both. But in recent years, studies have been revealing a different picture, one in which teens are neither as innocent nor as promiscuous as we think. They know about sex, but they are not necessarily having it. Here are the new teen facts of life.

A 2005 survey by NBC News and *People Magazine* revealed that 27 percent of teens aged 13 to 16 say they are sexually active. This includes 21 percent who have touched someone else's genitals, 12 percent who have had oral sex, and 13 percent who have had intercourse. Less than one half of one percent said they had ever been to an oral sex party of the kind celebrated in urban legend. This is much less sex than is presented by the media image of teens: in the movie *American Pie*, 75 percent of the four boys trying to get laid on prom night succeeded. But it is more sex than is postulated by the hopeful parents of teens. Of the parents surveyed by NBC/*People*, only 15 percent believed their own teens had been sexually intimate—about half the proportion of teens who had been intimate.

Behind the relatively low numbers for teen sex lies a prolonged trend. According to a study by the National Center for Health Statistics (NCHS), sexual activity declined significantly for younger teenage girls and for teenage boys between 1995 and 2002, and teen contraceptive use improved. The proportion of never-married girls aged 15 to 17 who had had sexual intercourse fell from 38 percent to 30 percent, while among their male peers the proportion fell from 43 percent to 31 percent.

This does not mean most teens are waiting until marriage. At age 18 to 19, according to NCHS, both boys and girls tend to become more experienced; in 2002, 69 percent of girls and 64 percent of boys in that age group had had sexual intercourse. But teens were delaying sex and having smarter sex. They were more likely to use contraception when they began having intercourse: 79 percent in 1999-2002, an increase from 61 percent in the 1980s.

The smarter teen attitude toward sex is consistent with the downward trend in teen pregnancy and births since the early 1990s. In 2002, according to NCHS, the birth rate among females aged 15 to 19 was 28 percent lower than in 1990. The birth rate among females aged 10 to 14 dropped to the lowest level since 1946. However, to put this in perspective, the United States still has the highest teen pregnancy and birth rates of any Western industrialized nation.

Teens are managing to stay the course not because they don't know about sex, but because they are choosing to wait. In the NBC/*People* poll, the majority (87 percent) of teens aged 13 to 16 had not had sexual intercourse, and 74 percent said they had not had sex because they made a conscious decision not to. Their reasons were many: they were afraid of pregnancy, sexually transmitted diseases, or their parents' reaction; they were following religious or moral beliefs; they were waiting for the right person; or they just believed they were too young.

Teens manage to keep their cool with sex even though they are bombarded constantly by sexual imagery and language on TV, in movies, on music videos, and on the Internet. A study by the Kaiser Family Foundation revealed that more than half of all TV programming, excluding news, sporting events, and children's shows, contained sexual content. The NBC/*People* poll revealed that 70 percent of teens aged 13 to 16 knew what oral sex was. In fact, they often use that knowledge to help them prolong the period until "real" sex: 4 in 10 teens said they had had oral sex to avoid having sexual intercourse.

As teens grapple with the messy issues of sex, they develop their own jargon. "Hooking up" is a "one-night stand"; a "friend with benefits" is a friend with whom one has casual sex but no commitment. Young African-American men sometimes distinguish between a "wifey," or regular girlfriend, and "shortys," casual sex partners.

Parents of teens often feel at sea about what their teens are doing sexually, yet in some ways the picture isn't as dark as it seems. Not only are most kids trying to be sensible about sex, many are communicating with their parents. According to the teens surveyed by NBC/*People*, 41 percent often talk to their parents about sex and sexual relationships, and 70 percent say they have gotten a lot or some information about sex and sexual relationships from their parents. That would warm the heart of most parenting experts, who urge parents to communicate with their kids about sex. The new teen facts of life are not all bad.

Index